# A HANDBOOK FOR CHRISTIAN PHILOSOPHY

## L. RUSS BUSH

ZondervanPublishingHouse
*Academic and Professional Books*
Grand Rapids, Michigan

*A Division of* HarperCollins*Publishers*

Handbook for Christian Philosophy
Copyright © 1991 by L. Russ Bush

Requests for information should be addressed to:
Zondervan Publishing House
Academic and Professional Books
1415 Lake Drive S.E.
Grand Rapids, Michigan 49506

**Library of Congress Cataloging-in-Publication Data**

Bush, L. Russ, 1944-
    A handbook for Christian philosophy / L. Russ Bush.
      p.   cm.
    Includes bibliographical references and index.
    ISBN 0-310-51821-0
    1. Apologetics. 2. Religion–Philosophy. I. Title.
BT1102.B79 1991
190–dc20                                    91-27534
                                            CIP

All Scripture quotations, unless otherwise noted, are taken from the
HOLY BIBLE: NEW INTERNATIONAL VERSION (North American
Edition). Copyright © 1973, 1978, 1984, by the International Bible
Society. Used by permission of Zondervan Bible Publishers.

*Edited by John Vriend and Leonard G. Goss*
*Cover by Lecy Design*

*Printed in the United States of America*

91  92  93  94  95  96 / AK / 10  9  8  7  6  5  4  3  2  1

# CONTENTS

*Preface* .................................................................9
*Acknowledgements* .....................................................12
*Introduction* ...........................................................13
    The Importance of Philosophy of Religion
    Self-examination
    Review and Evaluation
    Brief Bibliography

## PART ONE:
## FOUNDATIONAL PRINCIPLES

1. What is Philosophy? ...............................................21
    Asking Why?
    Who Are Philosophers?
    Finding Answers
    Why Study Philosophy?

2. How to Study Philosophy .......................................33
    Five Questions
    Philosophical Issues
        Metaphysics
        Morals
        Epistemology

3. Learning to Think Logically ....................................45
    Deductive Logic
    Inductive Logic
    Fallacies Associated with Induction
    Using Logic in Biblical Exegesis
    Logic in the Bible

4. Recognizing Worldviews ............................................69
   What is a Worldview?
        Knowledge and Reality
        Moral Values
        Meaning and Purpose
        Human Nature and Relationships
   Five Fundamental Questions
   Three Major Worldviews
   Summary

5. Testing Worldviews ...............................................81
   The Test of Logical or Rational Consistency
   The Test of Empirical Adequacy
   The Test of Explanatory Power
   The Test of Practical Relevance
   Conclusion

# PART TWO:
# TOPICS OF SPECIAL INTEREST

6. The Existence of God: Another Look at the
   Classical Proofs .....................................................95
   Divine Revelation
        Faith vs. Reason
        Faith and Reason
   Three Basic Types of Rational Theistic Proofs
        Religious Experience
        Rational Proofs: Apriori
        Rational Proofs: Aposteriori
   Rational Proofs: Another Look
        A Preliminary Evaluation
        A Biblical Proposal

7. Creation: A Reasonable Alternative .........................117
   Naturalistic Evolution
   Theistic Evolution
   Special Creation
   Testing Models of Origins
   The Problem of Verification
   The Scientific Mind
   The Problem of Interpretation
   Creation, Evolution, and Thermodynamics
        The First Law
        The Second Law
   Science, Religion, and Truth

**8. God and Evil: Part One** .......................................151
Does Evil Exist?
Evil in Western Philosophical Thought
    Platonic Idealism
    Augustinian Idealism
    Idealist Theodicy
Philosophical and Religious Alternatives Regarding Evil
    Fatalism and Determinism
    Pessimism
    Nihilism
Theistic Finitism

**9. God and Evil: Part Two** .......................................171
The Classical Formulation Reformulated
Eight Elements of a Biblical Theodicy
    Satan
    Eschatology
    Punishment and Retribution
    Discipline
    Probation
    Revelation
    Mystery
    Redemption
A Christian Response to the Problem of Evil and Suffering
Summation and Postscript
*Appendix One* ...........................................................191
    *The Authority of Holy Scripture*
*Appendix Two* ...........................................................195
    *Elements of Theism as a Worldview*
*Appendix Three* ........................................................205
    *The Irenaean Theodicy*
*Glossary* .................................................................215
    Expanded definitions and contextual notes on specialized
    terms commonly used in religious and philosophical writing
*Subject Index* ..........................................................325
*Name Index* .............................................................333
*Scripture Index* ........................................................337

# PREFACE

In a world moving increasingly toward "crisis unlimited," we need all the trained minds we can get with broad-ranging cross-area orientations. This is a day of single-discipline specialists, but under their leadership humanity's problems have become, if anything, more serious. Someone must take the time to learn to see relationships in an interdisciplinary sense. Someone must seek and find the unity of God's truth both in the Word and in the world. Why should not that someone be the Christian minister?

Of all the classical theological disciplines, the philosophy of religion is by far the most inter-disciplinary. Christian philosophers study not only the history of Western thought but also the teachings of the other major religious groups in the world. Relevant studies in the relationship between science and faith, attempts to conceive an appropriate explanation of the problem of evil and suffering, a general analysis of theological method, and the use of logic and reason both in exegesis and in proclamation are subjects naturally included in the philosophy classroom of the Christian school. Worldview studies strengthen the curriculum by helping students grasp the comprehensive nature of the issues we face in our world today.

The most significant changes in humanity's past seem to have come from those who had insight, those who broke the mold, who were broadly educated, who were aware of the larger world. A case could be made for the thesis that the greatest and most beneficial aspects of humanity's past have come from those who have seen the world in the greatest context—as a purposeful creation of holy, divine, infinite-personal intelligence. Such a context gives real (not illusory) purpose to human life. This worldview is most fully elaborated in the Judeo-Christian Scriptures which center on the self-revealing words and actions of this divine Creator.

If human beings really are made in the image of their Creator, and if they really have been given the responsibility of dominion over the creation, then extensive cross-disciplinary knowledge and insight would seem to be required. The ancient account in Genesis has God telling humankind to "keep (guard, protect) the garden," which we have often failed to do. Nevertheless, humanity's high calling is always to be the ruling protector of this world. The mind is humanity's greatest resource. To know is humanity's greatest challenge.

God created us capable of gaining knowledge, and he created a world to be known. If students turn their backs on a broad education in the traditional sense, it would be like turning away from friends or from those who have meant so much through the years. It would be like demonstrating apathy toward water in the middle of a desert. Such apathy is as inexcusable as atheism (cf. Job 38-41; Psalm 14, 19; Romans 1:18-22).

Humanity's mental potential can never be exhausted by any single vocation, however complex. The human mind is one of the colossal mysteries of the universe. To study, literature, philosophy, art, and history is to study the human mind as it has expressed itself in the past. The only goal more worthy would be the study of the Creator's mind as it has been revealed.

What is needed is a fresh look at the biblical worldview. In making the universe, God populated it with creatures made in his image. Human beings are to have dominion over all that God has given them. As there is a place for witnessing and for preaching as a holy calling, so there is a great need for apologetics, because God's truth has been challenged. But there is also a place for a knowledge of truth just because all truth is God's truth.

All that we learn brings us closer to a knowledge of all that God has made. Humanity's keen mind, as expressed in philosophy and in the arts, is never so distorted by sin that we cannot discern in it something of God's image. The human mind, as expressed in the sciences, portrays God's glorious creation. As expressed in history, it manifests God's

10

patience, love, justice, and willingness to give to human beings freedom and responsibility. Thus Jesus called upon his followers to love God with all of their mind. May it be so, Lord! May it be so!

oOo

Originally, the intent of this handbook was simply to provide a little vocabulary help to my students in basic seminary courses in Philosophy of Religion at Southwestern Seminary in Fort Worth, Texas. I recommended it especially to theology and religious education students who found themselves bewildered by the new theological and philosophical vocabulary they encountered in their reading and in their classes. Obviously the nature and purpose of the volume expanded somewhat during the course of several years of teaching. The glossary is still here, but I have also added introductory essays on a few significant issues of concern to Christian thinkers. Time for a major revision (looking toward publication) came during a sabbatical study leave in Washington, D. C. Final revisions were done during my first year of new responsibilities at Southeastern Seminary.

May the Lord bless the minds of those who read these pages. May those minds honor Christ by exalting him above all else, and thus heed Paul's warning in Colossians 2:8.

L. Russ Bush
Wake Forest, North Carolina

# ACKNOWLEDGEMENTS

This little handbook has been more than fifteen years in the making. Several thousand students have endured various recensions. Many have offered substantive comments for improvements. Some say the work of improvement is not yet complete, and I do not want to deny that.

My colleagues at Southwestern Baptist Theological Seminary in Fort Worth, Texas, always helped me to think with care and competence. I would especially like to express appreciation to John Newport for his influence upon me while I was at Southwestern. My new colleagues at Southeastern Seminary in Wake Forest, North Carolina, have no less kept the standard of excellence before me. Neither group should be blamed, however, for my lapses from that standard.

Nancy Owen, Barbara Walker, Debbe Hill, Sharon Edwards, and Mary Anne Barroz did the typing with skill, care, and concern for detail. I am grateful to them for their many hours of labor.

I also want to thank my wife, Cindy, and my children, Josh and Beth, for their patience and encouragement. As a family we also want to thank the wonderful folks at Capitol Hill Metropolitan Baptist Church in Washington, D. C., for all that they meant to us during our time together. God's good gifts never cease. Thanks be unto him.

# INTRODUCTION

Why should anyone study the philosophy of religion? Lists of reasons could be given, but those lists would probably be memorized by students the night before a test and then forgotten. Lists of reasons are not what learning is all about. The ability to memorize is not the equivalent of the ability to learn. Grades are necessary if we are to evaluate the various levels of student achievement. But it is commonly known that those who make the highest grades are not necessarily those who are most successful in life. Still—and this is also true—the student who cannot achieve good grades frequently cannot succeed in life. Grades do tell us something of value, and they are most easily given on the basis of the recall of facts. Thus it is natural to teach and test by giving lists of facts and reasons. In this case, however, a list of reasons is not the real answer to the original question.

Why should anyone study the philosophy of religion? Some people think there is no positive answer to this question. Maybe the subject is not worth studying. After all, only a liberal theologian would ask critical questions about the Christian faith. So let us rephrase the question.

Why should a Bible-believing Christian study the philosophy of religion? A brief essay on "The Importance of Philosophy of Religion" is presented here for you to read as one approach (out of many) that could be offered as a possible rationale for the study of philosophy of religion. In the mind of some this essay may seem foolish. To others it will create a spark of interest. It is an extended argument designed to guide the reader in thinking through a definite line of reasoning. The very process of thinking through the argument will be a good mental exercise.

13

# THE IMPORTANCE OF PHILOSOPHY OF RELIGION

An existing mind is one of the most significant facts of our experience. Only a mind can be conscious of its own existence, and only a mind can have any awareness of various facts of experience. A "mind" must exist, because anyone reading these words and contemplating their meaning is exercising that which is here referred to as "mind."

Of course it might be argued that there is no such thing as mind. In that case no one could be reading and contemplating these words. Moreover, it is difficult to discover just "who" might offer such an argument or to "whom" it might be offered. Naturally if "they" should be correct, it would not matter what is said here anyway.

If, on the other hand, it is self-evident that mind does exist, then it would be possible to argue that some ideas must also exist since ideas are meaningful mental conceptions. Upon reflection, most thinking minds conclude that all ideas are not of equal importance. Usually some things are believed to be more important than other things. Such evaluations presuppose some idea or set of ideas by which the evaluation of relative importance is made. The process by which we study and attempt to understand and evaluate (and act upon) ideas is therefore a most basic human enterprise. We cannot avoid the process. The only real question is how seriously we will approach the task.

Religion is not only a set of activities. It is also (and some would say, essentially) a set of beliefs (ideas held to be true by one or more minds). To state and define those beliefs is a valuable and desirable goal for those who adhere to them. This is the task of "theology" in the case of a theistic belief system. At the same time, however, it may be even more basic to ask what method (what pattern of thinking) has been used to arrive at those beliefs. What claims can be made as to the truth-value of those beliefs? Is religion (or a system of religious beliefs) an adequate basis for making decisions relating to human activities?

How can anyone know the answer to questions such as these? How could one know whether or not these are the proper and most important questions to ask?

How should one evaluate religion? What are the important (life-changing) ideas? What and how important are the issues addressed by religion?

What value should be placed on a mind? How seriously should ideas be taken? Is it true that (and how could we know whether or not) the mind is "one of the most significant facts of existence."

Philosophy is characterized by this sort of basic, analytical questioning of ideas. If ideas are important, then philosophy is important. If ideas are not important, perhaps it would be important to discover that fact and to establish a basis (a set of ideas?) that could support such an evaluation. This latter process, however, would be self-defeating. How could one use ideas to show that ideas as such have no value? Thus ideas must have some value. Is this not an existentially undeniable rationale for philosophy as an academic discipline? It cannot be consistently denied that ideas have some importance, and philosophy is the study of ideas. Therefore, it cannot be consistently denied that "philosophy is of some importance."[1]

This same principle may be specifically extended to the philosophical study of religion and especially religious beliefs. Ideas are important, but religious ideas claim to be ultimately important. While such claims alone do not prove their validity, they would seem to demand study owing to the possibility that the claims could be justified. Some might refuse to study these ideas because of total ignorance of them. Others are simply guilty of ignoring them. The former can no longer be completely true if your mind exists.

---

[1]Not all philosophical study is of equal importance, because not all methods of study are equally valuable, but more significantly we must recognize that all ideas are not of equal importance.

## SELF-EXAMINATION

Now check yourself for comprehension by answering these questions without looking back at the previous essay. Remember to answer the questions according to what the essay says regardless of whether or not you think the essay is correct.

**True-False**

_____ 1. Value judgments are always based on concepts which can be analyzed.

_____ 2. Religion should not be the subject of philosophical study but is simply to be believed.

_____ 3. Religious ideas are important, but they make no exclusive or ultimate claims.

_____ 4. To ask why one believes is more basic than to ask what one believes.

_____ 5. If ideas are important, then philosophy is important.

**Briefly state the main argument offered as an answer to the question: "Why should anyone study the philosophy of religion?"**

_____

_____

_____

_____

_____

_____

_____

**Multiple choice:**

____ 1. "Mind" exists
   A. because there is no alternative view.
   B. by definition
   C. because it is existentially undeniable.

____ 2. Philosophy is
   A. a specific set of facts.
   B. a method of thinking.
   C. a self-defeating idea.

____ 3. Theology is
   A. an unimportant task.
   B. a relatively unimportant task.
   C. an essential part of all theistic belief.

____ 4. Philosophy teaches that
   A. religion is not an adequate basis for de-
      cision making.
   B. mind is only an illusion.
   C. ideas must be taken seriously.

____ 5. The argument leaves the reader
   A. with the choice of ignoring philosophy
      of religion.
   B. with no alternative except to study phi-
      losophy.
   C. with the choice of believing in God or
      of believing in nothing.

## REVIEW AND EVALUATION

After some introductory comments, you were introduced to a brief essay on the importance of studying
philosophy and, in particular, philosophy of religion. Then
you took a test in order to measure your level of understanding. Did you find the test easy? Or was the test hard or
confusing? What about the essay itself? After looking at it a

second time, did it seem easier to understand? (Remember that a Glossary is at the back of the book.) Do you agree with the essay's conclusions? Did you think the reasoning was valid?

Congratulations! Regardless of the answers you gave to the questions in the paragraph just above, you have now engaged successfully in the mental discipline called philosophy. You have thought about the ideas presented in an essay which discusses the nature and importance of religious ideas. You thought analytically, asking yourself first if you understood the essay and then if you agreed or did not agree. This is a simple introduction, but it is nevertheless an example of the kind of thinking that a philosopher of religion might do. In the next chapter we will look into these things a little more deeply. Welcome to an exciting adventure.

## Answers:

True–False: 1. T; 2. F; 3. F; 4. T; 5 T
Multiple Choice: 1. C; 2. B; 3. C; 4. C; 5. B

# PART ONE:

# Foundational Principles

# 1

# What is Philosophy?

*Asking Why*
*Who Are Philosophers?*
*Finding Answers*
*Why Study Philosophy?*

A philosophy course in an evangelical Christian school creates for some people a situation that may be described by an analogy with Daniel in the lion's den. Daniel did not want to be in that lion's den. None of the lions wanted Daniel in there. The lions would have eaten him if they could, and Daniel survived only by the grace of God.

Students may see themselves as "Daniels" being challenged by the lion-like philosophies of men. Professors, on the other hand, may see the students as lions and may pray for God to shut their mouths. Home churches may think of themselves as being like Darius. They made a "decree" that their children should go to college and especially that their young ministers ought to attend a seminary. Then they find out that these young Christians will be required to take a course in philosophy. They send their students on to the school anyway, but they anxiously pray; and then on graduation morning they come to ask, 'O Daniel, has your God preserved you from the lions?'

Probably no other field of study has been so frequently

criticized by Christian people as the field of philosophy. Yet if one were to ask the average Christian "What do philosophers talk about?" they probably could not answer with assurance. "I think philosophers are liberal," says one. "Philosophy will destroy your faith," says another. "Go on to the class," says yet another, "but just remember that you don't have to believe everything you hear."

Sound advice, or so it seems. But what is it that students might hear that will destroy their faith? Exactly what is the content of a course in philosophy? The question sounds simple enough. Why is it so hard to get a simple, straightforward answer?

It is difficult to explain what philosophy is because philosophy is not a self-contained discipline. Philosophy is more a method of thinking than a specific thing being thought. It is a way of thinking more than it is a specific idea. For example, the term "philosophy" is frequently attached to some other field of study. There is a philosophy of science, a philosophy of art, and a philosophy of history. There is also a philosophy of religion. When someone studies the "philosophy" of something, the content of the course is determined by the specific discipline involved, but the method of study is different from what might be done in the normal study within that discipline. The questions asked by the philosopher are more foundational, more basic, than the questions normally being asked by the practitioner of the discipline.

History can serve as an example. Most modern educational systems require some study of history. One may study the American Civil War or the History of Europe in the Middle Ages. In each case the course would include a survey of the events during the period of time designated. Not every event would be included in the study, however. Only those events that were considered to be important would be included. But wait a minute! How exactly does one decide which events are important? All historians seek to explain the events they are studying. But what is the proper way to explain events? Are events in history "caused" in the same way "scientific events" are caused? What is the nature of valid historical explanation? Are there historical "laws" comparable to scientific "laws," or is history better understood if we use descriptive methods patterned after the kinds of explanations that are appropriate in setting forth the meaning and value of art? Is there one and only one "true" explanation of the flow of events in history? Why do various historians provide different explanations for the same events? If we all had the same information, would we all come to the same conclusions? Is there a pattern in history? Are things moving in a certain direction or toward a definite goal?

History refers to the sum of human events, but in practice no one ever knows or thinks of each and every event. "History" in practice refers to those events that are made known to later generations by written accounts or by the preservation of artifacts and information from the past. Thus, historians try to produce a truthful, sequential account of particular past events. (Chronology is often but not always a necessary element of valid historical accounts.) Philosophy of history, on the other hand, is a study of the basic assumptions that make the study (and the valid and appropriate telling) of history possible.

From this brief illustration, it is already apparent that philosophy is a discipline that asks very basic questions, that seeks to clarify the underlying assumptions of various fields of study. There are, however, some basic assumptions or some fundamental questions that are common to all fields of study. These are the issues that define the so-called "philosophic enterprise."

## ASKING WHY?

It is common for people to think of philosophy and philosophers as being characteristically abstract and out of touch with reality. Nevertheless, what philosophy actually deals with is very important to all of us.

Everyone believes something about life. Some people may not spend much time worrying about it, but it does make a difference what we believe about the nature of the universe or the spectrum of human affairs. Those who do not ask or who do not care to ask the basic questions of life will never develop a perspective from which to determine the significance of their own activities and ideas.

Anyone who asks "Why?" is asking a question that

23

ultimately leads to basic philosophical issues. What "ought" we to believe and/or do? How do we know? What is truth? Why does not everyone agree about things? How can we know who (if anyone) is right? How should we distinguish between two viewpoints? How reliable are our opinions?

Many people simply accept without question certain traditional beliefs. Some people never question a reported scientific discovery or theory. Religious ideas are sometimes believed without question or analysis. Philosophers insist that all these things should be subjected to intensive analysis. If the idea or theory is found to be based on solid evidence, and if the views are consistent with other accepted truths, then the reasonable person may conclude that it is justifiable to believe the proposed idea or theory. But without such evidence or without rational support, the reasonable person may question the validity of some proposed idea.

Job accepted the theory that the universe was controlled by a good God. Yet he experienced a series of events that seemed to challenge those ideas. How could God be good when Job (God's servant) was suffering so? Job listened to the various theories expressed by his friends. (The discussions are classic examples of philosophic discourse.) Job's friends express traditional ideas about the nature of ultimate reality, and Job has to rethink these traditional ideas. The accepted system of belief was not adequate to account for what Job knew to be true. Several possible alternative theories are considered throughout the book, but none seems to satisfy. Thus Job concludes that human reason may not be adequate to deal with some of the basic issues of his life. He maintains his faith in God, for God personally reveals his sovereign presence, but Job never received the answer he sought to the intellectual problems raised by his experience.

In spite of Job's failure to get his answers, all who read the account are helped to examine their own life, and many gain new perspectives on their problems. Socrates, at his trial (399 B.C.), suggested that the unexamined life is not worth living. Many spend their life in the pursuit of wealth and fame. But are those things really important? Job found out that true values are not the material pleasures of life. What

24

really counts is discovered only when the most serious kind of questioning is directed toward the most serious issues of life.

Evil and suffering may be the most noticeable problem faced by people throughout history, but by no means is it the only one. The existence of evil raises the even more fundamental question of the nature of ultimate reality. In a very real sense evil would not even be an intellectual problem unless ultimate reality were thought of as being orderly and meaningful. If one believes that the universe is fundamentally a random conglomerate of chaotic matter, then the appearance of evil or massive suffering would have to be accepted as a natural and normal part of our situation. If the universe originated in a "Big Bang," then order and rationality need to be accounted for rather than the existence of randomness and evil.

These questions about the actual nature of the universe are generally grouped under the heading "Metaphysics." There is no absolute separation, however, between metaphysical questions and moral questions. Assuming that ultimate reality is chaos, what should we do in life? Or assuming that order is fundamental, how ought we to live?

Is there a great mind that directs the flow of events? How could we discover whether mind has produced matter or whether matter has produced mind? How do minds work anyway? Do they follow natural patterns of cause and effect? What theory of learning is best? What educational methods are best in light of "who" people are? Does it really make any difference how we teach the Bible in Sunday school? Are some types of sermons more effective than others? Why?

On what authority do we make religious claims? How can we justify our acceptance of that authority? What principles should be followed to guarantee the proper interpretation of that authority?

The philosopher of religion will not be satisfied with just any answer to these questions. He or she wants the right answers. The majority opinion may be wrong. The rational person wants to know what the best answer is, and that answer comes only after thoughtful consideration.

# WHO ARE PHILOSOPHERS?

Some of the world's greatest thinkers have been religious leaders, such as Augustine or Aquinas. Descartes was a mathematician and a devout Catholic. John Locke, a Protestant, and Karl Marx, an atheist, were political thinkers. Nevertheless, all of these writers have been called philosophers.

Many philosophers have been academicians; that is, they taught in the schools. For example, Kant and Hegel have had an unusual impact on the modern world through the influence they had upon the academic world. Others, such as Rousseau or Hume, had other arenas for their work. Nevertheless, western philosophy traces itself to the educated elite among the ancient Greeks.

But philosophy should not be treated exclusively in terms of a special series of names of writers that ought to be studied. Philosophy is more than just a study of historical essays. Philosophers are people of all kinds who ask a certain type of question and who seek to understand reality at various levels.

Have you ever wondered, for example, about the unusual parallels that we find in history? The Reformation in Germany is paralleled by the Renaissance in Italy. One is essentially theological and the other is related to architecture and art, but both are a rebirth of learning and both change the subsequent course of history. Both look back to their own original "sources." In the religious context this is a return to Scripture; in the artistic context this is a return to classical Greek art forms.

Another example of intellectual parallelism can be seen during the last century. Hegel's developmental pantheism dominated the nineteenth century intellectually. Old Testament higher criticism in its modern form blossomed in nineteenth century Germany and displays a striking resemblance to Hegelian ideas. In 1859 Darwin proposed a believable mechanism for a theory of biological, evolutionary development that also parallels Hegel's dialectic. Post-millennialism grew in popularity among theological conservatives during the late 1800s, just as Hegel's optimism dominated the philosophical world. All of these ideas claimed that

26

they were based on independent, careful, and impartial study of the relevant data. Yet they all seem to have a common optimism about progress in history. Simple ideas or simple life forms were thought to be older, but complex ideas or complex life forms were thought to be relatively recent developments in the inevitably progressive nature of things. Are we really to believe that all these ideas, which unquestionably are different from the ideas in previous centuries, were unrelated to what might be called the "spirit of the age"? How can one fail to see that a study of the dominant philosophy of an era is essential to a full understanding of that era?

Each of the ancient civilizations had legends and mythologies by which they explained the world. Today most of those ideas are no longer accepted. In fact most science books are out of date if they were published more than twenty years ago (in some cases ten or five). These ancient mythologies or these older textbooks conflict with theories held today. Yet people generally accept current theories as being true. Why are the ancient ideas no longer accepted? Is it because they were based upon insufficient evidence? Is it because they could not account for facts that people subsequently discovered to be true about the world? What makes us think that the ideas we accept today will not fall into disrepute just as ancient ideas have done?

Generally speaking it was a philosopher who first challenged those "traditional" beliefs of the ancient civilizations. Much to the dismay of their contemporaries, the philosophers raised controversial issues. They pointed out inconsistencies. They demanded proof. They sought better theories.

Philosophers are doing this today. Many people do not like having their notions challenged. Scientists do not like having their theories challenged. Historians do not like having their explanations challenged. Psychologists do not like having their ideas challenged. Most especially, professional people do not like someone outside their specific specialty doing the challenging. Christians do not like having their beliefs challenged. So everybody "dislikes" the philosopher because he or she has no hesitance about raising questions. A philosopher does not consider any specialty to be off limits to probing questions. Philosophers are not always right in their conclusions. They have prejudices and personal perspectives, just like everyone else. They do not always ask the right questions. But they do ask important questions, and they do provoke thought, and that is not always bad.

## FINDING ANSWERS

Philosophy is famous for asking questions. But philosophers also (one hopes) find some answers. They do not always claim certainty for their answers. Sometimes they come up with "warranted assertions" or "justified opinions." Seldom do they claim to have final or absolute answers. This in itself causes a kind of dismay among their contemporaries.

Most people seek definite and simple answers. If a philosopher explains that the problem is more complex than people think it is, or if he or she points out weaknesses in every answer that has yet been suggested, people frequently have an emotional response. They become defensive and begin to justify themselves and their beliefs. Apparently, the most common human need is the need to "save face." No one likes to admit to being wrong. The evidence can be totally against them, and they still plead innocent. Few will admit to making a mistake. Even fewer will admit that they hold "false assumptions." But it is an obvious fact that people disagree; someone must be wrong (unless one concludes that there is no right or wrong; in which case even that conclusion could not be right).

Philosophers are also frequently wrong. There is no magical truth formula that makes philosophers right in every case. In fact the clearest examples of ideas being tested for truth come from the history of philosophy. Aristotle disagreed with his teacher Plato. Descartes and Locke held opposite views on the nature of the mind and the question of whether the mind contained innate ideas. Hegel and Kierkegaard took opposite positions on the nature of life and history, while Marx simply accepted Hegel's system but replaced the spiritual element by a material one. All of these

28

views cannot be right. All might be wrong, but all cannot be right!

One tremendous value of studying philosophy is not that you learn to agree with the latest thinker, but that you can learn to see various viewpoints. Ideas have consequences, and philosophy tends to force these ideas and their consequences to be clearly spelled out. Philosophers think and write in such a way that they work out the details of their views. We can see where various ideas lead by reading philosophy. We can see positions critiqued by other clear and careful thinkers. We can see implications that we might not notice otherwise. We can expand our own ability to understand ideas. We can learn the strengths and weaknesses of various theories. We can, we hope, learn to express our own ideas in their strongest form. We can learn not to open ourselves up to unnecessary criticism that comes because of sloppy speech, writing, or thinking on our part.

## WHY STUDY PHILOSOPHY?

Philosophy has an instrumental value. It is a tool that can help us to better understand our world. Philosophy as such is not a set of answers. It is a method of seeking answers. It does not answer all questions, but it does raise and seek answers to the most basic questions. Who am I? Where am I going? Why am I here? What is the nature of reality? What should I do? How can I know truth?

These are the fundamental questions of life itself. Metaphysical, moral, and epistemological questions dominate us whether we have ever heard that terminology before or not. The philosophers have influenced us whether we know a single one of them by name or not. We do not think like previous generations. Our attitudes are different, our concepts are different, and our worldview is different. The philosophers brought about those changes. In some instances it has been for the good. In other instances we may be much worse off than we would have been otherwise.

Why study philosophy? In order to make us use our God-given minds; in order to make us clarify our ideas and viewpoints; in order to help us know what the questions are to which Christ is the answer. All truth is God's truth. As we are better able to perceive the issues, as we are more informed about the nature of truth, as we clarify the "why" questions of life, we express our God-created uniqueness, we prepare ourselves to fulfill our Lord's commission, and we enable ourselves to fulfill a task assigned to us in Holy Scripture (cf. 1 Peter 3:15).

Paul warns against false philosophy. He knew what he was talking about. He knew exactly why that philosophy was dangerous. He even describes the basic assumptions on which it was built (cf. Colossians 2:8). Evidently he had made a thorough study of it. Then he offers an alternative, a philosophy built on Christ, and he describes the merits of that philosophy in great detail.

Philosophy is a way of thinking that emphasizes precision, analysis, careful consideration of the alternatives, and rational consistency as well as empirical adequacy. Philosophy concentrates on the basic presuppositions that underlie all thought. Its field of inquiry may be science, history, religion, or something else. But in every case its standards, rigid demands, and careful logical procedures are the same.

So often, where one starts has a great bearing on where one ends up. At least the starting point has a lot to say about the intellectual path to be taken. The role of reason is also an important point of evaluation in a system of thought. The test for truth is a crucial issue that must constantly be evaluated. These and other vital issues make up the everyday pattern of thought for the philosopher. Even if the Bible is believed to be infallibly true, the philosopher may still legitimately ask, "How do we know that it is true?" (This question may truly seek an answer rather than merely express doubt.)

Finally and invariably the issues return to epistemology (one's theory of knowledge itself). Philosophy is not limited to the question of knowledge as such, but it is never far removed from it. How do we know what we know? That is an important question.

Life can go on for the one who never asks the "why" questions. But can that life be worth living? So many people of all ages simply deny the gift of rationality as they refuse to be bothered with the problem of justifying what they believe. Hasty or lazy thinking may be common, but is it worthwhile?

Philosophers say no. Job could have cursed God and died. But he chose to rethink his beliefs. In doing so he grew in maturity, and he received God's high approval.

The philosophical task is not easy, but for those who treasure the gift of rationality that God has granted mankind, it is a necessary, profitable, and even a spiritually maturing task.

# GLOSSARY

Advancement
Agnostic
Analogy
Ancient Near East
Aristotle
Classical Period
Critical
Cynic
Dialectic
Enlightenment
Epicureanism
Epistemology
Existentialism
Hedonism
Hellenism
History
Idea
Interpretation
Knowledge

Language Analysis
Middle Ages
New Age
Pantheism
Philosophy
Plato
Popular Culture
Postmillennialism
Reformation
Religion
Renaissance
Scholasticism
Secular
Socrates
Stoicism
Theism
Truth
Value
Verification Principle

2

# How to Study Philosophy

*Philosophical Issues*
*Metaphysics*
*Morals*
*Epistemology*

When one reads a textbook or an essay in philosophy there are always certain questions that should be asked.

## What Am I Reading?

What does the title of the book, chapter, or essay mean?

Is this writer famous for holding or presenting a controversial opinion? What (if anything) do I know about the writer?

Is this an essay defending some particular point of view?

Is it an attempt to simply describe the beliefs of others (a textbook)?

Which parts of the reading are descriptive and which parts express the author's own evaluation?

33

What is the subject being addressed by the author? Is this subject relevant to my life? To the lives of other people? Who?

Is this reading treating an important subject? Why or why not?

## What Does the Terminology Mean?

Are there terms in the text that I do not understand?

Did the writer give the definition of the term earlier in the essay or in some other chapter in the book?

Do I understand the definitions as they are stated by the author?

Is a glossary of terms and definitions at the end of the volume?

## What Is (Are) the Writer's Conclusion(s)?

Can I distinguish between factual statements and statements of opinion?

Do I understand why the author wrote this material?

Is the author able to express ideas clearly? Does the writer set forth specific conclusions and defend them or is the conclusion left open-ended so as to let the reader make up his or her own mind about the matter?

## Why Did He or She Come to That Conclusion?

Does the author seem to have the facts straight?

Are there other authors that reach different conclusions about the same issues?

Does the author acknowledge other views and does he or she fairly characterize the views of others?

Is the author's reasoning valid?

**Do I Agree?**

Why?

Why not?

## FIVE QUESTIONS

According to the Bible, God made human beings in a special way. The biblical language is very picturesque as it says "Let us make man in our own image and after our likeness." Few theological terms have been so frequently studied and so differently interpreted as the term "God's image." But surely if it means anything, it means that man is somehow similar to God. God is the original; man is the copy. A true copy does not need to be a duplicate. Man is in every way limited and God is in no way limited, yet some basic and fundamental similarity exists.

Animals are not said to have been made in God's image. Thus the similarity of human beings to God seems not to be primarily in those aspects of their being in which they are similar to the animals. Their physical finiteness and biological functions apparently are closely related to animal life, but their mental and spiritual capacities clearly distinguish them from the animal world. Animals have emotions; they love and protect. Animals have a memory; they learn both by trial and error and by imitation. But the human mind is not just slightly more complex than the "smartest" animal's. It is qualitatively different.

Human beings are self-conscious; they have an awareness of a relationship to God, an ability to engage in extremely complex communication at the literal level as well as in a vast network of figurative levels, and each person is uniquely somebody. No two people have exactly the same personality. Each human being is unique and each person recognizes his or her uniqueness.

Since our Lord commissioned us to teach his truth, we must first learn his truth. But all of our human uniqueness comes into play at this very point. How should we study? And how do we learn? There are two basic answers to the second question: (1) We learn by our own experience which

35

we interpret in our minds, and (2) we learn by reading what others have written or by hearing what they say or by seeing what they do. Human knowledge, such as it is, is thus either (1) first-hand knowledge or (2) it comes from someone else's experience. For the purposes of this discussion the second category will be limited to written sources that are available for study.

So brief an essay as this cannot even attempt to get into the complexities of answer number one. The nature of experience and the various methods of seeking true interpretations of our experience are some of the primary themes of the whole field of philosophy and especially philosophy of religion. At this point it will simply be assumed that true interpretations are possible.

Answer number two is similarly complex because each writer has either had an experience which he/she is interpreting, or he/she is relaying the various interpretations of others, or he/she is comparing and evaluating interpretations. Philosophy, as an intellectual discipline, is very much concerned with the process of evaluation. Philosophical questions are for the most part "why" questions rather than "what" questions (though often one cannot properly ask the one until the other is correctly known).

American students are rather adept at gathering facts by the time they reach post-secondary schools. Nevertheless, philosophy is never merely fact-gathering, and many students do not find their course work in philosophy to be easy because of the nature of the inquiry itself. Yet there is a level at which some guidelines for the study of philosophy can be given, and, for our purposes, this level will be sufficiently important. **The questions many students ask are: "How do I know what I am supposed to learn? How do I know what is important? How can anybody understand philosophy anyway?"**

Let us go back and look in greater detail at the five suggestions given earlier. First, **what type of reading is involved?** There are various types. Some books, called "secondary" sources, are descriptive of the thoughts and writings of others. "Primary" sources are those written by the philosophers themselves. Sometimes these writings are very simple. The importance of an idea is not measured

36

solely by its complexity. At the same time it is true that profound ideas are usually more complex than our ordinary casual conversation. So it is essential that we concentrate when we read and study. Reading philosophy can seldom be effectively done while our attention is diverted to other things, and it should especially not be attempted while watching television. Serious thinking cannot co-exist with wholesale trivialities.

What is being read? One should look at the table of contents, at the title and subtitles, and at the overall structure of the material. What basic issues are being discussed? Some of the most frequent issues addressed in religious philosophical writing are theories about the nature of ultimate reality, the nature of man and morality, and theories about how one gains knowledge. What is ultimately real, does God exist, what is humanity's place in the universe, and how does one know truth?

In order to concentrate on the reading, one must recognize where the writer (or the person being studied) comes in the history of thought. Did he or she write prior to the modern era? Was the writer a Renaissance figure, a nineteenth century thinker, a medieval scholar? Is he or she a modern theologian, an existentialist, a realist?

Each historical period of thought seems to be dominated by certain trends. For example, the nineteenth century clearly was caught up in theories of optimistic progressivism. Progress was the key idea. It is not that other centuries had no optimistic thinkers, but the nineteenth century seems to have been especially intoxicated by the idea. To recognize such a trend is not the same thing as proving it to be false. There is always the possibility that true insight might not be limited to our generation. Thus it is a very superficial analysis to say, for example, that Darwin was wrong (or right) simply because he was a product of his century. His evolutionary theories were surely consistent with the temper of the age. So much so in fact that it should cause us to carefully analyze the adequacy of his interpretive system. But an interpretive framework is not necessarily false simply because it is consistent with an intellectual trend in history. However, it should be subject to the most searching analysis if it is in fact a theory that is closely aligned with a certain type of thought that characterized a particular historical era.

John Dewey, a famous and influential philosopher of education, was born in the very year of Darwin's publication of *On the Origin of Species*. Dewey is obviously persuaded by naturalistic theories of reality, and his educational theories are direct applications of Darwinist principles. One will not fully understand Dewey or modern educational theories if one does not recognize these historical and intellectual relationships. Furthermore, no thorough critique of Dewey should fail to mention the influence of Darwinism on his ideas. He is not wrong (or right) merely because of these influences, but our final evaluation of Dewey (or of any important thinker) must recognize the context of the writer's thought in order to fully understand what it is that we are reading.

What am I reading? When, where, and who? All of these questions are important. We should study the details, yes, but we must always put those details in the broadest possible perspective.

Do not be overly critical at first. Read to learn. Even the atheist or the heretic may teach us something if only by raising questions to which we are forced to find answers. Frequently, however, in our fear of being kidnapped by false philosophy, we never even hear the questions being raised. Thus we never find the answers, and we fail to preach those answers except by accident. Paul does warn us against false philosophy, but we can not heed his warning if we have no concept of what we are to avoid. False philosophy may not obviously oppose Christ. Sometimes the most dangerous philosophy of all is that which seems on the surface to be compatible with the gospel but upon close analysis is found to be deadly. One cannot remain ignorant of philosophy and thus be protected. The best defense is a clear and certain knowledge of the enemy's thoughts.

Understanding the thoughts of the philosophers is exactly the point of the second general question that should guide our study of philosophy. **What does the strange language of philosophy mean?** First, remember that every academic discipline has its own terminology. Even a hobby has a specialized vocabulary. Philosophy as an academic

38

discipline is not to be feared simply because of the unusual language.

Every student needs a good dictionary. Better yet, every student should *use* a good dictionary. Beyond that, students need to read good introductions. Usually these introductory surveys will provide clear discussions of key terms and ideas. A specialized glossary is an invaluable aid for the beginning student. The best way to learn the terminology is to get the definition and then read a discussion that puts the term in context.

Any discussion in philosophical literature is likely to end up by taking a position or at least making some type of evaluation. Sometimes the supposedly neutral or objective description of an idea will be so worded as to make it seem strong or weak. In other words, argument, persuasion, analysis, and evaluation are so much a part of philosophical thinking that the student must constantly be on guard. **Always ask what the author's conclusions are.** Never assume objectivity. Remember that conclusions are not necessarily wrong. It is not wrong to have opinions, but it is a poor student who reads a philosophical essay and does not recognize what conclusions have been drawn.

This leads to the fourth major step in studying philosophy. **Ask why those conclusions were drawn.** What reasons were given? It will always be helpful to mark these reasons in the margin of the text or to write them out to make them more clearly visible. Frequently there are also unexpressed reasons. All minds work with sets of presuppositions. Attitudes and fundamental viewpoints are not always expressed openly. This is not in every instance an attempt to deceive. Some basic attitudes are so deeply ingrained that a person may not even recognize the possibility of other perspectives. Those things that seem too obvious to mention are exactly those things for which the good student will look. What are the author's basic presuppositions? What are his stated and unstated reasons for drawing certain conclusions? It is often just as important to know why someone has certain opinions as it is to know what these opinions are. For example, it is more important to know why neo-orthodox theologians disagree with Thomas Aquinas than simply to know that they do disagree with him.

As a final stage in the study of philosophy, one should reflect upon the first four stages. After we have clearly recognized exactly what type of literature we are reading, having fully understood the material, and having recognized the author's conclusions **our task now is to make a personal evaluation**. Are the author's conclusions valid? What are his or her strong points? What are his or her weaknesses? Are some of his or her views correct while others are not? What reasons can be given for other viewpoints? Remember that emotional statements such as "I don't agree" are of little value by themselves unless the speaker is infallible. What we need are reasons why we do not agree or, better yet, reasons why some other view would be better.

# PHILOSOPHICAL ISSUES

Below are listed a few of the representative issues that are included in the field of philosophy.

## Metaphysics

What is the universe?

How did the universe come to be?

Can reality be classified as a unity or is it fundamentally plural?

Is ultimate reality stable or is it constantly in flux?

Is matter or mind more basic?

What is the relationship between mind and matter?

Is there such a thing as free will?

Are all things determined?

What is the nature of cause and effect?

Does God exist?

Why does anything exist at all?

What is real?

## Morals

Does a moral law or a moral reality actually exist?

How do we explain the existence of evil?

Are there any ethical absolutes?

What is the nature and source of "oughtness"?

Are ethics subjective or objective?

Is there a universal norm for moral activity?

How should we act? How should we live?

Why should anything be judged right or wrong?

What is right?

## Epistemology

What is knowledge?

What can be known?

How do we achieve and recognize reliable knowledge?

What is the status of universal ideas?

What is the source of knowledge?

How are appearance and reality related?

Can we reach certainty in any area of thought?

Are there any absolutes in any realm of reality?

Is reality objective or subjective?

What is the status of knowledge claims?

Do minds have innate ideas?

Are any of the various theories of knowledge valid?

What are the basic principles of logic?

How can we recognize fallacies in reasoning?

What evidence do we have for or against the existence of God?

41

How could we know if there is or is not an infallible source of religious truth?

What place does faith play in coming to know truth?

How can there be so many different opinions about the same facts?

How is faith related to reason?

Are there different kinds of truth?

Can two contradictory things both be true?

Is religious truth a unique type of truth?

What would it mean to believe that truth is unity?

Why believe anything at all?

What is true? What is truth?

## GLOSSARY

Absolute
Aesthetics
Axiology
Being
Contradiction
Determinism
Dualism
Epistemology
Essence
Ethics
Evidence
Existence
Faith
Flux
God
Innate

Knowledge
Matter
Metaphysics
Nihilism
Objective
Ontology
Person
Pluralism
Reality
Reason
Relative
Religion
Semantics
Subjective
Substance
Teleology

42

# A BRIEF BIBLIOGRAPHY OF SELECTED SOURCES FOR FURTHER STUDY

Brown, Colin. *Philosophy and the Christian Faith*. Downers Grove: InterVarsity, 1968.

Browne, M. Neil and Keeley, Stuart M. *Asking the Right Questions: A Guide to Critical Thinking*. 3rd ed. Englewood Cliffs: Prentice Hall, 1990.

Bush, L. Russ. *Classical Readings in Christian Apologetics: A.D. 100-1800*. Grand Rapids. Zondervan, 1983.

Craig, William Lane. *Apologetics: An Introduction*. Chicago: Moody, 1984.

Cunningham, Richard B. *The Christian Faith and Its Contemporary Rivals*. Nashville: Broadman, 1988.

Evans, C. Stephen. *Philosophy of Religion: Thinking about Faith*. Downers Grove: InterVarsity, 1983.

Geisler, Norman. *Christian Apologetics*. Grand Rapids: Baker, 1976.

Hoffecker, W. Andrew and Smith, Gary Scott, eds. *Building A Christian World View*. 2 vols. Phillipsburg: Presbyterian and Reformed, 1986, 1988.

Holmes, Arthur F. *Contours of a World View*. Grand Rapids: Eerdmans, 1983.

Hunnex, Milton D. *Chronological and Thematic Charts of Philosophies and Philosophers*. Grand Rapids: Zondervan, 1986.

Moreland, J. P. *Scaling the Secular City*. Grand Rapids: Baker, 1987.

Nash, Ronald. *Faith and Reason*. Grand Rapids: Zondervan, 1988.

Newport, John P. *Life's Ultimate Questions*. Dallas: Word, 1989.

Ramm, Bernard L. *A Christian Appeal to Reason*. Waco: Word, 1972.

See also references cited in footnotes throughout the various chapters of this book.

**3**

# Learning to Think Logically

*Deductive Logic*
*Inductive Logic*
*Fallacies Associated with Induction*
*Using Logic in Biblical Exegesis*
*Logic in the Bible*

A person who lives by habit or by uncritically following the traditional social customs of his or her peer group is not a philosopher. One begins to philosophize when one begins to reflect upon his or her experiences, beliefs, and/or traditions. Critical reflection is the motivational key to philosophy.

If one sets out to evaluate the basis and nature of his or her own conduct or the conduct of others, then one is engaging in moral philosophy. Reflection upon the nature, the function, and/or the purpose of the universe itself (as a whole or in terms of the things that make up the various parts of the universe) makes one a metaphysical thinker. To turn inward and reflect upon knowledge itself (analyzing the assumptions that support various beliefs and studying the structure of rational thought) is to involve oneself in epistemological issues.

Logic is basic to all of these categories of philosophical thought, because in every case conclusions of some kind are drawn on the basis of reasons or in light of the implications of the relevant cognitive evidence. Logic is a guide to the various methods by which reasons or statements of evidence are properly related to conclusions.

Are there any "laws" of thought? Are there any guidelines to teach us how to think properly and how to arrive at truth? Rational beliefs are not necessarily true merely because they are rational. Nonrational beliefs are not necessarily false. But rational beliefs are strengthened by their rationality, and nonrational beliefs must have some other persuasive element if they are to be justifiably accepted.

A person may hold a true opinion, the grounds for which he or she may not recognize. Ancient people correctly anticipated a regular sunrise and a high tide and a cold winter long before the actual reasons for the predictability of these phenomena were understood. One might also hold an opinion which seems at the time to be based upon adequate evidence but, upon further analysis, is found to be based upon inadequate or non-existent reasons. Such a belief would appear to be rational when in fact it is nonrational. (It would be difficult to give current examples of this since we would have no obvious way to recognize such beliefs, but there are many historical examples.) It is also possible that one may have a belief that is supported by various reasons, with no known evidence to the contrary, and yet it may turn out to be false though it would appear still to be rational. For example, it is not irrational to believe in universal salvation or in conditional immortality, but these beliefs may well turn out to be false even though they are rational and are supported by some strong reasons. Traditional belief in the existence of a permanent state of perdition for those who die unrepentant is also rational and based on strong reasons. Clearly we need some guidelines to help us through this maze of "thinking."

How do we distinguish a good argument from a poor one? As we have said above, rationality is not the same as truth, and nonrationality is not the same as falsity. Yet it would not make sense to seek truth without following rational procedures.

Rational beliefs are those known to be directly support- ed by strong reasons and persuasive evidence. Rational inquiry is a process of discovering which beliefs are rational.

46

Various disciplines have established different kinds of knowledge to be sought. Each field of study, such as science or history, has its own subject matter, and correspondingly each has its own method of inquiry. But the principles of rational thinking are common to all types of inquiry.

"Logic" as the term is being used here should not be thought of as a branch of psychology but as a branch of philosophy. In other words, logic is not merely a descriptive study of how people actually think; it is a persuasively prescriptive study of how people ought to think. Logic is a philosophical inquiry into the "laws of thought" in the sense that it tries to discover and state the necessary relationships between various kinds of statements.

A so-called "stream of consciousness" is the most common type of thinking, but logic deals with the special type of thinking known as "reasoning." This type of thinking is characterized by the production of reasons as evidence for some conclusion. The reasons must be related to the conclusion in such a way that the conclusion can actually be inferred from them. In other words, the conclusion must follow from the reasons given, even to the point of being required by those reasons.

Ordinary thinking frequently follows a simple pattern of suggestion or of an association of ideas. People seldom engage in logical thinking in the sense being described here. Nevertheless, if our thinking is to be reliable we must learn to recognize distinct ideas. We must learn to discover the necessary relationships between our initial ideas and the further ideas that are entailed by the ones already being considered. In this way we seek to discover what is right and what is wrong. This "seeking in order to find" is especially important in religious studies.

Sometimes this process is mentally exhausting. It is especially hard for those whose normal conversation is the clever repetition of the ideas of others. But let us not limit ourselves to gossip, news, or chitchat. Even among professionals, careful reasoning and logical analysis are often not employed. The content of many sermons is the content of commentaries parroted. Many public prayers are rearrangements of a standard list of phrases. Many group Bible studies are merely discussions of standard topics (along with a few illustrations of these topics) related to the actual theology of the Bible only by a process of casual mental association. Some of us need to be more creative. Clear thinking, however, is a first step toward creative thinking.

There is a great difference between a walk for pleasure and walking toward some definite destination. A destination will motivate us to stay on the right trail. We may be tempted to turn aside to see this or that, but if we have somewhere to go we are less likely to wander around daydreaming. The destination of philosophical thinking is the answer to some genuine question. The formulation of an argument is the process by which we seek to answer the proposed question.

The term "argument" is ambiguous. In this context it has nothing to do with emotional disagreements, disputes, or quarrels. A logical argument consists of a group of two or more propositions that are related to each other in such a way that one of them follows from the other(s). Initial propositions are called "premises." The final proposition that is supposedly entailed by the premises is called the "conclusion." Premises are statements of the "reasons leading to" or of the "evidence that supports" the conclusion.

Logic is a study of the rules of inference. Logic sets forth descriptive ways that we can know when a conclusion actually follows from the premises. The primary issue in pure logic is the nature of the relationship between the premises and the conclusion. The question of the truth of the premises is another matter. Truth is an important philosophical issue. But logical correctness or incorrectness is unrelated to the truthfulness of the premises.

To summarize the discussion so far: logic is the study of the "laws" or principles that govern rational thinking. To show that a conclusion necessarily follows from the premises of the argument is not the same as showing the conclusion to be true. There are other factors involved, not the least of which is the necessity of showing the truth of the premises. But logic points out definite rules that can be applied to determine if an argument is valid; that is, if the conclusion follows from or is required by the premises (whether or not the premises are true). Validity (logical correctness) and invalidity (logical incorrectness) describe the logical relationships involved, not the truth content. Nevertheless, logical analysis is a valuable procedure. It does lead us to believe that if the premises are true, then the necessary conclusion drawn validly from those premises should be true (in the case of a deductive argument) or that the conclusion is probably true (in the case of an inductive argument).

# DEDUCTIVE LOGIC

A valid deductive argument is one in which the conclusion logically cannot be false if the premises are true. In other words, the conclusion necessarily follows from the premises. A definitive characteristic of deductive arguments is that all the information or factual content of the conclusion must be contained in the premises. The conclusion of a valid deductive argument is nothing more than a clarification or an explication of the information contained in the premises. For example:

**All adult human beings have sinned.**
**I am an adult human being.**
**Therefore, I have sinned.**

The first premise names a category (adult humans) and makes a true statement about all (each one) of the members of that category. Since I am one of those members, the statement must apply to me. If all (every) A is B, then whenever an instance of A is identified, it will be necessary to acknowledge that this A is B. Let us look at another example, however, that seems to be logically valid but does not lead to an acceptable conclusion.

**Nothing good can come out of Nazareth.**
**Jesus came out of Nazareth.**
**Therefore, Jesus cannot be something good.**

Logically the argument is perfect. All of the information found in the conclusion (marked by the logical sign "therefore") is already contained in the premises. The first premise is a universal statement of which the second premise is a particular instance. Thus the subject of the second premise must necessarily partake of the universal characteristic affirmed in the first premise. If the premises are true, the conclusion must be true. The conclusion might be true even if the premises are false, but other reasons would need to be given in order to prove or disprove that. As it stands, the conclusion is true if the premises are true. There is no alternative. The conclusion is required by the premises. One (or both) of the premises may be false. If so, then the conclusion is not necessarily true. But the argument is nevertheless a valid deductive argument.[1]

Deductive validity is an all-or-nothing affair. There are no degrees of validity. Either the premises entail the conclusion or they do not. Another example may show this more clearly.

**The Messiah will be raised from the dead.**
**Jesus was raised from the dead.**
**Therefore, Jesus is the Messiah.**

Obviously this argument is invalid and fallacious even though Christians believe that the premises and the conclusion are all true. The form of the argument is not valid, however. As it is stated, this is something like saying:

**All dogs have fleas.**
**My cat has fleas.**
**Therefore my cat is a dog.**

There is nothing necessary about the conclusion at all, even though the conclusion does not include any new items of information. The description of Jesus in the conclusion of the original argument (that he is the Messiah) may be true (in fact we are convinced as Christians that it is true), but it cannot be shown to be true by these premises alone. Both

---

[1]Bible scholars recognize this argument from the first chapter of John's Gospel. Nathanael was aware that the Messiah was to come from Bethlehem, not Nazareth, and since he knew only that Jesus was from Nazareth, he did not believe that Jesus could be the Messiah. Interestingly, Jesus persuaded Nathanael that he (Jesus) was the Messiah without explaining about his birth in Bethlehem. Nevertheless, the truth of the conclusion in the argument above depends upon the truth of the premises. In this case, in relevant ways, both premises are either false or at best only partial truths. Jesus could be and in fact was the Jewish Messiah.

premises are particular statements. They may or may not be related. Lazarus was also raised from the dead. Does that make Lazarus the Messiah? But the raising of Lazarus was different from the raising of Jesus, says the Christian. That difference is not stated in the premises, however. At best these premises would lead to the conclusion that Jesus could possibly be the Messiah. But the term "possibly" is enough to rule out certainty; the argument, therefore, is not deductively valid. Both of the premises and the conclusion of the claim about Jesus may be (in fact they are) true, but the argument is nevertheless logically invalid. Some other premises must be added to make the argument valid.[2]

A deductive argument never leads only to a probable conclusion if the argument is valid. Deductive logic is a form of necessary inference. Mathematical argument is deductive. Euclidean geometry deduces its theorems from various axioms and definitional postulates. Valid deduction leads to certain conclusions. If the premises are propositions that correctly express the nature of reality, then the conclusion also directly relates to the true nature of things. Ambiguous or false premises lead to uncertain conclusions. Invalid deduction leads to uncertain conclusions. Deduction is a valuable mental tool, but it does not address every relevant issue.

## INDUCTIVE LOGIC

An inductive argument is one in which the conclusion is probably true if the premises are true. In other words, the conclusion does not necessarily follow from the premises, but it probably does. A definitive characteristic of inductive arguments is that the conclusion contains information that is not present or goes beyond the scope of the premises. The conclusion of a correct inductive argument is intended to extend the range of our knowledge beyond the information contained in the premises. For example:

---

[2]Remember: truth and logical validity are distinct concepts. They are often related, but they are not synonymous, and they must be carefully distinguished.

**Adam sinned.**
**Cain sinned.**
**Seth sinned.**
**. . . etc.**
**Therefore all have sinned.**

This conclusion makes a universal statement about all humans. The factual premises, however, do not technically justify this conclusion. Every human is not named, and even one unnamed or unknown exception would seemingly challenge the reference to "all." We would have good reason, however, to believe this particular conclusion to be true even if we were not aware that this conclusion was a divine affirmation (a revealed premise).

By induction we compile a list of factual statements and draw from those particular facts a more general (even a universal) conclusion. The particulars support the conclusion, and when the facts are relevant and substantial, they give compelling evidence for and add persuasive force to the conclusion. In an inductive argument, however, the conclusion always goes beyond the technical limits of the evidence.

Consider the following argument:

**Experience and experiment show that what goes up must come down.**

This inductive argument was believed to be true throughout recorded history. But today even a child can tell you about earth orbits and planetary fly-bys and "Voyager" and the rest. On the other hand, consider this bit of theological reasoning:

**Every relevant archaeological discovery has confirmed the historical truthfulness of the Bible.**
**Therefore, the Bible is historically inerrant.**

By way of contrast with the valid deductive argument, it is quite possible for the premise of this inductive argument to be true and for the conclusion to be false. The premise actually means "Every . . . discovery so far. . . . " If at some future time an archaeological excavation uncovered something that proved that some historical portion of the Bible was incorrectly recorded or that false affirmations had been made concerning historical events, the conclusion would be seen to have been false all along. If there are historical errors in the Bible, then the conclusion is false even if the premise is (and in the future remains) true. The fact that no historical errors have been proven so far, and the fact that archaeology has shown a broad and a genuine historical reliability to be characteristic of the biblical materials does, however, lend a great deal of weight to the conclusion.

The conclusion is supported by the premise. The conclusion, nevertheless, makes a statement that goes beyond the actual evidence given in the premise. There are many historical claims in the Bible that do not relate to any archaeological studies so far conducted. Further, there are many historical claims in Scripture that would not likely be capable of archaeological confirmation or disconfirmation. It may surely be that the conclusion is true (and most evangelical Christians believe that the Bible is historically truthful without any mixture of error), but this premise alone (regarding archaeological confirmation of historical claims) is not enough to guarantee the truth of this conclusion.

It is important to realize that the closer the archaeologists come to that point at which they will have exhausted the relevant possibilities for further study, or the closer they come to an exhaustive confirmation of the relevant biblical claims, the more probable the conclusion of inerrancy becomes.

The possibility of error in this or in any other inductive argument lies in that "extra information" in the conclusion that goes beyond the information contained in the premises. When or if the premises become universal with respect to the conclusion, the argument would become deductively certain. An inductively drawn conclusion will be based on various degrees of strength or various levels of probability depending upon the amount of support the premises provide for the conclusion. An inductive argument would be invalid if the premises were deceptive or if they did not support the conclusion. We debate inductively drawn conclusions, because we do not all agree on the likelihood of completing the induction successfully with the conclusion remaining intact and unaltered.

# FALLACIES ASSOCIATED WITH INDUCTION

The simplest and most common type of inductive argument is known as "induction by enumeration." A conclusion about all instances is drawn from premises which refer to a certain observed number (fewer than all) of the possible instances. This is a correct form of the inductive argument.

Food inspectors, for example, use a "spot-check" method. They do not examine every can of beans. They take a sample number of cans and check them. If the sample cans are found to meet the health standards, then all the cans will be assumed to meet the same standards.

**Every bean observed in the sample was found to meet the health standards.**
**Therefore, all the beans in this group meet the health standard.**

"All," "every," "each," and "no" are universal terms meaning either 100 or 0 percent of the instances. These terms, however, are not always used in a universal generalization. In the example above, the premise is that some percentage of the total number of beans other than 100 or 0 percent was actually observed. This makes the conclusion a statistical generalization. Thus the conclusion will only be as probable as the premises are representative. If only two peanuts were tested and both were bad, the conclusion might be drawn that the whole bagful is bad. But it may also be the case that the only two bad peanuts in the whole bag were inadvertently chosen to be tested. (This error could be avoided if a larger data sample were tested.)

The process just described of drawing a conclusion from a non-representative sample is the fallacy of "jumping to a conclusion."[3] Technically this version of "jumping to a conclusion" involves the "fallacy of insufficient statistics." Prejudice arises from sweeping generalizations made on the basis of an insufficient survey of the evidence. The common gripe about the postal service is a classic example. On the basis of a few delayed letters the whole system is judged to

---

[3]A "fallacy" is a logically incorrect argument.

be incompetent. No one seems to remember the hundreds of thousands of mail items that do not get lost and that do reach their destination on time. To say, "the postal system doesn't work" is to jump to a conclusion arising from the fallacy of insufficient statistics. It is more precise to say, "The postal system doesn't always work in the proper way." [Or perhaps even better: "The postal employees do not always work the system properly."]

Another common fallacy that arises with induction by enumeration is called the "fallacy of biased statistics." Not only must the data be sufficiently broad in the sense of a large percentage of instances, but it also must not be chosen in such a way as to destroy the genuine representativeness of the data samples. We may never be certain that our data is truly representative, but we should strive to avoid bias. Racial prejudice frequently arises when people commit this fallacy. To remember only the obnoxious characteristics of some individuals within a minority group, and to ignore or deliberately forget the instances where this characteristic does not appear, is to be guilty of the fallacy of biased statistics. To ignore certain types of behavior among one's peer group but then to criticize that same behavior among others is to be prejudiced and guilty of bias. The most common instance of this fallacy is when someone ignores certain types of evidence because it seems to conflict with a previously accepted belief system.

Christians are frequently accused of failing to avoid this fallacy. The critics point out that our testimonies always tell of the instances where a Christian was saved from disaster or aided when in trouble. But we do not frequently tell of those who prayed for help that never came, those who were defeated time and again, or those who died in the foxhole in spite of their vows. On the other hand, Christians claim that the unbeliever has a blinded mind and that he or she refuses to look at the massive evidence that supports the claim of truthfulness for Christian beliefs. Partial truths, limited experience, and closed-mindedness are always weaknesses of any presentation.

Inductive reasoning is open to many other problems. It must be remembered that any argument that leads to a conclusion about the future on the basis of past or present data is by nature inductive. Through inductive reasoning we know that night will follow day, that the next winter will include some cold days, and that next year's honey will be golden brown, sticky, and sweet. The scientific method is theoretically an inductive approach. Thus science is susceptible to change because it is not based upon deductive certainty. The best theories or the best established laws are always technically less than certain.

Yet this lack of absolute certainty in many cases has nothing to do with the psychological certitude an individual may have regarding the truth of a belief. We may lack deductive certainty and yet be persuaded to say, "I know whom I have believed."

## USING LOGIC IN BIBLICAL EXEGESIS

Instances abound where logical reasoning and rational arguments are presented in Scripture. Only a few will be examined here, but these will be developed in such a way that one who learns the methods of logical analysis will be able to apply the same techniques to other passages as a part of the regular hermeneutical task. Let's look at a noncontroversial scriptural passage that most Christians understand and accept as a valid argument.

> [Jesus] said to them, "If any of you has a sheep and it falls into a pit on the Sabbath, will you not take hold of it and lift it out? How much more valuable is a man than a sheep! Therefore, it is lawful to do good on the Sabbath." (Matt. 12:11-12)

First, it is necessary to restate the argument into a standard form so that it can be analyzed. The first question assumes a positive reply. Thus for the purpose of logical analysis it may be stated as follows:

> (1) Anyone of you who has a sheep that falls into a pit on the Sabbath will take hold of it and lift it out.

The second statement is an exclamation. The word "how" is used to intensify the comparative. Thus the proposition may be restated as follows:

> (2) A man is very much more valuable than a sheep.

The conclusion is already stated in the passage in a straightforward propositional form.

**(3) Therefore, it is lawful to do good on the Sabbath.**

Anyone looking at (1), (2), and (3) can see that the argument is not very clear. The conclusion includes a statement about what is "lawful," yet the premises do not speak directly and explicitly of the law at all. How can the fact that a man is more valuable than a sheep ever prove that it is lawful to do good on the Sabbath? The conclusion does not obviously follow necessarily from the premises. Yet apparently this is not intended simply as an inductive argument. The conclusion is stated as if it were a certainty. The argument proposes to prove that it is lawful to do good, not that it is "probably" lawful to do good. The argument (1) (2) (3), hereafter called Argument "A," is in a deductive form, but it is either invalid or there must be some hidden premises. One of the most valuable aspects of studies in logic is the recognition and discovery of unstated premises. Sometimes what people do not say is as important as what they do say.

Let us try to spell out some of the hidden premises.

**(4) Leviticus 23:3 forbids work on the Sabbath.**

**(5) Deuteronomy 22:4 commands the Israelites to help lift up any fellow Israelite's donkey or ox that they see that may have fallen along the roadside.**

**(6) God is consistent and does not contradict himself.**

**(7) Therefore, to obey Deuteronomy 22:4 is not to disobey Leviticus 23:3.**

This conclusion (7) can be justified only on the basis of a further hidden premise. It assumes:

**(8) Leviticus 23:3 and Deuteronomy 22:4 are laws revealed by God (cf. 6).**

We may now restate (7) to read:

**(7') To help lift an ox or a donkey that has fallen is not to violate the law against work on the Sabbath.**

57

This still does not help us very much because Argument "A" plus (7') is still not a formally valid argument. A sheep is neither an ox nor a donkey. A further premise must be included.

(9) The meaning of the law is not limited strictly to the literal wording of the law.

Premise (9) makes it possible to affirm:

(10) To aid a fallen sheep is to obey the spirit of the law as set forth in Deuteronomy 22:4.

(11) Therefore, to aid a fallen sheep is not to violate the prohibition against work on the Sabbath.

Conclusion (11) actually assumes (9) to be restated as: (9') To obey the spirit of the law is to obey the law correctly.

Argument "A" plus (7') and (11) now says in its logical restatement:

(12) Helping a sheep in trouble does not violate the law of the Sabbath.

(13) A man is more valuable than a sheep.

(14) Therefore, it is lawful to do good on the Sabbath.

According to the basic principles of deductive logic, (12) and (13) should lead to the conclusion:

(15) Therefore, helping a man in trouble does not violate the law of the Sabbath.

To be quite technical about this we must go on to say that this conclusion (15) can be drawn only if the following hidden premises are recognized:

(16) Helping a sheep in trouble on the Sabbath does not violate the Sabbath ban on doing work because of the value of a sheep.

(17) Exceptions to the Sabbath law can be justified depending upon the value of the entities involved.

It is interesting to note at this point that the Deuteronomy passage does not specifically claim to be an exception to the Sabbath law. The Pharisees who were hypercritical and who argued for literal strictness in their interpretation of the law perhaps understood Deuteronomy 22:4 to be an exception to the rule of Leviticus 22:3 partly because of (16), (17), (6), and (8).

In this discussion, the various propositions have frequently been simplified as the argument progressed, but one hopes that each restatement could be properly defended if that became necessary. The problem now is to show that (14) and (15) are equivalent propositions. If that cannot be done the argument will remain invalid. In this case the context does help. Jesus presented his argument "A" in response to a question: "Is it lawful to heal on the Sabbath?" Immediately after delivering his argument 'A,' Jesus healed a man with a withered hand on the Sabbath.

> **(18) "Doing good" in this context means "to heal" and thus "to help" the man who was in trouble (needed healing).**

Now (14) can be stated:

> **(14') Therefore, it is lawful to heal on the Sabbath.**

But a further problem jumps out at the careful logician. Did (12) faithfully translate (11) which actually meant to help lift a fallen sheep. In fact (5) refers to lifting the animal that has fallen by the roadside, whereas (1) speaks of a sheep in a pit. Thus it must be shown that (1) may legitimately be translated to (12). This would be somewhat complicated, but the cultural context and premise (9) should be sufficient to persuade us that the Jews were willing to accept (1) as equivalent to (12). But we know that the Pharisees did not consistently apply (9). At times they were very literalistic. In this case, however, they evidently did use (9) because Jesus uses (1) with (12) as the implied meaning. He evidently expected no argument from the Jews at that point.

Healing a withered hand is somewhat different from lifting a sheep from a pit, but again the implied meaning is not the literalistic one but the broader one of giving whatever kind of aid is actually required according to the situation. Giving this aid does not violate the Sabbath if the recipient of the aid is at least as valuable as an ox or a donkey. So the argument finally appears as follows:

(19) Exceptions to the prohibition of work on the Sabbath can be made if the work is strictly to provide aid for a creature in trouble that is as valuable as a sheep.

(20) A man is a creature that is more valuable than a sheep.

(21) Therefore to aid a man in trouble is an acceptable exception to the prohibition of work on the Sabbath.

(22) The extra valuableness of a man makes the work of aiding a man even more obviously an exception to the prohibition of work on the Sabbath.

(23) Therefore, it is certainly not a violation of the law to heal a man on the Sabbath.

This final form also contains hidden premises. An obvious one is:

(24) To heal a man is to render aid to a man.

But perhaps we are only a few technical steps away from showing that Jesus in fact did use a valid argument to defend his action of healing on the Sabbath. Do not trivialize such an analysis as this! To set forth all the steps in the argument is to discover exactly what was being said. It may be that some people can see all these implications immediately. But any false premise could make a deductive argument such as this one lead to a false conclusion. To show the full truthfulness of the argument Jesus uses, it is necessary to show that every premise (hidden or explicit) can be justified.

This type of analysis may also help us to think more deeply about the text. We may even be able to go beyond the commentators and do some creative thinking on our own. Surely we will understand more fully what Jesus was saying after making a study such as we have outlined above. It is very interesting to see that Jesus was actually working with premise (9) or (9'). This is consistent with his teaching in Matthew 5:27-28 and in other places.

Notice that the essential argument is contained in (19), (20), and (21). Premise (22) is an example of *afortiori* argumentation leading to the implied conclusion (23). In other words, Jesus actually meant more than he literally said.

This insight could lead the expositor to vocally emphasize the verb "is" in (3) when reading the passage aloud. By this oral interpretation the preacher can convey the intended meaning more clearly. A secondary vocal emphasis would fall on "good" to imply that there is a deeper meaning here too.

What else can this logical analysis teach us? The use of an *afortiori* argument should call attention to itself. Premise (22) is surely a part of Jesus' statement, but upon what is it based? Why is it true that a human is more valuable than a sheep? Modern naturalistic science claims that human beings are nothing more than highly complex animals. Is value as Jesus thinks of it to be equated with increased complexity?

The context again helps our exegesis here. The person Jesus was about to heal was a man with a physical deformity. He had a shriveled hand. The contrast is not between a poor animal and a fine, healthy man. This is a man for whom we would feel sorry. Yet it is this pitiable man who is "much more valuable than a healthy sheep." In the historical context of the first century A.D. Roman empire, this man would not be considered especially valuable.

In Israel, and in the theological context of the Jewish world, and in the strictly biblical framework within which Jesus worked, a man was similar to the animals and yet different from them.

**(25) Things which are similar may be properly compared.**

On this basis (9') is able to allow the translation of (7') into (11), because a sheep is an animal and both a donkey and an ox are animals. Because all these animals are useful to humanity, the substitution is possible. Without trying to be too technical, however, we must not overlook that:

**(X) A Jew would not help a pig out of a ditch on the Sabbath.**

**(Y) A pig is an animal.**

So the transition from "donkey and ox" to "sheep" is not simply their similarity as animals. They are even more similar than that. Deuteronomy 14:4 names the ox and the sheep as "clean" animals that may be eaten by the Jews. This distinguishes them from a pig. Further, the donkey, the ox, the goat, and the sheep were animals of particular value to Hebrew society. But ultimately these points (though relevant) are not the only way to address the issue. Premise (10) can be justified by something more than just (9) or even (25). The real basis seems to be as follows:

(26) Context determines meaning.

(27) Deuteronomy 22:1-2 commands an Israelite who sees a neighbor's sheep or ox go astray to take them back and not to ignore the situation.

(28) Deuteronomy 22:3 commands the same thing as number 27 except the animal involved is the neighbor's donkey.

(29) Deuteronomy 22:4 mentions only the donkey and the ox.

(30) Deuteronomy 22:1-4 make up a single contextual unit.

(31) Therefore, the meaning of Deuteronomy 22:4 is determined by the context.

(32) The context includes parallel commands for the Israelite's response to a situation involving his neighbor's donkey, ox, and/or sheep.

(33) Therefore, the full meaning of Deuteronomy 22:4 includes the sheep.

Thus (10) is justified by the biblical context as described in (27), (28), (29), (30), (31), (32), and (33) plus the hidden premise (9). Trying to discover the basis of the *afortiori* premise (22), however, demands even more analysis.

As we saw earlier, Jesus would not have been thinking in terms of valuableness apart from his theological presuppositions.

(34) Things are not distinguished by those ways in which they are the same.

(35) Men and animals are the same in that their physical origin is from the ground (Genesis 1:24 and 2:7, 19).

(36) Men are the same as animals in that both are living souls (Genesis 1:20 and 2:7).

(37) Both die and return to the dust (Genesis 3:19 and Ecclesiastes 3:19-20).

(38) Therefore, mankind and animals are not absolutely distinguished by their physical natures.

To put that in modern terms, physical complexity is not an adequate criteria for value judgments in the deepest sense. Jesus affirmed human value but on a different basis than mere physical complexity. Theologically, humankind is described as having at least one characteristic that distinguishes us absolutely from the animals.

(39) Comparisons of value are made at points by which things differ.

(40) Humans are made in God's image (Genesis 1:27 and 9:6), whereas animals are not.

(41) To be in God's image gives humankind the right of dominion over the animals (Genesis 1:26, 28).

A set of hidden premises that lie behind (40) and (41) is that:

(42) What God says is authoritatively true.

(43) What Scripture teaches is what God says.

(44) That human beings are uniquely created in God's image and have dominion over animals is what Scripture teaches.

(45) Therefore, (40) and (41) are true.

(46) The right of dominion is given to all human beings and applies to all animals.

(47) The possession of a unique image of God by human beings is an adequate basis for making a qualitative value judgment over against an animal that lacks the image of God.

(48) Therefore, a human being in the image of God is qualitatively more valuable than an animal.

By this process we see that (22) is theologically based and would be accepted by those who agreed with (42) and (43) plus, of course, (44) and (47).

It is even more fascinating to notice that Jesus had just used an even more obvious *afortiori* argument in the immediately preceding verses (Matthew 12:1-8). So the type of logical argument found here has its own supporting context.

One final note is perhaps worthy of mention. When the average Christian reads argument "A," he or she immediately grasps the force and the correctness of the logic. Our minds are capable of recognizing the validity of the argument even though we are not conscious of the actual steps involved in showing that validity. A computer solves a problem by (rapidly) going through every single logical step necessary to solve a problem. The human mind, however, functions in a different way. This does not automatically prove the Christian view of humanity, nor does it resolve the mind/body debate in philosophy. But it does provide a bit of inductive evidence that supports the Christian view of humanity's uniqueness.

Faith is that mental/spiritual step we take beyond the inductive premises to affirm the certainty of our conclusion. We know whom we have believed. The so-called "inner witness" of the Holy Spirit is one of God's ways of communicating with the human mind.

## LOGIC IN THE BIBLE

Matthew 12 is by no means the only place where definite logical forms are found in Scripture, but it is a rich chapter. Jesus employed his authority in many ways. Of course he spoke of the Holy Spirit's work in drawing people to faith, and he appealed to the authority of the Old Testament to validate his ministry. But he also assumed that people could follow his logic. Jesus held a high view of what his listeners were able to do. He assumed that ordinary people could not only understand his words but that they also could recognize the logical implications.

Matthew 12:26 is a clear example of *reductio ad absurdum*. The logical form of this argument is quite simple. To prove some propositions (p) to be true, you first assume that (p) is false (written "not-p"). On the basis of that premise we deduce a valid conclusion that is known to be false. Since a false conclusion follows by valid deduction from "not-p," the proposition "not-p" must be false. If "not-p" is false, then (p) must be true. The statement of the Pharisees was that Jesus cast out demons by the power of the prince of demons. Jesus said that it would be ridiculous to think that way. Satan could not establish his kingdom if he empowered people to work against himself. It is absurd to think that Satan would drive Satan out of places where he already had control of a human life. The proposition Jesus wants to prove to be true is that he is driving out demons by the power of God. He shows this by demonstrating that not-p (that he drove out demons by Satan's power, not by God's power) leads to unacceptable conclusions.

Matthew 12:28 is an "if-then" statement. If Jesus is empowered by God, then his actions were in accordance with God's will. The kingdom is where God's will is done. Thus by clear implication, Jesus proclaims the presence of the kingdom by virtue of his personal presence.

Another well-known logical form is the "excluded middle." The law of excluded middle is a tautology and thus is always true. By logic alone tautologies can be shown to be true if the words being used are meaningful. As an example of an "excluded middle" proposition, we could say: Either Newton was a physicist or Newton was not a physicist. There is no middle position in such an either-or situation. It is logically true. The middle position has been excluded by the form of the proposition itself. Jesus used this logical form in Matthew 12:30. "Either a man is with me or he is against me." Jesus excluded any middle position.

Paul also is adept at using logic. A very profitable written exercise for the reader would be to take 1 Corinthians 15:12-18 and write out each premise and each conclusion. As a minimum beginning it would be seen that Paul believed that:

(1) **Contradictory statements are not both true.**

(2) **Christ died on the cross.**

(3) If Christ has been raised, then it is false that there is no resurrection.

(4) If there is no resurrection, then the dead are not raised.

(5) If the dead are not raised, then Christ is not raised.

(6) Our faith and our testimony is that Christ has been raised.

(7) If there is no resurrection, our faith is futile and our testimony is false.

These examples do not begin to cover the many places in the Bible where a careful logical analysis can be helpful in interpretation. By no means is this to imply that proper exegesis should be limited to logical analysis. But where the exegete sees reasons leading to conclusions and can find careful arguments, he or she is able to see the exact nature of the logical forms employed. Romans 14:5 gives very sound advice to the Christians of that day and this: "Each one should be fully convinced in his own mind."

# GLOSSARY

Ad Hominem
Afortiori
Antecedent
Antinomy
Aposteriori
Apriori
Argument
Assumption
Axiom
Concept
Conditional Statement
Contradiction
Contrary
Critical
Deduction
Explicit
Fallacy

Fallacy of Irrelevance
Implication
Implicit
Induction
Inference
Irrational
Judgment
Knowledge
Logic
Paradox
Particular
Petitio Principii
Philosophy
Predication
Premise
Presupposition
Proposition

66

**Rational**
*Rationes Aeternae*
Reason
*Reductio ad Absurdum*

Self-stultifying
Syllogism
Valid

**4**

# Recognizing Worldviews

*What is a Worldview?*
*Knowledge and Reality*
*Moral Values*
*Meaning and Purpose*
*Human Nature and Relationships*
*Five Fundamental Questions*
*Three Major Worldviews*
*Summary*

> My brothers, if one of you should wander from the truth and someone should bring him back, remember this: Whoever turns a sinner away from his error will save him from death and will cover many sins (James 5:19-22 NIV).

According to James, a sinner is someone who has wandered from the truth. A sinner is someone who needs to be turned away from his error. This emphasis upon truth is a very important concept in the New Testament. According to John 4, Jesus taught that people are to worship God in spirit because God is a spiritual being, but Jesus added that we must also worship him in truth. The one who turns a sinner away from his error saves that sinner from the enemy of death and from judgment. As James phrases it, he "will cover many sins."

So often in modern life, Christianity has been pictured as being one lifestyle among many. In fact, the term "alternate lifestyle" has become a commonly used phrase to describe various ways in which people choose to live. But Christianity is not just a lifestyle. Christianity is built on something bigger than that. The biblical emphasis on truth includes moral standards, but it also includes intellectual ideas. Truth is more than morals.

Christian theism, rather than being a lifestyle, is more properly described by the term *worldview*. That may not be a phrase that is commonly used in ordinary conversation, and some people may not understand what it means. Nevertheless, people have a worldview even if they do not realize that they have one. People may not articulate their philosophy, but they do make assumptions about the way things are. In fact, a worldview is the philosophical framework that makes it possible to think at all.

## WHAT IS A WORLDVIEW?

A worldview is that basic set of assumptions that gives meaning to one's thoughts. A worldview is the set of assumptions that someone has about the *way* things are, about *what* things are, about *why* things are.

For example, most people assume that something exists. There may be someone, perhaps, who believes that nothing exists, but who would that person be? How could he or she make such an affirmation? Sometimes in studying the history of philosophy, one may come to the conclusion that some of the viewpoints expressed actually lead to that conclusion, but surely no one ever consciously tries to defend the position that nothing exists. It would be a useless endeavor since there would be no one to convince. Even more significantly, it would be impossible to defend that position since, if it were true, there would be no one to make the defense. So to defend the position that nothing exists seems immediately to be absurd and self-contradictory.

People simply assume that some things exist, and they work on that assumption. They do not defend it to themselves or to others; they simply assume it and work on that basis. It is possible, of course, for someone to analyze this assumption and give reasons why we believe something exists. But few people take time to think through such reasons.

Worldviews are built out of assumptions of this kind. Whether a person has or has not articulated reasons for believing that something exists, he or she nevertheless does have a concept of existence and is working on the assumption that something rather than nothing is actually there. The more significant and more controversial question, of course, is: What is it that is actually there? What is real? People do believe that something exists, but what is that something? And how does one know what that something is?

## KNOWLEDGE AND REALITY

To express these questions in philosophical terminology, one may speak of the metaphysical question: What is the nature of reality; what is actually there? Something exists; what is that something? In addition one asks the epistemological question: How does one know what exists, and how can someone know what is there? The way people answer these philosophical questions shapes and is shaped by their worldview.

The epistemological question may be the more fundamental one. If people will explain how they know what exists, and how they arrive at their conclusions, the explanation will provide insight into the kind of worldview they have. If they suggest that we know things strictly by sense experience, or if they claim to know some things by rational intuition, or if they try to articulate some other way by which they believe that we can gain knowledge, then they will have expressed how they assume that knowledge is achieved. The way they believe that knowledge can be achieved flows directly from their worldview. The assumptions upon which people work constitute their worldview.

On the other hand, metaphysical assumptions are often more obvious to those not trained in analytical philosophy. For example, some people will suggest that the answer to the metaphysical question is that only impersonal matter is there. This is the answer given according to the world-view called **naturalism**. Ultimate reality is thought to be nothing more than material, physical reality. Apparently, these naturalistic thinkers believe that if one has enough time (and, of course, many modern scientists claim that several billions of years are available), and if one adds a chance process (one that is moving or changing in a random way), then order will result. Naturalism assumes that it will be able to explain the formation and the continuation of the world by adding up impersonal matter and great lengths of time and a random-chance process.

The world, of course, seems to contain mind and personality, purpose and meaning, but naturalism attempts to explain all of these features of real life in terms of a natural development. From impersonal matter, using random processes over an extended period of time, naturalism claims to be able to achieve personality, thought, the complexities of the earth's ecological system, symbiotic relationships, and the myriads of other intricate and interdependent things that make up human society and the natural world.

Naturalism is a worldview that assumes that matter alone is ultimately real. Physical reality is the only thing that actually exists. All of reality can be located in space and time, and it can (even must) be studied by the scientific method. According to this worldview, all knowledge can be gained purely through experimental evidence.

There are other worldviews that take an entirely different stance on the ultimate nature of reality. One of the most common, pantheism, a form of idealism, assumes that the world is ultimately spiritual; that matter is essentially an illusion; that the essence of all reality is a divine spirit, or at least some great mind; and that matter is an extension of that mental or spiritual essence. Eastern philosophy is frequently built upon this type of metaphysic. Hinduism, for example, is a pantheistic religion that teaches that physical matter is an illusion.

Worldviews are more than lifestyles. They include moral codes, but they also include the assumed answers to questions that many people do not even ask in an articulate way. The primary question has always been: what is really real? Or to say it another way: What is truly true? It is self-defeating to deny the existence of one's own mind. But what actually and ultimately, if anything, is out there outside of one's mind? Of what is the world made? What is truly real?

Christian **theism** affirms that God has revealed himself to be there, that God exists. God is not just a thought or a projection of society or an illusion of the mind. He really is there, and he has made himself known to us. God is ultimately real. He is an actual being, that is, a Being which has no potential remaining to be fulfilled. God is perfectly complete in his own essence. Christian theists consider the world to be limited and contingent and held in existence by God's power.

Others would put an "s" on the word "god." **Polytheism** holds that "the gods" are real. This is the pagan or the animistic worldview. There are many gods, and they have many things to do and to say.

Then for many others living today, what is ultimately real are the gods of fate and chance. Physical **determinism** is metaphysical reality for thousands of people.

In brief review, then, these are some of the basic metaphysical options: that God exists; that an all-pervading spiritual force exists; that some personal, spiritual beings exist; or that matter itself is the only reality.

## MORAL VALUES

A third question, no less significant, is: What ought one to do? This is the moral question. People do act, and they relate to one another. Cultural and environmental factors are surely involved. Naturalism, however, assumes that all of life has developed strictly through natural processes. Therefore, however things are is the way things ought to be. What other standard could there be? Naturalism has no alternative reality with which to compare things. Whatever things are physically is what they are. There is no "oughtness" apart from "is-ness." If a distinction between "what ought to be" and "what actually is" were to be made, it could only be through the application of selfish or pragmatic principles. This pragmatic ethic, however, could never claim normativeness except in the particular context where it seems to be successful. Such success cannot always be predicted ahead of time. Even when success is assured, however, the goals toward which one strives have no necessary or exclusive claim on the acting agent. Thus, "oughtness" loses at least its urgency and more likely its significance altogether.

Christian theism, on the other hand, does not assume

that what one ought to do is determined exclusively by what actually is the case in space-time terms. A Christian believes that God himself is the source of moral standards. God is not identified with the world in Scripture. In fact, he is said to be the standard by which Christians are to judge the world. So if one looks at one's own life or at physical reality, and if what one finds there does not meet certain standards which are a part of God's revealed nature, then a Christian may legitimately say, "This ought not to be."

The question of "oughtness" should never be reduced to the question of "what is" in the physical universe. The attempt to make such an identification is sometimes called the *Naturalistic Fallacy*. Christian theism assumes that "oughtness" is related to God's character and to God's purposes. The biblical doctrine of sin, however, is intimately related to the concept of a moral fall, a historical break in divine-human relationships caused by moral rebellion on the part of human beings against God's character and God's revealed will for humankind. Judgment is being expressed on account of the fall of humanity. This judgment affects human relationships to God, to other people, and to the created order. Moral values inevitably flow from such worldviews.

## MEANING AND PURPOSE

There is a fourth question that shapes and molds or is shaped and molded by a worldview: Is there any meaning or purpose for life or for history? The general worldview of the nineteenth century, for example, was extremely optimistic. In fact, many people believed it was possible to achieve a peaceful world and a satisfied society. They were going to resolve all of their problems. They were going to wipe out disease. They were going to take away the drudgery of work by inventing new labor-saving devices. They were going to be able to communicate all around the world, and by building communications networks they hoped to establish peaceful relationships with all places in the earth. The outlook was so optimistic that many Christians expected the kingdom of God to appear immediately. Optimism simply exploded all over the latter years of the nineteenth century.

The twentieth century, on the other hand, lost that optimistic worldview and turned in the opposite direction. The new worldview has been extremely pessimistic. There have been many catastrophes, many wars, many setbacks, and many difficulties. To many it looked as if the world's economic situation was at a point of crisis. The international balance of power seemed to be on the brink of collapse. Peace negotiations often seemed to offer little hope for lasting peace. In many places diplomatic relationships seemed to be on the verge of breaking down.

During most of this century the whole world seemed to be in turmoil and the people have grown increasingly pessimistic. On the other hand, during the last years of the 1980s and on into the early 1990s, the sense of destiny changed again, especially as events in eastern Europe brought a measure of optimism back to the public mind. Things may have changed again even in the short time between the writing and the publication of this book.

Which way is the right way to view world events? Can someone honestly look at the world in an optimistic way as if history were moving forward and were about to accomplish and achieve new heights of greatness? On the other hand, is it correct to be pessimistic and to expect modern society to collapse in the next decades? Is it possible to look at this as if world history were just working through a cyclical pattern? Some, of course, have always said that history regularly and inevitably passes through optimistic and pessimistic periods in a predictable cycle.

Worldviews are the fundamental assumptions of thought life that enables a person to begin to formulate answers to questions such as these. Christians through the years have argued that history does have a meaning and a purpose, that it is going somewhere, that Someone is in control, that there is a reason why things happen, and that there is an ultimate destiny for human life.

## HUMAN NATURE AND RELATIONSHIPS

A fifth group of ideas that reveal the content of a worldview may be summed up by the question: What defines human nature? To make that more personal the question may be stated: What defines me? If one believes that humankind is essentially a machine, then human relationships will be understood in one way. If one believes that human beings are basically naked apes, then human relationships and human responsibilities and human society will be understood in a different way. If one thinks that human beings are personalities made in God's image, another view of society and human life will emerge.

## FIVE FUNDAMENTAL QUESTIONS

How does one come to know truth? What is really real? What ought one to do? Is there any meaning or purpose for life and history? And what does it mean to be human? These are not trivial questions. They affect lifestyles. They affect attitudes and motivations for both work and play. They determine what one thinks about TV programs. They affect how people respond to commercials and advertisements. They determine how people relate to the images of human life presented in the movies. They affect job performance and job satisfaction. They set the parameters for assigning value to areas of academic study.

These questions also guide scientific inquiry. If a person believes that the universe is essentially the product of random forces over infinite periods of time, he or she will have a different motivation and perhaps a different process by which to attempt to deal scientifically with the physical world from that which might be the perspective of one who believes that the world was deliberately created by a purposeful, meaningful, intentional acting Being.

These questions influence the way people deal with economic theories or the way they handle business ethics. Questions that are so closely associated with the basic set of assumptions from which people think and reason are not trivial questions. They are significant questions in every area of human life.

## THREE MAJOR WORLDVIEWS

There are three major worldviews, though there are several different versions of each, and perhaps some would want to call each modification another worldview. For the sake of simplicity, however, we will use the general three-fold classification.

The first worldview is that of **IDEALISM**. Idealism has both an eastern and a western philosophical tradition. Within western philosophy, idealism arises from the teachings of Plato. Platonic philosophy has changed somewhat through the years. Characteristically, however, Platonic idealism affirms that spiritual realities and physical realities are in two separate realms, with spiritual realities being the more important, the more fundamental, the ultimately determining factors.

Idealism in general teaches that ideas are more significant than physical things and that, in fact, ideas mold and shape physical things. Platonic idealism generally is rather impersonal. For Plato, ideas were not gods, they were simply ideas. They existed, but they were impersonal.

Eastern idealism is mostly pantheistic (and thus monistic rather than dualistic). God and the world are considered to be two names for what is essentially the same reality. This is a true idealism, however, because the world is considered to be an expression of God's thoughts. It is not thought of materialistically. In both traditional forms of idealism, ideas are really what make up, shape, and form the world.

The second view, **NATURALISM**, is perhaps the most common worldview among modern scholars in the West, and it is having an ever increasing influence in the East. Naturalism is based on the assumption that all reality is located within space and time and can be understood exclusively by the scientific method. According to this view, nothing other than physical reality exists.

The naturalistic worldview would include, of course, several varieties as subcategories, such as **materialism** or **positivism**. One possible subcategory is humanism which puts a high value on human life and on human ideals. It does seem, however, that this "value" is smuggled into the system, because ultimately human life, according to naturalistic assumptions, is simply a product of natural forces. How could some natural forces have any more intrinsic value than other natural forces? This question is generally left unanswered, or else it is answered by purely functional criteria which are much less than satisfactory.

Another modern subcategory of naturalism is *process* thought. This view is built upon the basic metaphysical concepts of Alfred North Whitehead. Of course, many other philosophers have been working in this area since Whitehead set forth the basic ideas. Several theistic forms of process thought have been suggested.

Essentially, process thought considers the world to be existing moment by moment in a continual state of change (process). History is that process which has already occurred (existing only in memory, now fixed and unchangeable). The future is made up of those potential possibilities that are still available. The future is open to the infinite potential of what might become an actual reality. The process itself (god) is able to actualize only that which is possible (available potentialities). Thus process theism has a finite god.

**Existentialism**, the view that people are what they do, and **nihilism**, the view that people have no value, are both the logical results of certain types of naturalistic thinking. Secularism is another version of naturalism.

Idealism with its several modifications and naturalism with its several sub-categories do not exhaust the possibilities, however. There is also a third major worldview known as **THEISM**. Subcategories of theism would include *Judaism*, *Christianity*, and *Islam*. Theists believe that mind is distinct from matter (as idealists claim), and yet theists believe that matter is real (in a way similar to the naturalistic view). Mind is original, however, and it is personal. Mind is ultimately located in a personal God who eternally rules the universe, and by whose Word the worlds were created.

Biblical theism teaches that God, whose existence is existentially necessary rather than merely logically implied, is a spiritual Being who has personality, love, and meaningful communication within himself. Since that kind of God does exist, rationality and meaningful thought are possible. With equal emphasis, theists affirm that the world has a physical reality. It is not an illusion; it is not merely an extension of God's essence, but it is something that is real over against God (so to speak). Matter has been created. It is something with which one can work in the laboratory. In fact, one must struggle against it in normal life.

Matter is a reality that is distinct from God and yet is totally dependent upon God. Every characteristic of this truly existing universe is dependent upon some characteristic of the God who truly exists.

## SUMMARY

Idealism, naturalism, and theism (along with various subcategories of each) make up the major worldviews of the modern world. Worldviews define the manner and the meaning of human thought life. Even those who do not articulate their worldview explicitly, nevertheless do think within a framework of meaning. Because truth is an issue for Christians, it is important to discern the elements of a worldview. Only then are we able to evaluate the content of our intellectual life and lifestyle.

These are five questions that address worldview issues: metaphysics, epistemology, morals, meaning, and essential human values. A study of worldview issues such as these helps us to turn from error and intellectual sin. When we identify a worldview, we can test it and seek the truth.

## GLOSSARY

Assumption
Christian
Common Ground
Common Sense Realism
Conservative
Determinism
Empirical
Empiricism
Epistemology
Essence
Existentialism
God
History
Humanism

Idealism
Islam
Judaism
Knowledge
Liberalism
Materialism
Matter
Metaphysics
Monism
Naturalism
Pantheism
Person
Personalism
Plato

Platonism
Positivism
Pragmatism
Process Thought
Rationalism
Realism
Reality
Romanticism

Scientism
Secular
Skepticism
Theism
Truth
Value
World-picture
Worldview

# 5

# Testing Worldviews

*The Test of Logical or Rational Consistency*
*The Test of Empirical Adequacy*
*The Test of Explanatory Power*
*The Test of Practical Relevance*
*Conclusion*

Naturalism, idealism, and theism are three major worldview categories. There are many subcategories and many modifications, but for the most part, what can be said about these major types will also apply to the various subgroups.

Simply being aware of these various categories is not enough, however, for they are mutually exclusive. Only one of them can be true. They cannot be combined, and they cannot be ignored. A person will inevitably think in terms of one or the other of these three views. Someone may, of course, have a mixture of ideas in his or her conversation, but when the issues of life become crucial, as they inevitably do, the distinctions in worldviews become crucial as well.

How can someone know which view if any is right? What is needed are adequate tests that can be applied to worldviews. Assuming that a person has analyzed his/her own thoughts or the thoughts of others and has detected the worldview involved, there are four tests that he/she should apply to determine the validity, the truthfulness, the intellectual value, and the relevance of that worldview.

## The Test of Logical or Rational Consistency

The first mark of truthfulness in a worldview is logical consistency. Truth correctly and fully expressed will be wholly consistent with itself and with all other properly expressed and correctly understood true propositions. A viewpoint that tries to express itself by affirming inconsistent propositions is self-destructive. If the inconsistencies involve essential elements, and if the inconsistencies are fundamental to the internal structure of the worldview, they defeat themselves by failing to affirm or by failing to cohere with that which must be affirmed if the view is to be considered as true by rational human beings.

Since Christians believe that only Christian theism is ultimately true, they would naturally expect a correct expression of their view to be internally consistent in every way. Christians also expect that naturalism and other worldviews, since they are not true, will ultimately express themselves in ways that are internally inconsistent and, therefore, self-defeating. A primary point Christian apologists often press against other worldviews is that only theism offers a fully sufficient basis for rationality itself. The epistemological question ("How does one know anything?" or more specifically, "Why does one use and how can one justify using reason?") is at the very heart of this test for consistency.

Naturalism, by definition, assumes that mankind's rational and mental processes have been derived solely from natural processes by the so-called struggle for survival and by random genetic changes over time. Over the years certain biological and environmental circumstances developed that supposedly caused humans to think the way they think. Our human minds and our conscious personalities supposedly developed as the complicated product of complex natural forces.

Thus naturalism implies that people think and reason the way they do because their natural environment has determined that they would think and reason that way. People have been "forced" (or better, predetermined) genetically, chemically, and environmentally to have certain attitudes and ideas. But if that is true, then why should anyone trust any of those ideas to be correct?

If some have been led (actually "determined") to believe a certain theory (any theory) because of their background and environment, and if they have no way of transcending that environment; if all of reality is physical, space-time reality, and if there is nothing other than that by which to judge and to evaluate ideas, then why should they trust their minds, or why should they trust reason at all?

Why should I, for example, ever believe that my ideas are true? How could I suggest to others that their ideas are not true? If naturalism were correct, the ideas of those who disagree with me and their ways of thinking would have been produced in exactly the same way that mine were; only I perhaps would have had some unique experiences that they would not have had; therefore we have come to disagree. But if I had had the same experiences and the same genes and the same background as they, would I not think exactly what they think? So why should I conclude that I am right and they are wrong? Why should I suppose that my experience is necessarily superior to someone else's experience? Perhaps my experience (wide-ranging though it may be) has misled me into believing something that is not exactly correct or true. To respond by saying that I have tested my experience by experiments and compared my experience to the reports of others does not solve the fundamental dilemma. It is the validity of rational inference itself that is at stake here.

The question is not simply the validity of my experience versus your experience. Experiences can be arbitrated if reasonable standards exist. Rather the question is the validity of the rational process itself. Persons who are going to use rational argument should be able to justify the validity of rational argument, or at least their worldview should support rational thinking, and it seems quite clear that modern naturalists cannot and naturalism as a system does not do that.[1]

---

[1]"New Age" thinking and other contemporary pantheisms and idealisms also fail to meet the test of rational consistency. Without a biblically theistic God, there is no sufficiently objective basis for rationality or rational inference. Furthermore, twentieth-century

Christianity, on the other hand, works on the assumption that rationality exists because there is a personal, all-encompassing rational Being who was existing before physical matter/energy or space/time reality ever existed. Christian theism further affirms that the space/time universe (in however many dimensions there may be) was produced by this personal, all-inclusive, rational Being. Human minds, moreover, have been created and produced by this same rational Being who made us in his personal image, thus able to think as he thinks and therefore able to understand this world which he has made. The human mind is able to perceive and recognize and truly understand the world, not because the world by its random processes has accidentally produced a biological organism with this kind of thinking process, but because the very One who created this world is the One who also gave mankind the thought patterns and the mental ability to perceive, recognize, and understand.

According to theism, reason is prior to nature. Reason orders nature. Reason is thus a valid tool for understanding nature.

Naturalism ultimately reduces reason to a physical force, a chemical process, and a psychological tool that has environmentally survived the genetic mutations of the ages. Naturalism thus has no basis for trusting reason, except pragmatic considerations. There is a catch, however. If we say reason is meaningful because it is useful (it works), then we have begged the question. "If useful, then meaningful" is a rational inference itself. If inference is already known to be valid, then we could use such an argument. But the validity of inference must be presupposed even to make the inference that inference is useful.

Naturalism leads to meaninglessness, and thus it is ultimately meaningless to affirm naturalism. If nature is prior to reason, then nature itself must be nonrational, and

---

advancement thought of all kinds has no sufficient explanation for the meaning of the life of Christ. Only trinitarian theism can logically have an incarnation of God the Son and yet have a transcendent Father and the relational bridge of God's personal Holy Spirit existing and interacting at the same time.

nonrational nature cannot rationally affirm itself to be real, much less true. Reason produced solely by nature is thus totally determined by nonrational forces and consequently cannot be objective, and thus not free, and thus is not truly rational.

Naturalism is self-defeating. The "advancement" of the 20th century is built on an illusion. Its foundations are inconsistent and false.

Christianity, on the other hand, claims to be built on the solid foundation of reality. It is logically consistent because it does not claim that reason is simply a product of natural forces. Christian theists are proposing that reason is a characteristic of God's essence, and that reason has been given to us by God. That thesis may be contested; in fact, non-theistic philosophers suppose that there is no God (of the rational or even of the non-rational kind) to give anything to anybody. But it is not unfair to point out to these thinkers that Christians at least have a sufficient philosophical basis for believing that reason or rational inference is valid, and Christians suggest that the modern naturalist has no sufficient or meaningful basis for believing that reason or rational inference is valid.

If the naturalistic worldview is correct, rational arguments against the existence of God are no more meaningful than are rational arguments for the existence of God. In fact, it would seem that rational argument would be relatively insignificant on the basis of a strict naturalistic epistemology. Clearly this is not the case. Naturalism claims "rationality" above all. Thus naturalism undercuts itself at a point of essential internal structure. Naturalism fails the test of rational consistency.

It is conceivable, however, for a system of thought to demonstrate a measure of rational consistency (given its assumptions) and yet still be false. Failing to achieve consistency is a mark of error, but it takes more than abstract consistency to demonstrate truthfulness.[2] Truth is not less

---

[2]Idealism is a worldview which assumes that some system of rationally consistent ideas exists, but these ideas are generally impersonal, and idealist philosophers characteristically offer no

than rational consistency, but it must also touch reality consistently and sufficiently.

## The Test of Empirical Adequacy

Adequate empirical support is certainly an essential test for the truth-value of a worldview. If someone has to deny established facts (or create non-facts) in order to defend his or her worldview, he/she is not likely to have the truth. If there are some things that really did happen, and someone, in order to defend his or her own position, argues that those things did not (or could not) happen, then he or she is not dealing with truth. He/she is simply expressing prejudice.

Christian theism, as a worldview, includes the claim that Jesus rose from the dead, thus demonstrating his deity, his messiahship, and his lordship over all things. Christians believe and persuasively argue that Jesus Christ actually rose from the dead. They believe that there is adequate and persuasive evidence for that historical event.[3]

---

viable way of establishing why they are there. Why do the "Ideal Forms" of Plato exist? How does someone know that one Idea is more important than another? How does the Idealist (like Plato or Hegel) recognize truth? The answer is simply by meditating and looking into his own mind. Idealism has no other answer. Nevertheless truth must be tested and known both by logical consistency and by empirical support.

[3]Rather than give the technical evidence here, I will simply summarize the main points and then direct the reader to books and articles that discuss this matter in some detail and that document the evidence in a more comprehensive and scholarly manner. The key evidences are (1) the evidence for his real existence as opposed to claims that the Jesus stories are legends or myths, (2) the evidence for his real and assured death, (3) the evidence for his tomb being empty three days later, (4) the eyewitness testimony that he was actually seen alive by some who knew him well enough to have detected a fake or a trick, (5) the utter failure of those who deny the Resurrection to provide adequate alternative explanations of the evidence, (6) the establishment and continuation of the church in both friendly and hostile territory based upon the preaching of the cross and the resurrection of Jesus, and (7) the willingness of the earliest church leaders to give their lives rather than recant their belief that Jesus had actually done what the

Thus they believe that one who denies the existence of God and therefore denies the reality of miracles, one who tries to live within a purely naturalistic or even a pantheistic kind of worldview, is forced to deny certain historical facts, such as the resurrection of Jesus from the dead, that actually did happen. Thus naturalism and pantheism and other non-biblical views do not meet the test of empirical adequacy. They do not explain all the facts.

On the other hand, a naturalist would perhaps suggest that a Christian was omitting certain facts, such as scientific laws, in his presentation of a miracle such as the resurrection. This would have to be studied. If the Christian is able to defend his or her view only by denying true facts, then unquestionably the Christian would have to modify these views or accept some other worldview. But such is not the case here. Laws of science describe actual repeatable, regular events. They can tell us how unlikely a resurrection would be (which we already admit), and laws can call to our attention alternative explanations. But if the evidence shows that the event did occur (and in the case of the resurrection of Christ it does), and if the alternative explanations are implausible (and they are), then it is naturalism that is guilty of prejudice, not Christianity.

No worldview can be established as true if it does not have adequate empirical evidence. If one must deny true facts in order to defend the view, or if he must affirm the unaffirmable, then he is not dealing with the true view. But Christians do not believe that they have to deny any facts,

---

resurrection claims. See Gary Habermas, *Ancient Evidence for the Life of Jesus* (Nashville: Thomas Nelson, 1984); F. F. Bruce, *Jesus and Christian Origins Outside the New Testament* (Grand Rapids: Eerdmans, 1974); James D. G. Dunn, *The Evidence for Jesus* (Philadelphia: Westminster, 1985); George Eldon Ladd, *I Believe in the Resurrection of Jesus* (Grand Rapids: Eerdmans, 1975); Carl F. H. Henry, ed., *Jesus of Nazareth: Savior and Lord* (Grand Rapids: Eerdmans, 1966); Frank Morrison, *Who Moved the Stone* (London: Faber and Faber, 1930); W. D. Edwards, W. J. Gabel, and F. E. Hosmer, "On the Physical Death of Jesus Christ," *Journal of the American Medical Association* 255:11 (March 21, 1986), pp. 1455-1463; Colin Chapman, *The Case for Christianity* (Icknield Way, England: Lion Publishing, 1981).

nor do they believe their affirmations to be without a foundation in reality. Rather, they press the point that the empirical data must be interpreted correctly, and they challenge the naturalistic interpretation, the idealistic interpretation, and all non-theistic interpretations of reality whenever they offer false interpretations.

When a person denies facts in order to build a theory, that person is not building a theory on truth. But if one's worldview has empirical adequacy, that is, if it is a comprehensive worldview, if the evidence from all areas of reality supports it, and if none of the correctly interpreted evidence contradicts it either internally or externally, then one has passed a strong test for the validity of his worldview.

## The Test of Explanatory Power

A third test, which is very close to the other two yet stands as a separate criterion, is that a worldview must have explanatory power. That is, it should explain those things that it claims to explain.

Why is it that human beings are not fully satisfied with material wealth? Why are human beings not satisfied when they have enough? On a naturalist view, it would seem that whenever someone gains enough, he or she would be satisfied. Naturalism teaches that all desires and needs come simply from natural physical processes. When those desires and needs are satisfied, why would that not make people happy? It is clearly true, however, that human beings are not happy just because they have enough physical or material wealth. They seem to need (or at least they strongly desire) more than they need.

Why do people desire meaningful relationships? After all, if men are simply animals, why can they not act like animals and find lasting satisfaction? Why not engage in sexual relationships with any and everyone at any time or place without guilt or shame and without feeling any need for further meaningful relationships? Dogs can do that; cats can do that. Why is it that so many people continue to think they have to have love and commitment involved in these relationships? And why is it that when people try to operate their lives apart from meaningful relationships, life tends to break down and disintegrate? Human life without love seems after a while to become empty and useless.

If naturalism is true, why do men struggle for equality? What difference does it make? If humankind has been produced strictly by natural forces, then why are people not content when they have an adequate environment in which they can survive in relative comfort? Why do they want more than is necessary for comfortable physical survival? Why is there a universal religious quest? Unless theism is true, there does not seem to be any satisfactory answer to these questions.

Christianity has an answer for these questions. Christianity is built on the assumption that more than physical reality is involved. Men are spiritual as well as physical beings, and they need spiritual satisfaction. Human longings and human desires are ultimately related to God. Human beings are made in God's image. Human relationships are not just physical relationships; they are also personal relationships. God is a personal being. There are certain elements of his character by which people relate to him and to other people and by which people compare those relationships.

Christianity does have an exceptionally strong and unique explanatory power. Christians can explain why people (even non-Christians) feel guilty when they do certain things. Because God exists, there are certain, transcendent, moral standards. Moral values are not fully reducible to environment or culture. Social customs are surely a factor in "guilt feelings," but there is more to the problem of moral guilt than simply "feelings." People are spiritual beings. Human beings have been made in God's image. That which violates the nature of God will inevitably affect humans. This explanation is strongly resisted by many, but it is a far more powerful and profound explanation than those offered by other worldviews.

### The Test of Practical Relevance

Last, and notice that this is last and not first, a worldview is to be tested by the criterion of practical relevance. Worldviews are not to be tested first on subjective criteria. They are to be tested first by logical consistency, empirical adequacy and explanatory power. But once one has demonstrated that a worldview does have logical consistency, that it does have explanatory power, that it does meet the standards of empirical adequacy, it is also important to know whether that worldview really has practical relevance. Water will quench thirst, and a true worldview will meet mankind's deepest needs. Only truth will ultimately satisfy.

People are looking for truth. Christianity not only is a strong worldview that can be tested and is not afraid of the evidence, but it is also practically relevant. It meets human needs. It provides purpose and direction for human life, and it solves human problems such as guilt. It enables human beings to establish meaningful relationships. It relates them to the world as the world really is.

One reason the energy crisis has become so serious is that we have not dealt with nature as managers handling something created by God but we have acted as if nature were simply a machine. We have pushed a button here and expected the machine to operate and produce over there. Yet nature is not and never has been only a physical machine. It cannot be treated that way or it will be destroyed.

We cannot build highways just anywhere purely on the basis of human desires or convenience. We must recognize that the earth is a complex, interdependent ecological system. This world is finely balanced and delicately attuned. It should be properly managed.

Human beings are to have dominion in the sense of being those who control nature and rule it for the purpose of making it useful and making it productive. But we have treated nature as if it were an impersonal, material, purely physical system that could be handled without any concern about a possible moral relationship to it.

Nature is not a purposeless machine. It is a physical energy/matter system created by God to accomplish his purpose(s). Human society has reached a crisis in dealing with nature because people have thought about nature from an incorrect worldview.

Human society and family relationships seem to be breaking down. Why? Because society has dealt with people not as personalities created in the image of God but as highly complex, sophisticated animals, consumers, or biological machines. Human beings do respond to stimuli. We are affected by their environment. But that is not the end of the story. People are not just animals. We do more than just consume energy. We are not machines. We are spiritual beings who have been created in the personal image of God.

Christianity is a worldview which, because of who people are, demands meaningful human relationships and proper societal structures and strong families. Human relationships are built upon and from divine relationships. In these ways and in a thousand similar ways, Christianity has practical relevance.

## CONCLUSION

There are four basic tests by which we can evaluate the strength of a worldview. Christian theism is logically consistent and empirically adequate. It has explanatory power, and it is practically relevant. If Christianity meets these four tests better than other worldviews, then Christianity should be accepted as a justified worldview.

## GLOSSARY

Advancement
Apologetics
Argument
Christian
Coherence
Correspondence Theory
Empirical
Evidence
Logic
Logical Postivism
Methodology
Naïve Realism
Naturalism

Occam's Razor
Probability
Proof
Rational
Reality
Self-stultifying
System
Theism
Theory
Truth
Verification
Worldview

# PART TWO:

# Topics of Special Interest

# The Existence of God: Another Look at The Classical Proofs

*Divine Revelation*
*Faith vs. Reason*
*Faith and Reason*
*Three Basic Types of Rational Theistic Proofs*
*Religious Experience*
*Rational Proofs: Apriori*
*Rational Proofs: Aposteriori*
*Rational Proofs: Another Look*
*A Preliminary Evaluation*
*A Biblical Proposal*

Though the uninitiated are often surprised to hear it, philosophers of religion study few issues that are more complex than the issue concerning God's existence. Biblical theism affirms the existence of a God who created all things other than himself and who holds all things in existence moment by moment, while naturalists deny the necessity of such affirmations. Naturalism is the belief that there is no supernatural reality. For naturalists, all of reality is located in space and time and is capable of being known through scientific methods of acquiring knowledge. Pantheists play the middle, so to speak, by affirming the same reality as naturalism though calling it God. Pantheism is the belief that everything is God. Naturalism represents modern western "Advancement" thinking, while pantheism is a characteristic view of eastern religious thought.

Process theology, a popular viewpoint in some circles in the twentieth century, is an attempt at compromise between natural reality as modern science perceives it and God. Natural reality, according to modern science, is not ultimately a substance or a static reality but rather an energetic, ceaseless process of change. Everything is changing and becoming; even God, therefore, is seen as bipolar. That is, God is said to have a potential pole (that which may be) and an actual pole (that which has been). The present is thought to be the moment-by-moment process by which God's potential realities become actual realities. God is identified as the process of existence itself. Like a mind that animates a body, so God is the life force that animates natural reality.

But process thought (sometimes called "panentheism," God is *in* all) has been strongly criticized by those who claim that it has no adequate explanation of how God's supposed potentialities can become actualized. There is no known example nor is there any known process by which pure potentials could ever actualize themselves. There must be an "actual" cause to make the "possible" happen. If God were partially "potential," there would have to be some actual cause (a God beyond the "potential" God) to make or cause the potentials to become actual. Things do not happen just because they are possible. Things happen when something actually causes them to happen. Chairs are potential within a tree trunk, but they do not actually occur just because they are potential. They must be caused to exist by an actual agent (a chair maker). But if there is a "God beyond God," a causal agent beyond the "divine" potential, then process theism is not describing ultimate reality, and thus it fails to solve the question of God's existence except in the sense that it points beyond itself to a more traditional form of theism.

Furthermore, if process thought were correct, it seems that purposefulness and/or randomness would be ultimately indistinguishable. Arbitrary natural laws could result from either or both. As a result, process theology has no apparent apologetic. How could one know that the "process" is properly described theistically rather than naturalistically? Since there is no obvious way to decide this question, something else is needed. Process thinking fails the test of comprehensiveness.

## DIVINE REVELATION

The Bible claims to be the preserved verbalization of that which has been revealed by a Creator God who exists. Holy

Scripture's historical narratives imply that the existing God worked in and through human activities to accomplish his purposes and to express his will. The didactic portions of Scripture imply that the existing God spoke to his servants (and through them to other people both contemporary and future) and thus revealed his thoughts, character, intentions, and will.

The Bible, then, claims to be a major piece of evidence that must be considered when one examines the question of God's existence. But a claim is not by itself proof. What we really need to know is whether the Bible (or any other sacred writing) could ever be sufficient evidence to answer the theistic question affirmatively. Does the Bible prove God's existence? Or to put the question more generally: Does special revelation prove that God exists?

On one level, the first response is to say, "Yes, of course!" If there is such a thing as special revelation from God, then God must exist (or at least he must have existed when the revelation was given). But the "if" haunts us a little. To affirm special revelation is at bottom nothing more than a sophisticated begging of the question. God must already exist if there is to be any special revelation. If God does not exist, then one is mistaken to affirm that there is any special revelation. If one uses personal experience as the "truth-test" to apply to conflicting claims of special revelation, insoluble epistemological problems appear. For example, it severely begs the question to use the experience itself to prove the truth claimed about that experience. If God does not exist, then one is mistaken to claim that one's experience is an experience with God. This is true no matter how persuasive the experience might seem to be. Moreover, naturalism offers a seemingly consistent interpretation of all human experience without arriving at religious or theistic conclusions. At least this is what modern psychology and sociology claim.

**Rational tests** for truth are sometimes offered in place of experiential tests. They are, however, equally inadequate, because we cannot achieve rationally inescapable arguments for the truth of any worldview. Our truth tests must be rational, because persuasion is a mental activity (at least in part). But rational tests do not produce rationally inescapable arguments. Other logical possibilities are always thinkable (even if they do not actually occur in reality).

## Faith vs. Reason

Many theologians have taken a fideistic approach to theistic affirmations. **Fideism** (from the Latin *fides*, which means *faith*) is the belief or the attitude that our knowledge of God comes purely by faith, not by reason nor through empirical evidence of any kind.[1] Human reason is thought to be inadequate (on account of sin, according to Reformed theology; on account of finiteness, according to modern Neo-orthodoxy). Thus it is thought that we must believe in God simply and strictly by faith. (Faith in this case is defined as affirmation apart from reason and evidence.)

The epistemological problems here are even more severe, however. Not only does this fideistic approach continue to beg the question, but it is a claim that can consistently be made within any worldview. A Buddhist could claim that Buddhism must be accepted by "faith." Even atheism could be accepted by this kind of "faith." In fact, any view at all can be held if one simply holds it by "faith" alone without any rational tests. Fideism, however powerful the spokesman, never proves that God exists. It simply affirms and proclaims God's existence. The fideist contends that God's existence cannot be proven; it can only be proclaimed. Begging the question becomes a virtue. Consequently, fideism does not rightfully make a truth claim at all. How could a fideistic claim ever be justified or established as true? Fideistic claims are not arguable on

---

[1] Faith, as the word is used in Christian orthodoxy, is different from fideistic faith. Biblical faith means the positive, accepting, obedient commitment to that which has been received by divine revelation. Faith is believing God's Word. Faith in the authentic biblical sense is never independent; it always has an object. Fideistic faith is the acceptance of something that cannot be shown to be true otherwise. Biblical faith is acceptance rather than resistance or suppression of that which God presents as true. God's presentation takes various forms, but it is seldom if ever without an evidential context. Christian faith is not an unreasonable or a non-rational faith.

strictly fideistic grounds. There is nothing wrong with
proclaiming the existence of God, but something is not true
just because someone affirms and/or proclaims that it is
true.[2]

Our fundamental question, therefore, returns. Can
God's existence be known? Is it even possible that the Bible
(or some other sacred writing) can be a special revelation?
The claim alone does not make it true. If we have no reason
to believe that God exists, then we have no basis on which to
interpret the Bible as a special revelation. To accept something for no reason is to have no control over what is or is
not to be accepted as true. Reason requires that significant
beliefs be based upon something. To act or believe for
absolutely no reason would be to act contrary to reason's
requirements. Thus, such beliefs would be irrational.

Now suppose someone were to argue like this: if reason
as such is somehow sinful, then we should try to be
irrational. We should accept the Bible without recourse to
sinful reason as a supporting factor. But notice, that position
itself is a rational conclusion. "If reason . . ., then we
should. . . ." If the premise that "reason is sinful" is true,
then to act irrationally would be the logical (rational) thing to
do in order to avoid sinfulness. This is surely confusing if not

---

[2]It is argued by some Christian fideists that the best evidence
for someone's existence is an affirmation of that existence by the
individual whose existence is being questioned. Thus they say that
God's self-proclaimed existence should not be questioned. This is
an interesting point to make and it is surely correct. But if we have a
book that claims that UFO's or "little green Martians" exist, we are
not likely to accept that claim simply because the claim is made.
Though God would have the sovereign right to demand that we
believe in him without confirming evidence, it is hard to see how
we could justly be held responsible for not believing unless we had
been given some adequate basis for believing. If the fideist responds
by saying that God made us so that we would naturally respond to
his self-proclamation, I would want to agree except for the rather
obvious fact that all do not thus respond. Furthermore, Scripture
rather clearly teaches that we are responsible for our unbelief. That
implies that sufficient evidence has been given for belief. What God
has provided, let no human being ignore.

outright contradictory. Can it be rational to act irrationally? Surely we need to start over and look for another approach.

**Faith and Reason**

A more reasonable approach is to take the existence of God simply as a hypothesis, and then see if such a hypothesis fits the facts. This is the **"systematic consistency"** approach of E. J. Carnell and others, and it has been very popular with contemporary evangelical scholars. The method is a kind of "combinationalist" approach. It makes use of an appropriate combination of rational, empirical, experiential, and pragmatic evidence. The hypothesis of God's existence is tested and found to be consistent with all the facts (when they are "properly" interpreted).

The Achilles heel of this approach, however, comes in the justification of the starting point. Why should one begin with the hypothesis that the God of biblical theism exists? Hindu philosophy begins with a radically different hypothesis and seems to be satisfied with its ability to "fit the facts." Naturalism uses this same approach and more or less cogently argues that the naturalistic hypothesis fits the whole range of facts better than a theistic hypothesis.

To argue over which facts support which theory best seems useless, because facts are not independent explanatory entities. Facts always gain their meaning ultimately from the overall framework of interpretation, not the other way around. In many cases the same "fact" of history or science, for example, can be interpreted either theistically or naturalistically. A miracle is a possible fact if theism is true, but a miracle claim is either not a fact or it is a misinterpreted fact if naturalism is the case. There are no purely neutral facts. All facts are interpreted facts, and they gain their subjective meaning from the worldview of the observer. Of course, not all worldviews are equally valid, and only one worldview actually describes the whole of reality. Thus there is an objective meaning for all facts, but our problem comes in how we know that objective meaning.

God's existence has not been inescapably proven by the apologetic of systematic consistency; it has only been cogently and persuasively affirmed in a comprehensive, rational setting. This is quite an accomplishment. But at this point one comes to realize the logical and the ontological priority of God's existence.

In other words, we must always remember that God's existence is not produced by any argument. God is either already actually there or else he is merely a figure of speech or perhaps only a valuable idea. His existence or non-existence is already a fact prior to our examination and does not in any way depend upon our examination of the evidence. Our conclusion about the cogency or lack of cogency of some particular argument is, strictly speaking, irrelevant to the question of God's actual existence.

Our personal knowledge of God's existence, however, is very much dependent upon persuasive claims, persuasive evidence, and upon whether or not God (if he exists) has made himself known by revelation to humans. Let us turn, then, to reexamine the classical discussions of rational theistic proofs to see whether a theistic hypothesis can be shown to have merit or not.

Is there any basis for affirming theism? If God exists, then it is certainly possible that there might be a verifiable word from God (such as the Bible). But how can one know whether or not God does exist?

## THREE BASIC TYPES OF RATIONAL THEISTIC PROOFS

There are three basic types or categories of rational arguments for the existence of God. The most persuasive of the three is the argument that God has directly revealed himself to someone. This argument, strangely enough, is persuasive but is technically the weakest of the three from the standpoint that it is based quite naturally in personal subjective experience and therefore does not offer sufficient, objective, justifying criteria. The other two types do attempt to offer sufficient rational criteria.

## RELIGIOUS EXPERIENCE

Though the **personal testimony** of a religious experience is a very common way by which people are actually persuaded that God does exist (and thus it may have some evangelistic value among those who do not question such things too deeply), it is essentially not arguable independently. That is, the evidence for God which comes from his direct revelation to someone is a type of evidence that is available only to those who have received this revelation. You cannot prove to someone else that God revealed himself to you, if the revelation was strictly private and special. All you can do is make the claim.

If the revelatory claims are to be transmitted to others through a verbal personal testimony or by means of a secondary source such as a written record (the Bible, for example), one would (in the nature of the case) be faced with the necessity of adducing non-revelational evidences to show that this personal testimony or this written record was in fact an accurately transmitted record of that originally claimed revelation. After settling the question of accurate transmission, the question of the authenticity of the claim would still be a further matter of concern.

While this so-called **revelational apologetic** has been a very popular approach, it does not seem to have the philosophical credentials that other arguments for the existence of God have, nor does it effectively bypass them in the public arena. In fact, it may be argued quite cogently that even the most persuasive, personal experience needs an external confirmation or an objective standard of interpretation. Otherwise the truth claims are expressed fideistically and thus beg the question of truth.

Experience may and undoubtedly does persuade the one who has it, but it is an apparent fact that seemingly identical psychological and physiological states can be produced by multiple causes. This state of affairs demands some ability to provide an external standard of interpretation in order to distinguish among these possible causes. To be blunt about it, how could one know it was God and not Satan (or drugs or hypnotic suggestion) that caused the experience claimed as "religious"? Something other than the experience itself must be used to make such a judgment. Evangelical Christians often remind believers to test "experiences" by the Word. Experience alone does not always conform to truth.

Two methodological approaches present themselves as philosophical alternatives to simple claims of direct, religious experiences. These methods are classified as *aposteriori* and *apriori* with reference to their starting point.[3] **Apriori** arguments begin with internal characteristics of humankind's mental nature. These arguments are rationalistic (in the technical sense). They try to demonstrate God's existence without appealing to sensory evidence, and thus they hope to provide a justifying context in which experiences can be tested and known to be from God. **Aposteriori** arguments begin with aspects of reality external to the human mind. These arguments are empirical in that they attempt to reason toward God from a starting point provided by sense-experience. Both types offer "reasons for believing" that God does indeed exist. Thus they intend to form a sufficient base for theistic affirmations and for theistic interpretations of experiences with transcendent reality.

### Rational Proofs: Apriori

Several attempts have been made to base the existence of God on **the moral nature of human beings** themselves. Humans are characteristically thinking, communicating, moral beings. People not only make tools, thus demonstrating their technological ability, but they communicate with a propositional language, and they set up rules of behavior, thus constituting their social life. Apparently there is a pre-rational moral conscience among all people. Good and evil may have different content in various cultures, but the basic categories are always there. Humans also seem to recognize a cumulative cultural tradition. History and the study of history is a unique characteristic of humanity. To be human is to transcend processes that contribute only to human survival. In fact, to be human is to be an aesthetic being; one

---

[3]*Apriori* refers to reasoning from assumed principles or from definitions. *Apriori* arguments start with ideas or concepts that are assumed, that are found within the human mind. These assumptions or presuppositions are already known prior to any conscious attempt to draw rational conclusions from them. *Aposteriori* refers to reasoning that is based on principles derived from the observation of facts. *Aposteriori* arguments start with principles drawn from experience and developed by induction from sensory data arising from the world that exists external to the human mind.

who will decorate, produce artifacts, make pictures or carvings even for (especially for) nonutilitarian purposes. These features of human nature seem to point to the conclusion that something more than innate natural principles of matter must exist. There seems to be a pull, a direction, a purpose that is built into the human personality, but it is one which does not seem to proceed out of the natural world as scientists have been able to understand it. Our moral and aesthetic nature must come from God.

This *apriori* approach to the existence of God is most commonly based on the moral nature of the human personality. The argument is not that everyone agrees upon particular moral standards, but rather that moral standards are innately a part of human personality. These moral standards take the same position in this argument that elements of design take in the teleological argument (as we shall see in a moment). That is, these moral elements seem to imply a moral source other than material forces alone. The conclusion of the argument based upon these unique elements of human nature is that there must be a superior, transcendent, moral, aesthetic, propositionally conscious personality who is the actual source of these elements of human personality.

Objections to this argument are usually built upon the logical possibility that an objective moral law is a psychological illusion or the possibility that moral laws do not need a cause or an explanation. These possibilities are highly unlikely, but they do seem to point to the need for another approach to supplement the theist's case. To argue that an existing moral source is necessary to account for the human moral conscience seems to demand an argument on grounds not strictly *apriori*.[4]

---

[4]Some, of course, may argue that logical probability and existential probability are equivalent. That is, they suggest that something is likely to exist or not likely to exist based on the logical probability alone. But this is certainly not self-evidently the case, and if we are to make such a claim, we would at least have to give our reasons. The basic problem of all *apriori* approaches is that the actual, existential existence of an idea does not follow necessarily from its logical probability, no matter how high it might be.

The so-called **ontological argument** is another well-known example of an *apriori* argument. The fact that people almost universally have at least some conscious awareness of God that prompts them to participate in theological discussions, that leads them to perform religious services, and convicts them of their own lack of perfection is taken as rational evidence for the necessary existence of God. By innate definition, God is the greatest conceivable being. A being that does exist is greater than the mere idea of a being that does not exist. Thus God, as the greatest conceivable Being, must exist. This idea of God is not produced by rational argumentation but rather is the *apriori* source of such argumentation.

Several of the objections to the ontological argument for God's existence center upon the question of what is necessarily real. Is the rationally inescapable the real? If so, the ontological argument is worthy of careful consideration. If, however, rational inescapability is not the guarantee of actual reality, the ontological argument could not stand alone as a persuasive argument for God's existence. It is logically possible that nothing exists (and, of course, that is always a logical possibility though it is an actual impossibility), therefore the rational force of all purely logical arguments is never sufficient to prove the actual existence of the conclusions. The *apriori* arguments seem to need the same kind of support that experiential arguments need. Perhaps that needed supplement can be provided by an *aposteriori* approach.

## Rational Proofs: Aposteriori

The *aposteriori* arguments begin with some existing feature of the world or of the universe and reason from that to the existence of God. The basic direction of these arguments is to persuade people that the universe is not self-explanatory. In other words, these arguments contend that contingency is an essential feature of the universe.

Their effectiveness as proofs depends, of course, upon whether or not the universe is a contingent reality, and upon whether or not this can be known. In other words, the argument is that in its essential character the universe is neither self-existent, nor self-explanatory, and thus the

105

universe itself is not a necessary being. The existence of a contingent reality (such as the universe) presupposes the existence of a necessary reality (one capable of causing and maintaining the whole contingent universe). Though one could conceivably speculate that reality may simply have appeared of its own accord without any causal source, this speculation has never been supported by any actual evidence. There is no experimental evidence at all that things in the universe arise from absolutely nothing. All of the hard experimental data support the view that things always come from something else. (Life comes from life, and effects have causes.)

The "something else" that causes or allows some event to occur also must come from another something and on and on. The seemingly necessary conclusion to all of this is that *since something is here now, there must be an eternal something sufficient to cause and maintain that which currently exists.* If the universe itself has characteristic and essential features that indicate its inherent dependent status, then one would be led quite naturally to conclude that there must be some eternal reality other than the universe itself upon which the dependent universe depends. This eternal reality would be either the necessary reality (the uncaused cause of all else) or it could conceivably be another contingent reality. If it were another contingent reality, however, the argument would simply continue until it did come to a necessary reality. Since something is here that is dependent (i.e. that could not be here unless something else were there first to cause and maintain it), then there must be an original something.[5] That

---

[5]Note that the argument is not just that the universe needs an original cause in time alone. If that were the case, the original cause might have existed in the past only. But the evidence for contingency is evidence for current contingency. The form and order of the universe are not only not self-originating, they are not autonomously self-adjusting. The question is not simply: Where did the universe come from? but also: Why does the universe continue to exhibit its current dependent form? The argument is that the explanation for the existence of the universe must not only be an original cause in time, but also a current, moment-by-moment cause, a presently existing cause.

ultimately necessary being is affirmed by Christian theism to be a "something" that provides life, personality, and meaning to and through the universe. Thus that something is a someone! This creative being is God himself.

There are several types of *aposteriori* arguments, and they have been carefully stated and quite thoroughly analyzed over many years. The **cosmological argument** is one of the best-known of the rational arguments for God's existence. It is based upon the actual existence of some contingent reality. Usually it is stated in simple form: there must be a First Cause of all that exists. Technically the contingency argument leads to an Uncaused Cause. This is referred to as the first cause only by default; there would be only one uncaused cause of the same universe. It is the current existence of things as well as the simple origin of things that must be accounted for, and it is actual reality, not merely possible things that must be caused.

Major objections to this argument include the counterproposal that an infinite series, (i.e. an infinite regress) of causes is possible. (This proposal is intriguing but almost certainly false and impossible.) Another objection is an alternate conception of the universe as a diverse, multiple entity, not a whole entity that needs a single cause. No convincing evidence for this hypothesis has been forthcoming, however. Another hypothesis is that perhaps the universe is a unique kind of reality that is dependent upon itself.

While these objections and others like them have served for some as persuasive excuses, the biblical theist agrees with Paul (Romans 1:20) that there is no adequate excuse for denying the existence of God nor for failing to worship him. Even those who affirm a self-dependent universe still must account for the fact that it is an existing universe rather than a non-existing one. Why is there something rather than nothing?

If there is such a thing as cause and effect (and it seems almost self-evident and at least reasonable to believe that there is) and if that relationship is in fact truly a causal one, then an effect would surely be contingent upon its actual cause. This can be accepted despite the false Humean supposition that "cause" is simply a mental habit, and despite the self-defeating Kantian compromise that "mental habits" are all that we have to work with anyway.

If the universe, then, can be properly described as in any sense an effect, rational thought about this fact would demand (as a necessary rather than merely a probable conclusion) that there must be a first, original, uncaused cause. This type of argument is often identified with the philosophical method used by Thomas Aquinas (though it is perhaps debatable how much Aquinas actually depended upon this kind of thinking). There is also a *Kalam* version of this argument that is increasing in popularity in the late twentieth century.[6]

A second type of *aposteriori* argument is the **teleological argument** or the argument from **design**. If in fact design does exist, that is, if the apparent design in the natural universe is not simply an illusion or only a mental projection of order, then the natural, reasonable, logical conclusion would be that a designer, a source of that design, must exist. The debate ranges over whether the universe does or does not exhibit features that are correctly described as design, and

---

[6]*Kalam* is the Arabic term for "word" or "speech," but it is also a title referring to Muslim scholastic theology. Medieval Arab philosophers tried to base theism upon logical arguments for the necessity of a beginning for the universe. The recent Kalam form of the cosmological argument usually emphasizes the modern scientific evidence ("Big Bang" cosmology) pointing to an actual beginning for the physical universe. If the universe began, then it would have had a cause (since Something cannot come from Nothing, and everything that has a real beginning must have a cause sufficient to bring about that beginning), and to produce the kind of universe that actually exists, that cause would have to be all-powerful and personal. The Thomistic version of the cosmological argument does not depend upon the fact of a beginning. Aquinas believed that it was possible for the universe to have been eternally maintained in its contingent state by an eternal Necessary Being. The Thomistic version does not deny a beginning. It does not depend, however, upon a beginnning. The scientific evidence in the mid-twentieth century does favor a real beginning for the observable universe. Not all assent to "Big Bang" cosmology, however, and Christians would be unwise to tie theism exclusively to naturalistic scientific theories that may change.

over what sort of reality would be necessary to produce design.

The debate seems to be almost endless because the theory of evolution in its naturalistic expression quite vigorously argues that apparent design is more correctly described as the natural product of innate natural properties within matter itself. The problem of evil and suffering in the world is also frequently cited as an argument against the teleological approach to nature. Evil is seen as an evidence either of disharmony and lack of design or else as evidence that the source of design must be imperfect at best or malicious at worst. Nevertheless, if it could be shown that a contingent design did in fact characterize the natural universe, that would lead logically to the conclusion that some intelligent source or some intentional force was responsible for it.

The biblical theist, William Paley, argued that the infinitely complex nature of the presently existing universe is good evidence that there is an infinitely complex being that has produced it. It is to be noted that a biblical theist does not necessarily believe that the universe is technically infinite in complexity. The created universe is thought to be finite, thus the teleological argument could not properly move by logic alone to an infinitely complex deity. (The concept of infinity is not at all clear to everyone who uses the term, of course, and thus the value of the teleological argument is not necessarily diminished by this logical reality.) The vastness, the intricate balance, the "anthropic" purposefulness illustrated by the precision of nuclear and cosmic relationships in the known universe is nevertheless taken as evidence for the greatness of that power and intentional will that must have produced it.

These evidences (and more) have traditionally been used to argue *aposteriori* for the highly probable rational conclusion that a creator God does exist. Some even suggest (and I think that I would agree) that a well-stated cosmological argument based on a principle of existential undeniability, for example, actually leads to the logical conclusion that this God necessarily exists.[7] Even so, though many people do feel the force of teleological reasoning, it is clear that only a few people actually come to believe in God because of technical reasoning of this kind.

## RATIONAL PROOFS: ANOTHER LOOK

Thus there are two basic forms of *aposteriori* arguments, namely the cosmological and the teleological, and two forms of the *apriori* arguments, namely the ontological and the moral arguments, along with the general argument from religious experience. Each of these arguments have been extensively analyzed, stated, restated and debated through the years by the scholarly community. Yet perhaps there is still room for another look.

It seems clear to me that *apriori* arguments cannot stand alone. They are not rationally inescapable because alternate logical possibilities do exist in the minds of men. Of the *aposteriori* arguments, the teleological argument is the most varied and in many ways the most interesting, but the cosmological argument seems to be the technically stronger one, because it can be premised by a contingent reality that unquestionably does exist. That everyone is not convinced by this argument is not necessarily due to the formal invalidity of the argument. Some people simply do not ask, or if they do, they do not consciously seek to answer, the ultimately significant metaphysical question: Why does this particular something rather than nothing exist? Many philosophers give no answer to this question. They claim that there is no answer. The only answer, of course, is the theistic one,

---

[7]Existential undeniability refers to the fact that some things must be affirmed, they cannot be denied. For example, one can say the words: "I do not exist!" but no one can actually affirm that statement because to affirm it is to refute it. Thus it is existentially undeniable that I do exist if I make any sort of affirmation at all. Moreover, I am clearly not a necessary being. Thus it is undeniable that some contingent beings do exist. This is an affirmation that seems to be undeniably true and thus it can serve as a valid premise from which to develop a cosmological argument.

but, surprisingly, we are not forced to affirm even that which our minds understand to be true.

## A Preliminary Evaluation

Kant's objection that all thought is somehow isolated from reality (noumena vs. phenomena) is a technical objection that is either false or else nothing can be known to be true. To take refuge in skepticism is always a philosophical option, but it could hardly be said to be the correct position. Rational arguments for the existence of God, whether valid or not, do make one very important claim: God is the source of rationality, and rationality is in touch with reality, because both are products and reflections of the creative rationality of God.

The cosmological argument claims that existence does not begin to exist irrationally. If the universe simply "popped" into existence and had no cause, then it might just as well "pop" out of existence tomorrow. Parts of reality may have miraculously "popped" into existence last year, or some of reality may have, for no reason, ceased to exist last month. No science could be sustained upon such an irrational metaphysic, however. Things can be meaningfully understood only if there is a rational stability to existing reality. Generally speaking, the laws of nature are regular. The universe can be understood because it is fundamentally rational.

The point at which the critics often seem to miss the real thrust of the rational proofs is this very claim about rationality itself. The traditional arguments for God, whether or not they formally demonstrate the unquestionable existence of God, are really attempts to support the validity of reason itself.

If, for example, the cosmological argument is not true, if it does not lead to any valid conclusions, if it is wrong and false and incorrect in its thrust, and thus if a rational Source of rationality does not exist, then on what basis could rationality be defended at all? This becomes very significant when one realizes that all criticisms of the rational proofs depend upon the validity of rationality. If rationality is not necessary, and if irrationality is equally as valid as rationality (or equally as invalid), then no argument against the rational proofs has any necessary validity at all. No one could use any logical argument to prove or to disprove anything. But if reasoning is valid and if a rational refutation of a theistic proof is to have any value, then logic and reason themselves must be based on something other than the irrationality of a reality that may for no reason pop in or out of existence without cause or consequence.

In other words, it seems that the very attempt to refute a rational proof for God is self-defeating, because, without God, reason could only be an innate property of irrational matter. Thus it has no claim on absolute truthfulness. In fact, on the basis of this approach to metaphysics, God may begin to exist tomorrow. Who could say that this would be impossible? Surely there could be no necessary, rational proof against such a possibility.

This totally irrational state of affairs is not often the conscious metaphysic presupposed by the philosophical skeptics, yet it is not logically excluded by their proposals. Rationality presupposes the existence of God, and nontheists use that very rationality in their critical attacks upon theistic proofs.

## A Biblical Proposal

There is, however, a more positive word to be said about all of this from the biblical theist's point of view. The Bible is not silent about the traditional philosophical arguments for the existence of God, though fideistic biblical theologians seem committed to ignoring this fact and regularly deny that the Bible even gives proofs for God's existence. God is always assumed, they say, by the biblical writers. What I wish to suggest is that the Bible does make a case for God's existence. The evidence for my suggestion is quite extensive, but I will give only one example.

Paul expresses God's revealed truth about this matter in his letter to the Romans. In Romans 1:20, Paul bases theism *aposteriori*. He seems to build his case both cosmologically and teleologically. God's eternal power can be seen from the form and design of the created universe. His deity is his uncaused existence, his unique non-contingent nature. These things make up God's invisible nature. The great "I am" is the necessary being from which all contingent reality derives. According to the Revised Standard Version:

> [18]The wrath of God is revealed from heaven against all ungodliness and wickedness of men who by their wickedness suppress the truth. [19]For what can be known about God is plain to them, because God has shown it to them. [20]Ever since the creation of the world his invisible nature, namely, his eternal power and deity, has been clearly perceived in the things that have been made. So they are without excuse; [21]for although they knew God they did not honor him as God or give thanks to him, but they became futile in their thinking and their senseless minds were darkened. [22]Claiming to be wise, they became fools, [23]and exchanged the glory of the immortal God for images resembling mortal man or birds or animals or reptiles. [24]Therefore God gave them up in the lusts of their hearts to impurity, to the dishonoring of their bodies among themselves, [25]because they exchanged the truth about God for a lie and worshiped and served the creature rather than the Creator, who is blessed for ever! Amen.

Notice in verse 20, the perception of God's eternal power and deity has been clear since creation. Thus Paul is unquestionably claiming that knowledge of God flows out of the created universe. The things have been made, he says. That is, they are not self-existent nor self-explanatory. People (vs. 21) responded either by idolatry or by some kind of naturalistic pantheism. This seemed to be profound and intelligent, but in fact it was morally foolish (vs. 22, cf. Ps. 53:1). Naturalism, pantheism, process theology, evolution, idolatry, and any other non-theistic view is a lie (vs. 25) and is inexcusable.

Paul makes a clear transition in chapter 2, and he supplements his cosmological approach to theism with a clearly stated *apriori* moral argument (verses 12-16, especially vs. 15).

> [28]And since they did not see fit to acknowledge God, God gave them up to a base mind and to improper conduct. . . . [32]Though they know God's decree that those who do such things deserve to die, they not only do them but approve those who practice them.

113

2:1 Therefore you have no excuse, O man, whoever you are, when you judge another; for in passing judgment upon him you condemn yourself, because you, the judge, are doing the very same things. . . . 12 All who have sinned without the law will also perish without the law, and all who have sinned under the law will be judged by the law. 13 For it is not the hearers of the law who are righteous before God, but the doers of the law who will be justified. 14 When Gentiles who have not the law do by nature what the law requires, they are a law to themselves, even though they do not have the law. 15 They show that what the law requires is written on their hearts, while their conscience also bears witness and their conflicting thoughts accuse or perhaps excuse them 16 on that day when, according to my gospel, God judges the secrets of men by Christ Jesus.

Having based theism cosmologically and having pressed the moral implications implicit in this worldview, Paul then turns to the fundamental reality of divine revelation. If there is a God, and if a moral law has been revealed, then it may be cogently argued that divine revelation exists.

3:1 Then what advantage has the Jew? . . . 2 Much in every way. To begin with, the Jews are entrusted with the oracles of God. [The written Word of God.] 3 What if some were unfaithful? Does their unfaithfulness nullify the faithfulness of God? 4 By no means! Let God be true though every man be false. . . .

Is there any further way to verify the reality of divine revelation? Is there a way to present this truth of God apart from the complexities of philosophical apologetics? Yes, there is.

3:21 But now the righteousness of God has been manifested apart from law, although the law and the prophets bear witness to it, 22 the righteousness of God through faith in Jesus Christ for all who believe. For there is no distinction; 23 since all have sinned and fall short of the glory of God, 24 they are justified by his grace as a gift, through the redemption which is in Christ Jesus, 25 whom God put forward as an expiation [a propitiation] by his blood, to be received by faith. This was to show God's righteousness, because in his divine forbearance he had passed over former sins; 26 it was to prove at the present time that he himself is righteous and that he justifies him who has faith in Jesus.

Faith is man's positive response to this revealed knowledge of God. Faith is not a mental activity that fills in the intellectual gaps of knowledge so much as it is a moral commitment to that knowledge that has already been intellectually grasped. Faith does not automatically or primarily solve intellectual problems. Faith is the means by which God solves moral problems, and faith is the hope (even against hope), and the belief that God will do whatever he has said he will do.

> 4:9 . . . We say that faith was reckoned to Abraham as righteousness. 10How then was it reckoned to him? Was it before or after he had been circumcised? It was not after, but before he was circumcised. 11He received circumcision as a sign or seal of the righteousness which he had by faith while he was still uncircumcised. . . . 18In hope he believed against hope, that he should become the father of many nations; as he had been told, "So shall your descendants be," 19He did not weaken in faith when he considered his own body, which was as good as dead because he was about a hundred years old, or when he considered the barrenness of Sarah's womb. 20No distrust made him waver concerning the promise of God, but he grew strong in his faith as he gave glory to God, 21fully convinced that God was able to do what he had promised. 22That is why his faith was "reckoned to him as righteousness," 23But the words, "it was reckoned to him," were written not for his sake alone, 24but for ours also. It will be reckoned to us who believe in him that raised from the dead Jesus our Lord, 25who was put to death for our trespasses and raised for our justification.
> 5:1Therefore, since we are justified by faith, we have peace with God through our Lord Jesus Christ.

Chapters 7 and 8 add the personal testimony of a conversion experience and describe the new life in Christ. Chapters 9-11 give historical evidences to confirm the Christian gospel, and the rest of the book is a practical exhortation based on the truth established in the preceding chapters.

This is Paul's inspired apologetic for the truth of the Christian worldview. The traditional arguments find a representative treatment, but each must be seen in its proper order and in its proper context. The Christian in today's world would do well to take another look at the classical proofs for the existence of God.

# GLOSSARY

Advancement
Apologetics
*Aposteriori*
*Apriori*
Atheism
Big Bang Cosmology
Cause
Contingent
Cosmological Argument
Evidence
Faith
Fideism
God
Hypothesis
Intuition

Kalam
Moral Argument
Natural Theology
Naturalism
Ontological Argument
Pantheism
Process Thought
Proof
Rational
Reason
Revelation
Skepticism
Teleological Argument
Theism

# 7

# Creation: A Reasonable Alternative

*Naturalistic Evolution*
*Theistic Evolution*
*Special Creation*
*Testing Models of Origins*
*The Problem of Verification*
*The Scientific Mind*
*The Problem of Interpretation*
*Creation, Evolution, and Thermodynamics*
*The First Law*
*The Second Law*
*Science, Religion, and Truth*

Metaphysically, why do things exist? Historically, how did things come to be the way they are? Questions like these concerning ontological and temporal origins always fascinate the human mind. We are interested in knowing where, ultimately, we came from and thus in knowing whether life has any real purpose or meaning.

In this chapter we shall discuss two alternative philosophies of origins. The first is related to some form of theism (though it can be discussed in non-religious language) and is referred to as the "creation model" of origins.[1] The other

---

[1]In this chapter, I will use the admittedly religious phrase "creation model." A non-religious description of the facts and interpretations that make up the "creation model" would be "the abrupt origination of species" or "punctuated individuation." This religiously neutral language merely describes various plant and animal types as having originated independently; that is, the evidence is that they did not descend from previous genetic pools or

alternative employs an "evolutionary model" of origins. (A "model" is simply an explanation or a set of scientific interpretations, a framework for describing supposed relationships between accepted sets of factual data.)

Creation attributes (explicitly or by implication) the

---

ancestral populations. Something must have caused these new beginnings of living kinds. Creationists claim that God was the direct cause. The scientific evidence for abrupt beginnings, however, can be described without using the theologically loaded term "creation." Were it not for court and school board decisions denying teachers the right to present this evidence in the state-supported government schools, we would not need terms other than "creation." Nevertheless, because creation implies a Creator, in the growing legal precedent excluding all reference to God in public life and especially in the public school classroom (in this case even implied references), use of the term "creation" in a science classroom to describe a viable scientific interpretation of undisputed facts has been seen by the secular courts as being somehow "unconstitutional." Thus "non-religious" language has been developed. The motivation is not to hide meaning or beliefs, but the concern is to find some way legally to present a very plausible interpretation of the fossil evidence and of the geological data. In 1987 (Aguillard vs. Edwards) the U.S. Supreme Court denied legal standing to the Louisiana Balanced Treatment Act (which required that the creation model be given a fair hearing in the science classroom). But in the ruling the court affirmed that teachers are free to examine and describe alternative non-evolutionary theories in the public school classroom. Since many school boards have continued to deny that right, other precedent-setting cases are still in the courts. Christians should earnestly pray that truth will not be excluded by law from the public schools of our "one nation under God." Nevertheless, it does seem that for the near future non-religious language will have to be used in public schools. Perhaps school boards can be asked merely to require that whenever origins are discussed in a science class, evidence that does not support the evolutionary model should be presented in addition to evidence that does support it. Such a requirement is fair and does not require "religious language" nor does it require religion to be introduced as an explanation. The overwhelming lack of transitional fossils is a fact regardless of the "explanation" given for this fact, and science classes should not omit relevant facts when dealing with controversial subjects.

origin of all things to an eternal non-natural cause (or causes). Evolution affirms (by assumption) a natural cause (or causes) as the source of the present configuration of things. According to the usual naturalistic interpretation of the latter model, there is no non-natural cause nor any non-natural reality that could produce either an absolute beginning of things or the present configuration of things.[2] There

---

[2]Notice these distinctions carefully. Technically we must recognize that "creation" speaks to the issue of origins, the absolute beginning of something (whether it be a living creature or the universe itself). "Evolution," on the other hand, speaks primarily to the issue of the development of things since their beginning. Some have claimed that the two models address different issues and thus are not in conflict. Such claims seriously show a misunderstanding of the two models, however. Creationists generally believe that when things were created they were in the same general form that we can observe today. Variations may occur and deterioration certainly occurs, but each major kind of thing is thought to have begun as a separate entity. Thus for a special creationist, the great variety of living things we see today did not have a common "ancestor" but were separate kinds from their very beginning. Evolutionists, however, do assume an essential process of variation and differentiation from a single origin (from a network of common ancestors and ultimately from a common chemical process in nature). Naturalistic evolution denies any transcendent reality. The only reality is nature itself. Theistic evolution affirms a transcendent Creator but nevertheless affirms a natural, orderly, development of all living things, perhaps including a real but scientifically "invisible" providence. Thus special creation and theistic evolution are true alternatives. They cannot be viewed as complementary notions, for each cancels out some of the main affirmations of the other. Evolution and theism do not necessarily cancel each other out, though this combination is seriously flawed, as we shall see. But evolution and creation as scientific models do cancel each other out. One cannot have abrupt origins of each major living kind and at the same time have all major kinds developing naturally and gradually one from the other. Conceivably there could be a third model that somehow includes more data and offers a better interpretation of the natural world, but practically speaking we seem to have only two real choices, and these two alternatives cannot be harmonized. We must use reason to evaluate the merits of each alternative and thus choose between them.

are many variations within these two models (including several attempts to combine natural development and theistic origination); however, the basic positions are clearly distinct one from the other and will be discussed separately below. Today the most dominant model is the theory of naturalistic evolution.

## NATURALISTIC EVOLUTION

Evolution is a scientific model that describes the development of orderly systems (whether of subatomic particles or of galaxies) by historical, progressive processes which are assumed to be inherent within matter itself. Matter and energy are, by some, considered to be eternal in their essential nature. The complexity which is presently observable in the universe is thought to have originated in randomness.[3] This change is not believed to have been

---

[3]"Randomness" is not a fully accurate word. The initial (hypothetical) explosion known as the "Big Bang" is indeed understood to be a real, dynamic explosion, and thus it would surely seem to have been chaotic. However, it is argued by some that the primordial mass which existed prior to the disordering "bang" must have been absolutely and perfectly orderly. This assumption is an attempt to save the "Big Bang" hypothesis from an obvious violation of the entropy principle. Order exists now: thermodynamic order naturally tends toward disorder: new order does not arise spontaneously from disorder: therefore, order must have been original. Creationists agree with this reasoning but find it difficult to recognize how it can solve the entropy problem raised by the naturalistic models of origins. An orderly universe exists now. Thus it must have had an orderly origin that significantly exceeded the current level of orderliness. God is the only fully adequate source of such order. It is not at all clear exactly what it would mean to speak of energy and matter as being hypothetically structured so as to be perfectly orderly. Even if we think only in general terms about a natural state of complete orderliness, no natural force is known that could produce or maintain such order. The hypothetical collapse of a previous universe would not result in such order. Order does not arise from true chaos. The new science of "chaos" is not proving that chaos produces order but rather that what we call chaos is not true chaos. What appears chaotic is often geometrically

accomplished by any "outside" or supernatural power. The development of all that we see and know today is said to have come about through the complex processes of cause-and-effect that are presently discernible by using the scientific method.

## THEISTIC EVOLUTION

Not every evolutionary model is atheistic. Theistic evolution is a suggested model which argues that a transcendent "direction" has been applied to these evolutionary

---

orderly in very complex ways. See James Gleick, *Chaos: Making a New Science* (New York: Viking, 1987). Creationists sometimes press the argument that the highest orderliness possible would by now have dissipated into true chaos if the universe had in fact been decreasing in orderliness at the current increasingly rapid rate of energy dissipation for the full twenty billion years hypothesized since the so-called "Big Bang" happened? Whatever the hypothetical pre-"bang" mass would have been like, an "explosion" would be a random scattering of mostly hydrogen atoms (if even they could be readily formed in such an "event"). These atoms would all be rushing away from each other in radial lines. Lacking external friction, it does not seem that these atoms would naturally form lumps or clumps, nor would these primordial atoms have any inherent rotational patterns, nor would there be any original chemical structures of any kind. Even if simple hydrogen stars did somehow form and eventually went supernovae thus spewing out into space complex atoms "cooked up" in their interior nuclear furnaces, the likelihood is that those heavier atoms would "naturally" be evenly scattered throughout the universe, not grouped into useful and suitable configurations for galaxy clusters, binary star systems, planetary systems such as ours, and environments suited for life. There is no sufficient or necessary reason to suppose that a "Big Bang" explosion would naturally result in any kind of an orderly pattern, much less the specific orderly pattern observed in the universe that does exist now, even less the highly ordered environment of the earth, and much much less the extremely orderly complexity that characterizes even the minimum chemical configurations on which life can ride. The human brain, for example, is said to be the most complex configuration of matter in the entire universe. Stars are utterly simple compared to a single strand of DNA.

processes. Theistic evolution, nevertheless, assumes that the scientifically describable processes are exactly the same as those described by the naturalistic evolutionist. The difference is that theistic evolutionists assert that some directing "pressure" is an essential element in the evolutionary theory itself.

A theistic-evolutionary explanation of reality, however, is difficult to maintain for several reasons. Clearly an attempt to establish itself as an intermediate position between the two basic alternatives, it is, nevertheless, a viewpoint for which there could be no supportive evidence. Theistic evolution as a model of origins is not testable, because it is ambiguous at each of the crucial points. If one accepts all of the naturalistic explanations for evolutionary development, then the claim that God is an essential element of the explanation is simply added to the theory for purely religious reasons. It makes no actual difference at all. Therefore such claims become "pure" faith, subjective choice, and arbitrary assumption. It is a "faith" that is not supported by any empirical evidence (the supposed evidence is all claimed equally by naturalistic evolution), nor is the theistic element necessarily related to any of the actual physical data.

Subjective feelings and/or contentless intuitions seem to be the source of this version of theism. It certainly does not arise from philosophical necessity. Even less does it arise from biblical exegesis.[4]

---

[4]There are numerous theological and exegetical objections to theistic evolution as a model to explain the origin of all things. I mention only that such a model cannot be derived from the text of Scripture unless it is first read into the text of Scripture by the interpreter. Genesis moves through definite stages of goodness ("and God [six times] saw that it was good"), not through a continuum of struggle, extinction, and mutation. Moreover, evolutionary theory is in no wise compatible with the biblical account of the origin of the human female. Eve is specifically named as the original human mother. Adam, then, had no mother. This, it seems to me, is exegetically indisputable. One cannot derive an evolutionary origin for humans from the biblical text. It simply does not teach or affirm such ideas. The evangelical Christians who hold to theistic evolution (and many do) usually argue no more than that the text

Evolution as presently conceived may or may not be the correct scientific explanation of biological or other natural change, and theism may or may not be the correct world-view. But if evolutionary models are empirically false, adding theism hardly makes them true. If, on the other hand, evolutionary development can be adequately account-ed for without involving the idea of God (i.e. if evolutionary models are true as the naturalists claim), then the affirmation of God's involvement in the process is superfluous. In essence Deism reappears as the underlying philosophical structure of the "theistic evolution" model of origins.[5]

## SPECIAL CREATION

The other major meaningful view of origins is often called the theory of special creation. This model suggests that matter, energy, man, animals, plants, stars, and the space-time universe itself were brought into existence by special creative (non-natural) processes[6] which are no longer operat-ing today.[7]

---

taken figuratively will allow one to hold evolutionary views. They rarely argue that the text actually conveys, affirms, and/or teaches evolutionary theories.

[5]Even if Genesis could not be accepted as a historically descriptive account, theistic evolution would still suffer from the philosophical weaknesses outlined briefly in the text. To affirm that evolutionary models will not work without a theistic involvement is to affirm that evolutionary models alone are not adequate to account for the origin of all things. Please note that the issue here is not whether evolutionary models have any explanatory power. They do! Evolutionary models may or may not adequately describe biological processes of change and development, but theistic evolution means nothing as a philosophical model of absolute beginnings (origins). Perhaps someone could argue for a creation model of origins and a subsequent natural evolutionary develop-ment, but this, in my opinion, is Deism (and thus is subject to standard philosophical critiques of that historical system of thought).

[6]Creative processes, by my definition, are non-natural. Nature did not exist prior to its creation, thus the cause of the origin of nature as a whole could not be natural. There was no prior reality in

This is the viewpoint reflected, in the first chapter of the Bible. There in Genesis God creates the heavens and the earth out of absolutely nothing; that is, out of no previously existing material, out of no previously existing physical

---

existence other than the supernatural God. Since the word "creation" is often used in popular speech to refer to the process of making something out of previously existing materials, the term "special" is usually added to distinguish this idea of absolute origination from evolutionary models. Popular speech also has a usage of "creation" that refers to a literary product or an artistic work or musical composition or something similar. Interestingly, this usage implies that something "new" has come out of the ideas in a human mind. This is somewhat analogous to the creation model of origins in that God's mind is seen as the original source of the existing reality we call nature, just as a man's mind is the origin of, for example, the melody or the plot in a musical or literary creation. In God's case, however, he not only composes the melody, he makes the instrument using materials that he brings into existence just for that purpose.

7This notion is often misunderstood. Processes that are not currently operating surely cannot be studied directly, and thus many assume that creation is thereby unscientific. This is a misunderstanding, however, for at least two reasons. (1) Evolution, as I define it here, is not an observable process, and it has not been demonstrated in the laboratory. In fact the notion that life can spontaneously arise from natural processes surely goes against all known evidence from currently operating processes. The experiments that have been done to show how amino acids may have been formed all assume atmospheric conditions that do not exist on the earth at this time and may not have existed on the earth at any time. Moreover, the amino acids formed under these conditions are quickly destroyed by those same conditions, and thus would not survive in a natural environment that might produce them. Evolutionists, however, do not conclude that evolutionary theories are for those reasons non-scientific. Creationist theories should not be ruled out *apriori* either. (2) There are currently existing evidences that can lead one to theorize about possible processes in the past that could produce the facts in question even when no comparable process is currently operating. Such reasoning is not unscientific unless it eliminates all testing procedures. As we shall see, some creation models are subject to scientific testing as are some evolution models.

force, out of no prior substance or energy field of any kind. Natural reality originates exclusively out of the intentional purpose of God's mind. Matter and energy have not existed eternally in any form. Rather they came into being at a specific moment by God's direct, creative, spoken command.

We assume that God spoke the world (the universe) into existence.[8] In the Genesis account God directly speaks to call forth each major category of reality. He produces light; he divides the water into seas and lakes; he causes the dry land to appear; he brings forth plant life on the land; and he creates the animal life on the earth and specifies that they were to reproduce "after their kind" (which they do).

At the end of the process God also produces human-kind, male and female, as a separate and unique creation (Gen. 1:26-30). Human beings are physically related to the animals and the plants and, in fact, the earth itself. God

---

[8]Technically speaking, the biblical account does not say "In the beginning God said 'Let there be the heavens and the earth.'" It only affirms that God created the heavens and the earth without specifying any process at all (not even the process of God speaking). The recorded speaking of God begins when He commands light to shine in the darkness that covered an existing earth so as to produce day and night there. The creative work of God that is described in Scripture, however, is a work performed by verbal command. God says, "Let there be . . . ," and it was so. This is the only description given of any creative process, and thus by analogy many theological interpreters have understood initial creation itself to be by royal edict. Since matter is not divine but rather is brought into existence by God's decree, most orthodox theologians have gone on to affirm fiat creation *ex nihilo*. This is not absolutely necessary for orthodoxy, however, since it is possible to conceive of an eternal God as being an eternal Creator. Thus it is logically possible to think of matter as always having been created, though such notions are speculative, and seriously lacking in substance. None of the really important issues are solved by this hypothesis. The universe as a special form of matter definitely had a beginning according to Genesis 1, and a significant amount of scientific evidence points to the same conclusion. Personally I find nothing in either Genesis nor any other book of Scripture that would lead me to suspect that this eternal matter theory might be true, nor do I see any scientific necessity for denying an origin for matter itself.

shapes the human body from the dust of the ground (the chemical elements of the earth) into a form capable of being united with a divine nature (which Christians believe it on one occasion was). The first human being, then, becomes a unique living being when God directly breathes into him the breath of life (Gen. 2:7). Thus, humankind is made in God's image, physically and spiritually, and is given a unique destiny. Humans are to be the stewards of the earth. They are told to have dominion over all things.

These special creative processes, however, cease on the seventh day. God finishes all of his work of creation and rests. The Bible suggests not that God was tired but that all special creative processes ceased, for God "rested" from all his work of creation (Gen. 2:1-3).

The creative processes were unique, and they were particular. God has not ceased to uphold[9] his creation (Heb. 1:3). Nor has God ceased to work redemptively (John 5:16-17). But he has ceased his work of creation, as we define and understand the concept.

God has continued to maintain the orderliness and the purposefulness of his universe (Col. 1:16-17; Acts 18:24-28). It is due to God's providential care that the forces of nature (such as gravity) are consistent and regular and that the seasons continue in accordance with his promises (Gen. 1:14, 8:22). Biblical creationists believe that it is God who originally established the orbit of the earth and who maintains the proper relationships between each of the parts of his created universe. The periodic chart of the elements found in chemistry textbooks is another marvellous example of the complex orderliness found in matter itself. Moreover, the ecological balance in nature and the appropriate physical relationship of the earth to the sun, along with the many other apparent characteristics of order and design which can be seen[10] in the universe, are to be directly related to the

---

[9]"Upholding" surely would include the conserving process of adaptation (within divinely established limits) that is so evident in biological systems that must respond to environmental changes.

[10]For a listing of seven or eight different kinds of design that can be observed by the human mind, see J. P. Moreland, *Scaling the Secular City* (Grand Rapids: Baker Book House, 1987), pp. 43ff.

praise of God's greatness and of his mercy toward us (Psalm 104).

# TESTING MODELS OF ORIGINS

According to the viewpoint of special creation, the processes of creation were directly related to the power of God's spoken Word. Scientists are not able to enter into the nature of God and his creative powers by scientific investigations in a laboratory or by physical experiments of any kind. Thus, it seems unlikely that naturalistic science, as such, would ever be able to demonstrate empirically the absolute correctness of the viewpoint known as "special creation." On the other hand, it is equally impossible for science, as such, to disprove the theory of special creation and, thereby, establish the theory of evolution. Nor is it possible for science, as such, to prove that the evolutionary model of origins is true.[11]

---

[11]Science by definition and by nature is the empirical and rational study of currently existing reality and contemporary processes. Models of origins, however, are suggested interpretations of the past. This is an important point to make, because even many scientists and science teachers seem to believe (mistakenly) that science actually studies the past. Science only studies the present, and then, in light of sometimes unstated assumptions, a scientist may offer reasonable interpretations of the past. All of the data, however, exist in the present. All of our scientific observations and experiments occur in the present. Even if one could see an instance of the spontaneous generation of life today, that would only prove that such an event is possible under current conditions (or under the conditions established in the laboratory experiment, which is occurring in the present), not that it actually did occur under past conditions (which may have been very different). One may, of course, choose to believe that it did happen that way in the past, but such a view could not be more than a belief. If an observer was present (in the past) and left us a written account of his observations, that could serve as historical evidence for us. No one has ever reported a valid observation supporting the theory of spontaneous generation, however, nor has anyone ever observed any animal or plant evolve naturally into another kind of animal or plant. The logic of it all is quite simple. Evolution is as much a

It is theoretically possible to provide meaningful evidence for an evolutionary development from some given original state to the present configuration of things (though conclusive evidence is hard to come by), but to provide evidence for a naturalistic origin or for an exclusively naturalistic development seems to be virtually impossible. It is hard even to conceive what such evidence could be.[12]

The two theories can be tested, however, in terms of their explanatory and predictive value. The assumption by which this testing can take place is that "the truth about reality will best explain all of the data," that is, comprehensively, fully, and without internal or external contradiction.

Before discussing this testing procedure in detail, there is one further point of clarification that must be made. One cannot successfully test an interpretive model until one understands exactly what the model is, what it means, and what it implies. Many have been led to believe that creation is a static model that denies obvious facts such as biological change, adaptation, and development. This, however, is a serious misunderstanding.

The conflicts that arise between evolution and special creation are not really arguments about whether or not development takes place in earth history. These interpretive models do differ in their understanding of the nature of that development, but those who follow the view of special creation believe that development takes place. They claim, however, that this development takes place within definable limits. The Bible clearly teaches that animals and plants were

---

"believed interpretation" of the evidence as special creation is. The models may be tested against the data, and one model may clearly explain more data in a more effective way than the other, but neither of these "believed interpretations" can ever reach the level of empirical and rational proof. Evolution would be more believable if there were numerous known examples of natural species transformation; however, there seem to be no undisputed instances and very few indeed that can even be pointed to as proposed (hypothetical) examples.

[12]It will surely not do to fly into space, look around, and announce the absence of God, as the Russian cosmonaut attempted to do on an early manned space flight.

created to reproduce "after their kind." This would not deny the possibility (even the likelihood) of some change, variation, and development within the general, broad category "kind." However, it would deny that all current life forms could have originated and developed from a single original life form. One "kind" of animal does not evolve into another "kind" of animal according to the viewpoint of special creation.

The identification of the scientifically describable limits for the biblical category "kind" is a subject that still needs further research.[13] Some creationists identify the biblical "kind" with the level of classification known in modern scientific taxonomy as the "family." Others argue that the biblical category "kind" is equivalent to the scientific classification "genus." When defined as "an interbreeding pool of genes," "species" may be the equivalent of "kind." Some modern definitions of "species," however, are perhaps more narrow than the biblical definition of "kind."

Thus, a creationist is likely to believe that there has been some change or development within the biblical "kind" if the evidence warrants such belief. (There is some evidential basis for believing, for example, that the modern dog breeds have developed from earlier dog forms.) But the creationist would be unlikely to accept a current evolutionary theory suggesting that modern birds have descended directly from ancient dinosaurs (for which, by the way, there is no conclusive or even plausible evidence[14]), because creationists

---

[13]A great deal of this research has been done already. See, for example, Lane P. Lester and Raymond G. Bohlin, *The Natural Limits to Biological Change* (Grand Rapids: Zondervan Publishing House, 1984); Frank L. Marsh, *Variation and Fixity in Nature* (Mountain View, CA: Pacific Press Publishing Association, 1976); A. E. Wilder-Smith, *A Basis for a New Biology* (Einigen, Switzerland: TELOS International, 1976); and John N. Moore and Harold Schultz Slusher, eds., *Biology: A Search for Order in Complexity* (Grand Rapids: Zondervan Publishing House, 1974).

[14]Archaeopteryx is supposedly the most primitive bird known, and supposedly it links modern birds to their reptilian ancestors. There are only six fossil specimens currently (1988) identified, and they all come from a unique upper Jurassic limestone formation in

expect reasonable limits to biological change, and they expect true theories to be supported by reasonable kinds of evidence. Creationists argue, for example, that cats do not, have not, and will not become dogs, nor does the empirical evidence show that cats and dogs ever developed from a common ancestor. The evolutionist, on the other hand, would suggest that all living forms have common ancestors at some point in the past.

These viewpoints can be tested by comparing the implications of these claims against the available evidence. For example, the existence of transitional fossil forms (i.e., intermediate fossil forms showing animals or plants in various stages of change or transition from one kind of life-form to another kind) is predicted by and thus would support an evolutionary model. In fact, evolutionary theory

---

Bavaria (traditionally dated by evolutionists as being approximately 150 million years old). The most recent specimen found was announced in the June 24, 1988 issue of *Science* by Peter Wellnhofer of the Bavarian State Collection of Paleontology and Historical Geology in Munich. This new fossil is the largest discovered so far, and there are clear feather imprints. In the past, scientists had agreed that in archaeopteryx the connecting bone between skull and jaw had a single lobe. This was seen as evidence that archaeopteryx was truly a transitional form, because most vertebrates have one such lobe but birds have two lobes. Thus here was the primitive bird, a bird with feathers but not yet having evolved its second lobe on that connecting bone. Wellnhofer, however, has been studying these fossils. Using an advanced X-ray technique known as "computed axial tomography" (better known as a CAT-scan), he has found, to his surprise, that the distinctly avian characteristic (the second lobe) is in fact found in this earliest known bird. (This is reported in technical detail by the researchers in the Spring 1988 issue of *Paleobiology*.) Though my conclusion is not drawn by the researchers (who are all committed to the evolution model of interpretation), once again the evidence seems to say that the bird kind is distinct and has been as far back as the evidence goes. There are no creatures which are half birds and half reptiles. Fully formed feathers and distinctively avian bone structures are already there in the oldest bird fossils that we can find. The bird kind and the reptile kind are not related by descent. Each are unique from the beginning.

virtually demands the existence of many fossils of this kind. However, no clear examples of such fossils have been found.[15] Only a few fossils are even claimed as examples of transitional forms, and none are undisputed. These are the famous "missing links." The fact of the lack of transitional fossils, however, can only support a creation model.[16]

Naming the lack of evidence will not make it evidence. The evolutionist names his lack of evidence "links" that are "missing." But how does he know they are missing? Maybe they were never "there" in the first place. Maybe each "kind" was, from the beginning, distinct.

How can the "lack of evidence" be given the status of an existing bit of evidence that is only missing? The answer is that the evolutionary belief-system requires the past existence of these "links," and so they are described as "missing"

---

[15]To be fair and to illustrate how difficult it would be to use fossil evidence alone to demonstrate the past existence of transitional forms, consider the following: (1) Of all the millions and millions of animals that have ever lived, most have not fossilized upon death; (2) all known fossil finds have been or can be classified and named, each fossil often being assigned to a specific species; (3) even a clear mixture of fossil traits would not prove that the form was transitional: consider what might be said if the duck-billed platypus were known only as a fossil. This true-breeding animal is not, however, a transitional form between fowl and mammal. For one thing it exists contemporaneously with both. It is an odd but nevertheless a true mammal. This lack of evidence has led many modern evolutionists to deny that they expect to find transitional fossils. This denial has naturally been far more prominent after the evidence showed none to exist.

[16]All the evidence may not yet be known, and strictly speaking all conclusions must (from the scientific point of view) remain open to reevaluation and revision if new evidence is discovered. Furthermore, the current lack of evidence is not by itself a fully conclusive proof against a theory, but surely the lack of evidence for a view cannot be taken as being support for the view. Lack of transitional fossils is a significant weakness in the evidential case for evolution. However, the creation model actually predicts this kind of data. Creationists predict that fully developed, discrete kinds have existed as long as living creatures have existed. This claim is consistent with all of the evidence now known.

since none have ever been found. Creationism, on the other hand, obviously fits the data at this point much better than evolutionary models do, because creationism claims that such transitional links do not now and never did in the past exist. Therefore, creation models imply the state of affairs that we find, but evolutionary models imply a state of affairs that does not seem to obtain.

Neither view is proven or disproven (absolutely) by such reasoning, but the two alternatives certainly can be checked against the available evidence. We test our models by asking which model fits the actual evidence best.

## THE PROBLEM OF VERIFICATION

Though neither evolution nor creation (as scientific or historical events) can be studied by direct scientific methods (since neither can be reproduced in the laboratory), it does seem that these two positions (as models for the interpretation of data) could be tested by comparing the meaning and implications of each model with the available scientific data.[17]

---

[17]Creation by my definition would be a unique, one-time event. Thus it would not be subject to experimental reproduction. Evolution, on the other hand, is often believed to be a demonstrable, scientific principle of development. If the principle of biological variation and change could be established in the laboratory (and, of course, such a principle has been established virtually beyond doubt), then the naturalist would argue that the theory of evolution has been established by that laboratory finding. Such a conclusion is drawn because a major assumption of naturalistic philosophy is that no explanatory discontinuity exists. Creation is unscientific, these naturalists affirm, because it introduces a discontinuity into the explanatory paradigm. To say "God did it" is to affirm a cause that is discontinuous with all other "natural" explanatory causes.

Evolution, however, has several significant discontinuities in its explanatory model. There is no demonstrable evidence that life can naturally or spontaneously arise from non-life. Personality does not obviously arise from the impersonal. These two innovations in the natural process seem to imply a personal, living cause. The existence of such a cause is at the heart of the creation model, but is excluded by naturalistic evolution.

The element of survival value serves as a major explanatory link in evolutionary theory, and yet highly significant aspects of human life (e.g., music) seem to lack any element of survival value. Music is often called an "evolutionary excess" in order to account for its existence. But even if that were true, such a theory does not explain its value and significance to human beings.

Moreover, contingency is a characteristic of all naturalistic explanations (since everything without exception is assumed to have a natural cause), but contingent explanations are never final or ultimately satisfying. By definition they cannot stand independently. Losing one's reason in the "mysterious cosmic swirl" is no answer either. If naturalism is true, the mysticism of Carl Sagan is as unscientific as any view could be. The interactions of matter and energy may be either complex or simple, but they are mathematically describable and thus thoroughly knowable. To turn to physical reality and treat it mystically is essentially pagan and idolatrous.

Furthermore, evolution like creation is a historical process. If it occurred at all, it occurred in the past. Transitions between species must have happened during specific time frames in each case. For example, the actual transition from invertebrates to vertebrates would have happened in a specific portion of the inaccessible past. But no one saw it happen, nor is there fossil evidence that documents the transitional stages. More significantly, even if one could produce such a transition in a controlled experimental setting today, that would at best prove only that such a transition possibly could have happened, not that such a transition actually did happen, and even less that it happened naturally in that specific way. The laboratory experiment, to be valid evidence of evolution, would have to produce specific, viable transitional forms that over time stabilize as a definitely new and fertile species; this transitional sequence must occur strictly in response to environmental factors that can reasonably be believed to have obtained at the appropriate time in earth's history; and corresponding fossils must be found to demonstrate that the sequence, thus shown to be possible, did in fact occur in nature. Nothing even approaching this level of evidence has ever been produced. There are no such fossils, and even this type of laboratory evidence would not easily avoid the charge that the transitions were produced as a result of the controlled environment of the laboratory. However, a controlled experimental setting is exactly what a non-theist does not have in the natural environment. Only a theist could think of nature as having been influenced or controlled by an intelligent force. The naturalistic evolutionist, therefore, would not prove his theory even if he could produce a transitional form in the laboratory. He must prove that thousands of specific transitional forms did in fact arise

While it is not likely that one could prove either of these theories to the absolute exclusion of the other, it does seem that the interpretative context and framework which they provide would be testable on the basis of their ability to correlate, explain, and predict the data which are observable. Certainly, aspects of both models can, therefore, be tested by scientific procedures.

It is important to realize that the theory of evolution and the theory of special creation are theories (or interpretive models) that primarily concern the formative history of existing reality and the present configuration of things. If one were a special creationist, it would not necessarily affect his or her ability to collect, correlate, or utilize any actual experimental or observational data. The special creationist would go about scientific activity in the normal way, just as an evolutionist would. Both would observe the data, collect it, and seek a reasonable, unified explanation of it. A special creationist would use that data in the same way that other scientists might use the data. He could be seeking a more reliable way of discovering oil deposits or minerals in the earth. He may be seeking a better insecticide or a more effective fertilizer. Perhaps he is seeking a more economical, viable energy source. He could be developing technological advances in electronics, or he could be formulating new concepts about astronomy, medicine, chemistry, or physics.

The special creationist differs from the evolutionist, not in his daily practice of observing, collecting, experimenting, developing, applying, etc., but in his explanation of what reality is. A special creationist would give a different reason from that of an evolutionist for why things ultimately are as they are. All good observers should be able to agree on what can and cannot be observed in a given context, but what

---

without any outside intelligent influence on the process. Such proof seems to be directly impossible since the intelligent scientist would always influence the experimental parameters of his or her own experiment. Thus testing for either creation or evolution as a model of origins must be done indirectly. The issue will be which model fits the available data best and which one offers the most reasonable explanation of all the relevant aspects of the question.

those observations mean is another question (though the fact and the interpretation are not unrelated).

If the special creationist's explanation is correct, then he should be able to apply his understanding to the observable data. Certain kinds of predictions could perhaps be made. If things have been specially created, then one might expect certain natural features to be present that one might not expect on the basis of a purely random development (such as symbiotic relationships; an ecological balance in nature owing to the providential care and design of the Creator; genetic stability; natural breeding barriers; distinct and systematic gaps between basic kinds of plants and animals even in the fossil record; elements of beauty that are unnecessary for survival; intricate, sophisticated systems even where simple ones would adequately serve basic survival needs, etc.).[18]

On the other hand, the theory of evolution offers an alternative explanation of existing physical reality. The evolution model also predicts an ecological balance (due in this case to a natural struggle for survival where that which is out of balance does not survive), but it differs from the special creation model in that (among other things) it predicts (and in fact depends on) unlimited genetic variability, breeding tendencies but not barriers, transitional forms between all kinds of life (and at least representative fossilized transitional forms should exist), meaningful and useful explanations of all biological development in terms of natural selection (that is, survival benefits), and evidence of continuity and gradual variations between all life forms in order, from simple to complex.[19] Much research and debate centers

---

[18]These things, of course, do exist in nature, and they are not the kinds of things an evolutionary model would readily predict. Belief in creation as Genesis presents it also leads one to expect that he or she will be able to understand and use those things which God has made, since they were made for the purpose of being understood and used. Humankind was given the right of dominion, and having been made in the Creator's image, Adam began the scientific task of naming the animals and later of producing food crops.

[19]These expectations have not been borne out by the scientific data collected so far. One can always give "after-the-fact" explana-

on these very matters. Special creationists frequently point out that these crucial evolutionary predictions are not obviously true.

Evolutionists, of course, also expect the evidence to support a great age for the earth. Special creationists may or may not believe the earth is ancient, but evolution would seem to require a great age for the earth. Since no actual natural change from one biological kind into another (which is fertile and thus self-sustaining) has ever been observed, the naturalistic theory has retreated (according to some proponents) into the view that evolution is happening, but that it is too slow to be scientifically observed. How undetectable change differs from no change is not clear, but evolutionists somehow still believe that this change happens, because their model requires it to be happening. Special creationism, on the other hand, does not predict change of this type and thus is not concerned to provide explanations for its lack of observability.

The age of the earth is significant for biblical interpretation but not for the special creation model as such.[20] Special creationists, however, often point out that "nonobservable" change is too slow to have produced the modern biological world from an original organic simplicity, even if the earth is

---

tions, but such explanations are always hypothetical. In other words one might suggest that giraffes grew long necks because they needed to reach tree leaves high off the ground. But if they had short necks like horses one could just as easily explain that. Anything can be "explained" after-the-fact. Scientific models must have predictive value if they are to have much significance for science. Gradual variations between kinds are not found in any meaningful (evolutionary) order, for example, in chromosome numbers or even in the genetic protein sequencing on the DNA molecule. Evolutionary theories do not seem to predict the data very well in these crucial areas. See, for example, Michael Denton, *Evolution: A Theory in Crisis* (London: Burnett Books, 1985).

[20]Some special creationists, though not all, have argued that certain natural processes seem to imply a relatively young earth. If they are right, the evolutionary theory would be seriously weakened. A young earth is not essential for the special creationist model, however.

as old as modern theories claim, and that the probabilities for disorder (rather than order) increase in direct proportion to the length of time the change involves. The longer the time, the more the likelihood for reproductive (genetic) error increases. Thus the likelihood of deformity, disorder, and decay increases.

Nevertheless, theories concerning the earth's age are crucial only to the theory of evolution. Evolutionists must have an ancient earth and an even more ancient universe. Nevertheless, whatever the age of the earth is, it remains true that the available evidence taken as a whole seems consistent with a creationist model, but it does not seem to support the evolutionary hypothesis with equal strength.

# THE SCIENTIFIC MIND

Evolutionary theories do not necessarily affect the way a scientist might collect or utilize any of his actual experimental data. Evolutionists may function as excellent scientists in many fields, just as creationists may. They normally do their scientific, experimental work in the same general way that a creationist does. The same natural laws and physical/chemical processes are recognized by both.

It is significant to note, however, that naturalistic evolutionists do not have the same philosophical basis to justify their work that a creationist does. If the human mind (which has survived the body's struggle with the environment) is simply the random, accidental result of a complex series of highly improbable, impersonal, unintelligent processes, then how could one trust that such a mind even possessed an accurate awareness of reality? Why should one believe that reason itself is trustworthy?

The naturalist sometimes replies that we know our minds are trustworthy because our ideas are functional (that is, our ideas can be satisfactorily put into practice). This answer seriously begs the question, however, because it assumes the very point at issue. Unless human reason were already known to be trustworthy, one could not with assurance recognize whether an idea was functional or not. If reason is not trustworthy, our ideas about what is and what is not functional could not be trusted.[21]

The creationist, on the other hand, believes that God created everything that can be located in space and time.[22] God knows what reality is, and he knows why it is the way that it is, because he knows what and why he created. Thus a creationist assumes that ultimately all truth is known by God.

Since truth is known (by God), it must be the case that truth can be known. If humankind were not like God at all, then perhaps truth could not be known by human beings. If, on the other hand, mankind is in some ways like God (that is, if the doctrine of humanity's creation in the image of God is true), then human beings could perhaps gain true knowledge about the world made by God. Some initial and crucial knowledge could be revealed from God to mankind, but the human mind (in a way like God's mind) could also directly observe, correlate and understand the world in which it finds itself.

Thus, a theist has an epistemology (a theory of knowledge) allowing for the possibility of achieving and recognizing real truth. If a naturalistic evolutionist believes in that same possibility, it is not because his evolutionary theories provide a valid basis for it. He does his scientific work as if it were possible for him to know the truth. This possibility of

---

[21]Naturalists often cannot "see" this point at all. They are "certain" that their "mind" is in touch with reality, because their "ideas" seem to them to "work." To tell them that this is only possible because reason is more fundamental than matter and that mind is truly original is to destroy all that is essential to naturalism. Thus, like a safety valve or a circuit breaker, the naturalistic mind will often "let off steam" (blast out in a verbal tirade against creationism as being unscientific) or "shut down" completely (denying the relevance of the point). Nevertheless, it remains true that a worldview that cannot justify the validity of reason itself is self-stultifying and thus false.

[22]God may have created some non-space-and-time things, but we probably could not know that, unless he were to tell us that he did it.

knowing truth is justifiable, however, only on theistic assumptions.

## THE PROBLEM OF INTERPRETATION

Since naturalistic evolutionism is actually a philosophical worldview (not just a biological theory), non-theistic evolutionists usually interpret everything according to evolutionary concepts. They explain all of their discoveries in terms of a random origin and of a chance development. Teleological explanations are rejected or revised. Naturalistic thinkers do not even have linguistic room for God or purpose. Everything is thought to have developed by natural processes from something else, and this goes on *ad infinitum*. There is no end to the process. Neither is there any absolute beginning point.

Even the so-called "Big Bang" is not always thought of as the absolute origination of matter and energy by naturalistic scholars.[23] The "Big Bang" is sometimes claimed to be the natural result of some unknown prior reality or of a previously existing universe that collapsed. This cyclical theory of eternal matter and energy is absolutely contradictory to the biblical concepts of singular creation and final judgment. However, it must be admitted that the available data is (to some extent) capable of being interpreted within an evolutionary framework.

The fact that such an interpretation is possible has—oddly enough—led many to claim that only non-theistic explanations are scientific explanations. Theistic explanations are said to be strictly "religious". But this can only mean that science is no longer defined in terms of a complete and

---

[23]A seeming exception to this rule is the American physicist, Edward P. Tyron, who suggested in 1973 that the quantum theory of physics would, under just the right conditions, allow the whole universe to have come into existence out of nothing. The naturalistic evolutionist, science writer Isaac Asimov, claims that many scientists would "very much like to believe" Tyron's theory if they could. Asimov and others seemingly would like to accept the *ex nihilo* creation of matter and energy while still denying theism. Cf. Isaac Asimov, "The Very Beginning," *American Way* (April 15, 1986): 17-18.

truthful description of reality. If it were so defined, then God could not be ruled out *apriori* as a part of a scientific explanation.[24]

Many Christian people have been anxious to identify the popular "Big Bang" cosmology with the biblical doctrine of creation. Sermons often identify the light of the explosion with the light of the first day in Genesis, etc. Such a harmonization between science and the Bible has a great appeal for some people. Unfortunately, the only significant thing the two cosmological views have in common is the affirmation of a beginning (the belief that the universe has come into its present form since some definable beginning moment in time). The almost universal acceptance of "Big Bang" cosmology among secular thinkers, however, does indicate that the evidence seems to be overwhelmingly against the eternal existence of the universe in its present form.

One cannot directly observe the "Big Bang" anymore than one can directly observe special creation. Nevertheless the "Big Bang" theory has been widely accepted in the scientific community because certain experimental evidence

---

[24]Of course, theists do not think of God as simply one describable element out of many which make up reality. Nor is God directly observable in the sense that a volcano or an elephant might be. He is in fact the ultimate and absolute source of all reality. His actual existence (his divine nature) is necessary while all other reality is contingent. In other words, God is the only reality that must exist. He exists independently. He exists whether anything else does or not. Natural aspects of reality depend upon other natural causes to form and shape their existence. Ultimately, however, the actual existence of all natural things depends upon the supernatural existence of God. This is a foundational assumption upon which a theistic-biblical view of science is based.

The naturalist, on the other hand, always argues for a theory of the universe that ignores this foundational principle. Philosophically the naturalist must argue that contingency is ultimate. This inevitably leads to relativism in every area of life including ethics and epistemology. This single principle perhaps characterizes modern secular man more than any other. Truth is lost if everything is relative. Knowledge is no longer a unified whole for the naturalist, but rather it has been fragmented.

has been found to be consistent with that theory. The creationist argues that all actual experimental evidence is also consistent with the theory of special creation.[25]

But the secular mind persists in denying that there can be any legitimate reference to God in a scientific description or theory. For numerous Christians this seems to be simply a philosophical precommitment on the part of the naturalistic scientist. It is not a necessary inference from any body of scientific data, and it is not a necessary presupposition for scientific research.

If God truly does exist, and if he did create the world as Genesis teaches, then one should not have to omit this fact when giving a scientific explanation, nor would one expect to find scientific data absolutely contradicting this viewpoint. Many evangelical Christians argue that no authentic, scientific data contradict the theory of special creation. Even more,

---

[25]Even the three-degree cosmic microwave background radiation could result from astral heat sources in a created universe, though in this particular case the isotropic radiation that has been found to exist does fit closely with expectations predicted by "Big Bang" cosmologists prior to its discovery. It is not unfair to note, however, that this background radiation is really the only convincing evidence "Big Bangers" have. The evidence for an expanding universe is consistent with "steady state" cosmologies and creationist views as well as "Big Bang" theories. Other suggested lines of evidence are consistent with more than one theory also. Some recent evidence seems to indicate that the "residual radiation" may not actually be isotropic. The universe may be warmer in some directions and cooler in other directions. If this evidence is significantly sustained by further research, we may see a return to steady state theories by many naturalistic scientists. Steady state theories have always been more appealing to naturalistic philosophy. Moreover, the "smoothness" of the radiation has become an unexpected problem. If there is no significant variation (and such seems to be the case if recent research is sustained and confirmed), then there is no explanation for the origin of massive galaxy clusters (which by observation are known to exist). When the implications of these new discoveries are fully realized, "Big Bang" cosmology may be replaced with another cosmological model. Only if we "do our homework" will theists have an opportunity to help shape tomorrow's cosmology.

the Christian argues that a significant amount of scientific data tends to support in unusually direct ways the biblical worldview. This is not a claim that special creation can be scientifically proven. It does remain an article of faith. But it is not a faith that is unsupported or a faith that is irrational, and it is no more of a "faith" than is the theory of naturalistic evolution.

Special creation is not a faith that stands in opposition to known realities. We are not required to take a "blind leap" of faith in order to believe in special creation. The creation model is in no way lacking in empirical support. Major components in the body of wisdom that supports special creationism are, for example, the well known laws of thermodynamics.

## CREATION, EVOLUTION, AND THERMODYNAMICS

If the biblical worldview is true, then everything that we learn about this world should be consistent with theistic faith. The things that have been made should point us to the reality of God (cf. Romans 1:20).

The special creationist theory of the origin of the universe is actually much simpler than the evolutionary theory, and, as we have seen, it fits many known facts and the observed data as well as if not better than other major theories. Some of the best-known facts from a scientific perspective that are directly relevant to the problem of testing the two models, and thereby deciding between them, are the universal laws of thermodynamics.[26]

Evolutionary theories run counter to and, thus, must constantly overcome the second law of thermodynamics.

---

[26]Thermodynamics is essentially a scientific description of heat flow. Engineers study these principles to enable them to build efficient workable systems of energy transfer. Thermodynamic laws can be expressed in technical language and mathematical formulas. They arise from the basic principles of natural law, however, and they can be described in commonsense observational language. My discussion here will not be at the technical level.

However, the first law of thermodynamics is seemingly consistent with both philosophical models of origins.

## The First Law

The first law of thermodynamics is the law of the conservation of energy. The total amount of energy in the universe remains constant. Under special conditions a transformation of matter into other forms of energy may occur, or matter may undergo chemical transformation (compounding, oxidation, dissolving, etc.), but taken as a whole and seen together, matter and energy are not now being created or destroyed, and chemical equations always balance.

This is consistent with the naturalistic idea that matter and energy are eternal, that they have never been created, and that they will never be ultimately destroyed. However, the law was formulated only to describe the presently observed characteristics of the universe. Thus it is also technically consistent with the idea that God at some point in the past created all existing matter and energy, but that he is now holding it in existence so that nothing new is being created and nothing is being ultimately destroyed. The first law of thermodynamics, therefore, is easily accounted for by both models of origins. The two models offer radically different interpretations of the law's significance, however.

The naturalistic model extrapolates the first law eternally in both time directions. Into the past the naturalist assumes that nothing has ever been created. Into the future the naturalist assumes that all things may (or will) change their form but that nothing will in essence ever be absolutely destroyed. These assumptions, of course, relate directly only to the essential nature of reality (space/time, matter/energy), not to the various forms in which it may be manifested. These naturalistic assumptions are directly contradictory, however, to the alternative of an original creation out of nothing and a final judgment that is based upon moral standards.

The special creationist, on the other hand, is equally comfortable with the presently observable evidence that supports the first law of thermodynamics. The special creationist, however, believes that the law is not eternal; that is, it has not always applied, nor will it necessarily always apply in the future.[27] Nevertheless, the first law of thermodynamics, for the creationist (whether he is a biblical creationist or strictly a scientific creationist) is an accurate scientific description of the present nature of reality.

Creationists deny that the first law is properly applied as an accurate philosophical assumption about the essential nature of reality. No apparent differences, however, would be observed in the present operation of the universe under this law whether special creation or evolutionary theories were accepted. Both groups of scientists work on the assumption that matter and other forms of energy are not presently being created or destroyed in chemical and physical reactions in the laboratory or in the universe. The second law of thermodynamics, however, is not so easily compatible with both models.

## The Second Law

The second law of thermodynamics is sometimes called the law of entropy.[28] Hot things cool off. Energy usage and heat dissipation are unidirectional. Every system, left to

---

[27]Creationists believe that there was an absolute beginning of matter and other forms of energy. Since that original creation, God has maintained everything that he created. This preservation is what the first law of thermodynamics describes. Matter and energy may change form, but their essential existence is not destroyed. In the future there may be a conclusion to this space-time universe. The Bible teaches that God will bring to an end the universe that he is presently maintaining, and that he will make a new heaven and a new earth (cf. Isaiah 65:17, 2 Peter 3:10, Revelation 21:1). Theologians often debate whether this is an absolute end and an absolutely new beginning, or whether it might merely be a transformation (including perhaps the suspension of those elements of the second law of thermodynamics that are destructive or harmful to life).

[28]My discussion here is not intended to be technical. The information is simplified for a general reading audience of nonscientists. One who finds my descriptive material on the second law to be superficial and perhaps lacking at some (or many) points is urged to examine the important article by Walter L. Bradley, "Thermodynamics and the Origin of Life," *Perspectives on Science and Christian Faith: Journal of the American Scientific Affiliation*, Vol. 40, No. 2 (June 1988), pp. 72-83.

itself, will become more disorderly as time goes on. Available energy will be used up. Things will wear out. Clocks will run down. This process seems to be an inescapable fact.

Things do not increase in order and complexity without a corresponding decrease in the order or complexity of the total system surrounding it. For example, our children grow up to be adults by eating, breathing, and exercising (among other things). However, they eat much more potential energy in their food than they actually use in their bodies. In practice, the increase in order and complexity in one system will always be less than the disorder that results in the larger system. Thus, the body is constantly eliminating waste.

Waste is a common characteristic of physical and chemical reactions. It is that which is not able to be completely used by the system. In an automobile engine, for example, there is an enormous amount of heat that must be removed through the radiator and the water cooling system. This heat is wasted heat; it is not being used to power the engine. It is extra energy that must be eliminated from the system because it cannot be efficiently used. This heat is rapidly dissipated into the air and finally into outer space. From the exhaust pipe in the back of the car the extra, unused, waste products of the internal combustion engine are expelled into the air as pollutants. Thus, all the originally available energy dissipates and becomes so disorganized as to be completely lost for all practical or useful purposes.[29]

---

[29]Available, useful energy is also lost and disorder increases in the total environment of any natural process. To accomplish the change from a simple living cell to a complex multicellular human being would require an enormous amount of available energy. This energy would have to be provided in the proper quantity at the proper times. A suitable conversion mechanism would be required in order to make use of the energy. A technology that could organize and appropriately concentrate all of this energy would be necessary. The energy introduced into the environmental system of the earth by sunlight alone is hardly an adequate explanation for the transformation of nonliving matter into biological life capable of reproduction and sustained existence. Sunlight would be deadly for biological life if it were not for the ozone layer in the upper atmosphere that filters out many of the harmful elements of the

Some engines are more efficient than others, but no perpetual motion machine exists, for there is always some loss of useful energy in any constructive process. It takes more available energy from fuel to run electric generators than one is able to get out of them. We can transform energy in one form into energy in another form, but we never get 100% energy conversion into work. There is always energy discharge even with the most sophisticated technology.

The evolutionary pattern, which is based on the belief that all modern, complex, biological life forms have come from simpler forms through processes dominated by chance, seems to creation scientists to be in direct conflict with this basic law of thermodynamics that is observable everywhere. Things do not naturally and normally increase in complexity. When someone plants a garden, someone must work diligently in order to produce the crop. Otherwise weeds will choke the vegetables. Weeds waste the available energy for growing food. If someone were not there to take care of the garden, very little food would be produced. Yet naturalists believe that the marvelous complexity and orderliness of living forms on this earth came about not because someone was directing the process, not because someone was initiating and caring for the development, but they say it simply took place randomly, accidentally, by chance through natural cause-and-effect patterns. Special creationists, on the other hand, believe in an original created perfection from which the natural unaided process would be degeneration rather than increased complexity.[30]

---

sun's radiation. Yet ozone is produced naturally by organic life. This leads us right back to the old "chicken and the egg" problem. Which came first, the ozone-layer or organic life? Neither one appears to be capable of independent existence.

[30]Perfection is understood here to mean that which is appropriate to its intended purpose. It is not necessary to describe the original created state of things in abstract terms of mathematical balance or in purely arbitrary categories of idealized existence. The perfection of the original creation is the suitability of that creation to fulfill God's purpose. Thus it may have been simple; it may even have needed to grow in complexity if that were to be God's purpose, but it would have to be fully capable of fulfilling that

146

By working within the limits of the gene pools, people can breed animals with distinctive characteristics. A good example of this is the work done to improve the meat or milk production in certain breeds of cattle. Or in another more common instance, men have produced a variety of specialized dogs for sport and for pleasure. If purebred dogs are not carefully protected, however, they will mingle with mixed-breed dogs and the "blood lines" will be lost. The natural unaided process would be to degenerate from the highly specialized purebred dog back to the common less specialized, mixed-breed dog. (Nevertheless, even common mixed-breed dogs have extremely complex genetic pools and are themselves highly specialized creatures.)

The naturalistic theory of origins would have us believe that all of the highly specialized genetic complexity present in the biological life forms of our modern world came about from an original simplicity which has been changed through normal, natural, unaided, chance processes to achieve the modern information-full complexity. It seems much more reasonable from the point of view of empirical observation to assume (as creationists do) that the original reality was in a highly-ordered, information coded, complex state from which there has been a slow but consistent degeneration

---

purpose in order to be called "perfect." Since a most obvious feature of this world is the tendency of complexity to simplify over time, one would need to show special cause to expect that the natural and intended purpose of anything would be naturally to increase in complexity. The rapid growth of variations in living forms does seem to have a stated purpose in Genesis ("to fill the earth"), but these variations are not comparable to an evolutionary rise in genetic complexity.

It should be noted that biblical creationism (as distinct from scientific creationism as such) might not consider all aspects of the second law of thermodynamics to be natural, original principles. Death is a result of sin according to the Bible, and the decay processes, the weeds, and the inevitable loss of available energy in useful forms is often seen as an imposed "curse" upon the earth (Gen. 3:17-19). We are in bondage to corruption. It is the future lifting of this "curse" that makes up a significant part of the doctrine of redemption (Rom. 8:18-23).

147

since the beginning. Only by man's noble efforts, for example, in medicine, in agriculture, or in ecology, has there been any retardation of this degeneration process.[31]

## SCIENCE, RELIGION, AND TRUTH

The Bible teaches that in the beginning when God created the world he considered it to be very good. At least in its essential features, the universe then may have been very much like the universe as we know it today. The changes that have taken place since creation have been changes of degeneration from a state of original goodness rather than of increasing goodness.

Evil has entered the world, and evil is always destructive. The scientific study of this degenerative process is not tied to an acceptance of a particular religious theory, however.

Is it "religious" simply to argue that creation and subsequent degeneration is a better explanation of the universe we observe than any and all theories of an unaided rise of order out of chaos? Naturalistic evolution's denial of any supernatural reality is equally "religious," then, because it simply reverses the argument and offers another ultimate reality and another response to evil.

---

[31]It is in this context that we find the real meaning and value of the formal principle of natural selection. Life is organized in such a way as to resist this degeneration and to preserve itself. Mutants are almost always degenerate forms. Natural processes work to eliminate those abnormal forms from the herd or the flock, etc. By eliminating unusual forms of life from the breeding circle, the various species instinctively act to preserve the original species form intact. Species will vary and adapt to changing environmental conditions, yes, but their natural instinct is to survive and to maintain a pure breed, so to speak. Creatures once thought extinct have from time to time been found alive today. The stability of the genetic reproduction process has thus been demonstrated, and it is quite remarkable. Natural selection is a conservation process, a biological activity system that resists the very kind of change evolution requires. Natural selection prevents the law of disintegration from destroying life. In theological terms it is the sustaining providence of God.

It must be remembered, however, that many people have an enormous distaste for the theory of special creation. They oppose it with deep emotional feeling. They consider anyone who might even suggest that special creation could be a viable position for scientific thought today to be some kind of an impossibly backward thinker. Special creationism is thought by many to be a holdover from a pre-Advancement (even a pre-Enlightenment) mentality, a mind-set of religious fundamentalism, or a reactionary, anti-progressive, anti-intellectualism.

Many modern thinkers are literally incensed that someone might suggest an alternate theory to the optimistic, progressive, upward movement of the evolutionary pattern. In fact their intense opposition to special creationist views sounds less like a scholarly, scientific, dispassionate discussion of data and interpretations and more like a defense of some important prior commitment on their part. Emotionally and psychologically it is almost as if they are defending their own religion. Of course, high emotion does not characterize every discussion of evolution, and certainly emotion or the lack of it is not relevant to the validity of the theory being proposed, but Christians must be sensitive to these emotional feelings when discussing these issues.

On the other hand, no Christian should feel intimidated by an evolutionist's opposition to creationist views. As Christians we are in principle open to any observable fact or any actual scientific data. All truth is God's truth. Creationist views, if they are true and correct, will not ultimately conflict with any correctly understood fact of reality.

The real issues between naturalists and theists are philosophical and religious. The controversy centers on how one interprets the data. The issue is not finally that one group denies the existence of certain scientific facts that the other group affirms. It is much more subtle than that. Ultimately it has to do with how one comes to know truth in the first place. On what basis do we interpret the data? What framework, what guiding assumptions, what worldview will we accept as being the true description of reality?

Theistic special creation is a reasonable alternative to the evolutionary hypothesis. Only theistic creation explains the fact of actual existence in light of the contingency of all observable elements of the universe as we know it. Only theistic creation provides a reason to trust reason. Only theistic creation adequately explains my moral consciousness of sin, my conscience. Only theistic creation gives a reasonable explanatory basis for my intelligence or for my spiritual desires.

The creation-model gives a reasonable basis for the rational interpretive framework necessary for success in scientific research. The creation-model is rationally consistent, empirically adequate, existentially relevant, and comprehensive. It is also taught in Holy Scripture.

For an evangelical Christian these are sufficient and persuasive reasons for believing that theistic views are correct and that naturalistic views lack crucial elements needed to support them. Where reason, evidence, and relevance meet in such a comprehensive way to support a particular worldview (as they do in support of biblical theism), it is not inappropriate to rest in the conclusion that such a view is true.

# GLOSSARY

Ad Infinitum
Big Bang Cosmology
Causality
Chaos
Cosmogony
Cosmology
Creation
Deism
Entropy
Evolution
Fiat
Genetic Fallacy
Hypothesis
Interpretation
Matter

Methodology
Model
Naturalism
Phenomenon
Reductive Fallacy
Religion
Science
Theism
Theistic Evolution
Theory
Thermodynamics
Truth
Verification
Vitalism

# 8

# God and Evil: Part One

*Does Evil Exist?*
*Evil in Western Philosophical Thought*
*Platonic Idealism*
*Augustinian Idealism*
*Idealist Theodicy*
*Philosophical and Religious Alternatives Regarding Evil*
*Fatalism and Determinism*
*Pessimism*
*Nihilism*
*Theistic Finitism*

Evil and suffering may well be the most complicated and the most serious of all of the intellectual issues that confront the Christian worldview. So serious in fact is this "problem" that some unbelievers have posed it as a logical "proof" of atheism (or at least as a seeming disproof of biblical theism).

It is assumed that:
   (1)   Evil is incompatible with perfect love and goodness.

Further, it is assumed that:
   (2)   God is perfectly loving and perfectly good.

This would lead to the apparent conclusion that:
   (3)   God desires to abolish evil.

The logic of this is as follows: God's love is perfect. That means his every thought would be fully in keeping with his basic character. If evil is defined as something that is not compatible with some essential characteristic of God's nature, then it would seem to follow that God's nature would lead him to oppose evil. If evil is defined in such a way that it does not stand in opposition to the concept of love and goodness, then it seems most difficult to understand why it should be called evil at all. Thus by simply understanding the definitions of evil and of goodness, we conclude that anyone who desired goodness would oppose evil. God surely desires the greatest good. Therefore God desires to abolish evil.

Moreover, it is assumed that:
(4)   God is all-powerful.
(5)   God is able to accomplish whatever he desires to accomplish.

Statements (2) and (4) would seem to be essential parts of the Christian definition of God. Thus:

(6)   Evil cannot exist. *

This seems to be a logical conclusion due to (3) and (5). However, (6) is not actually the case since:

(7)   Evil does exist.

What possible explanation can be given for this state of affairs? Christians believe (2) and (4), and thus they accept (3) and (5). But they also recognize that (7) is true. The dilemma seems to force us to deny either (2) or (4). Some, of course, have denied (7). To express this problem in its classical form, the following diagram can be used.

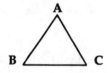

A = God is completely good.

B = God is all-powerful.

C = Evil exists.

Any two points are certainly compatible, but the problem comes when one tries to affirm all three points. Each point is defined in the broadest possible way.

*Evil* refers to all kinds of evil: sin, suffering, pain, sickness, distress, deformity, cruelty, abandonment, natural disasters, accidents, decay, fear, death, war, loneliness, violence, Satanic temptation, oppression, etc., and, to some,

152

even hell itself is thought of as evil since it is a place of eternal punishment.

*God's power is understood to be absolute.* God has no limits on what he is able to do. Of course, most theologians admit the limits of logical contradictions or actual impossibilities (for example, God cannot lie, or cease to exist, or become less than or more than one God). God can, nevertheless, do whatever he wants to do. He is not limited by finite boundaries nor by external forces.

*God's goodness is understood to be absolute.* In him is no evil at all of any kind. He is perfectly loving, merciful, sinless, and pure.

A and B are believed to be true about God because we believe that God has revealed these things about himself in Scripture. C is an undeniable fact of experience (and is affirmed in Scripture as well). Thus it seems that either our experience with evil is deceptive, or else God is not what Scripture teaches that he is. In the latter case, God (as he has been traditionally defined) does not exist. An attempt to treat this problem with a view toward defending God's goodness in light of the existence of evil is called a "theodicy." An effective theodicy will at least reduce the problem of evil to the point where it no longer functions as an "atheistic proof."

Perhaps it is appropriate to examine C first in order to discover something of the nature of the problem. Then it will be helpful to briefly summarize and analyze a few of the attempted 'solutions' for the problem of evil that have been offered throughout history by philosophers, theologians, and other religions. In light of insights gained from this survey, a reevaluation of the problem will be attempted in the next chapter, and a survey of biblical principles relating to this problem will be included.

## DOES EVIL EXIST?

There seems to be a *prima facie* case for evil. Bad things happen, don't they? At the very least it must be said that people think that evil exists.

A young mother nursing her firstborn is visited by the doctor who has to tell her the child has suffered brain damage as a result of the difficult delivery process. The child will never learn or be able to experience normal human relationships. Even more, the bone damage will likely cause physical pain for the child every day of its life. Surgery could help, but the parents have no money. The husband is a minimum wage unskilled laborer. The mother had no opportunity to get an education and is essentially unemployable.

On the Gulf Coast a major storm blows in and totally destroys a new home. The young family is poor, and the husband has been doing most of the work himself. They have only minimum insurance and had spent all their savings for the building materials.

A wealthy industrialist is faced with the necessity of having both kidneys removed. He has plenty of money and can well afford the expense of external machines to keep himself alive and active. But life is now very difficult for him and will obviously be cut abnormally short.

Surely these things are evil.

In the jungle a mighty python slowly coils itself around a screaming rabbit. A black panther stalks a baby gazelle. A grass fire out of control destroys hundreds of nests and many hundreds of animals are burned alive. In the ocean a shark seldom rests as it searches for weak and helpless fish. Does evil exist?

One idea that immediately comes to mind is that we must make some distinctions in all this. Surely earthquakes and hurricanes are not the same as brain damage and both are different from economic difficulties. Then again the natural conflict of the animal world is not the same as a runaway fire. Yet somehow the obvious fact that things could be better than they are (at least we can rather easily think of a happier description than the true description) leads to the conclusion that this is less than the best possible world. Evil does exist.

To suggest that evil should not be defined simply as a description of a less-than-perfect state of affairs is simply to treat the problem semantically. Call it what you will. Bad things happen. To say that "some good comes" from those things is simply to treat the problem pragmatically. But the amputation of my leg is not good just because it teaches me

154

the seriousness of snake bite or even if it motivates me to seek a better antidote for snake poison. That some good comes is a blessing that prevents total despair. But it does not remove the fact of poisonous snakes, nor does it replace the leg nor remove the stares and whispers of others. Evil does exist.

Perhaps evil can be overcome, but it does exist. Perhaps it can be reduced in force by a changed attitude, but it is always there. Even the most devout and faithful members of the church may suffer with bone cancer or a brain tumor. Evil does exist.

It is late at night. The singing and the warmth of the service of praise and worship still lingers in the mind of eighteen-year-old Jennifer. Bob is away on business and the apartment is solemnly quiet and still. This is the first time the couple has been separated since their recent wedding, but he will be back tomorrow. A nice hot shower and then to bed.

What is that?

The blackness of the room is impenetrable.

Jennifer stiffens, and she feels her heart begin to race. It did sound like someone walking down the hall. Was it Bob? He would surely have called.

The door slowly opens, and a stranger appears. He has a knife and a grin one could never forget.

No! No! This can't happen.

Help! Don't hurt me!

Please!

Please!

Bob is called to the hospital. Entering the room he hurries to the side of his young bride. She is only partially conscious. The doctor has described the brutal assault, but Bob is still unprepared.

Her beauty forever destroyed; an insane attack; perversion and lust the only apparent motive.

Does evil exist?

Not all are as dramatic, but examples of immoral behavior are everywhere in our world. War, murder, and rape seem to be overpowering in their impact, but it is only a matter of degree to go from these horrors to things such as stealing or vindictiveness or greed. Evil does exist.

Several years ago a copyrighted story appeared in a Texas newspaper concerning a young Little League baseball player. Usually he played infield, and sometimes he pitched. But it was just a practice game and he begged his dad, one of the coaches, to let him play catcher. Why not? So his dad relented. A wide pitch, a tipped ball, and the little fellow reached out to catch it. But the ball bounced off the tip of the bat and hit him behind the ear.

The father was quoted as saying:

> "I rushed over to him, and he stood up and took off his mask. He said, 'Dad, I'm not feeling too good.' With that, he fell to the ground unconscious. . . . He never came to."

Just a child! Hit in one of the few places not protected by a helmet or catcher's mask. Are we to praise God for allowing this "accident?" Can we believe in the goodness of God at all? Did God not have the power to prevent that young boy from drowning at the Christian youth camp? Could God not have prevented the auto accident that took all but one member of that gifted Christian family? Could not God have prevented conception in the case of that incestuous rape? Could God not enable us to discover the polio vaccine a few years sooner? Why must there be melanoma or Alzheimer's? Why must there be volcanoes and earthquakes? Why must there be addictive drugs? Why do fire ants and mosquitoes and killer bees exist? Why must viruses be so difficult to treat? Why do so many who have so much nevertheless feel so depressed and unsatisfied? Why is happiness so hard to find? Why does torture and cruelty continue? Why is there so much evil?

For an atheist these issues are real enough, but they pose no great intellectual problem. Chaos and randomness are the most fundamental categories of naturalist philosophy. The problem for atheism is how to explain the apparent order and the structure of the universe. Why does goodness appear at all? But this is easier for an atheist to explain perhaps (not philosophically but psychologically) than the problem of evil is for the theist. Natural selection at least offers some "explanation" for the "fitness" of creation, but can a good God account for the existence of evil?

Yet evil does exist.

# EVIL IN WESTERN PHILOSOPHICAL THOUGHT

Western Philosophy has been dominated historically by philosophical Idealism. Idealism may be defined as that viewpoint which denies that mind has originated from or may be reduced to matter. In other words, idealism affirms that mind (or reason) is an original and a fundamental feature of the universe.

## Platonic Idealism

Plato personifies the idealist point of view. For Plato, ultimate reality can be grasped only by reason. Ordinary experiences of sight, smell, taste, touch, and hearing relate to a world that is subject to change. Truth, however, is not subject to change. Therefore, experiences of a temporary or changing character could not be ultimately related to truth. Plato saw physical reality as being shaped by true, unchanging Ideas, but the physical entities themselves were like shadows or copies of the real entities. Plato believed that universal Ideas actually existed in a spiritual realm, a world of permanence and truth. He taught that only through rational meditation are we able to gain a vision (an awareness) of the realm of eternal Ideas, the basis of all true knowledge.

For Plato the material or physical elements of the universe are eternal, but in its natural state the universe is purely chaotic and random. God, for Plato, is not the originator of matter itself, but he is the "Force" that impresses the form and structure of the eternal, rational Ideas onto the material universe. Since Goodness was the most significant of the abstract Ideas, it would seem obvious that everything ultimately would relate to the Good. Therefore, for Plato everything that God produced would be somehow related to the Good. So it could be said that randomness and chaos are the natural state of things from which "God" used the Idea of the Good to produce structured, ordered things.

Some parts of the dough will reproduce the shape of a cookie cutter better than other parts. But in no case do you have a perfect reproduction of the cookie cutter. In a similar way, Plato thought, the stuff of the universe would not accept more than a limited or imperfect reproduction of the Good that is being stamped on it by the Demiurge (his term for the god-like "Force"). Evil, then, belongs to the natural physical universe, and goodness belongs to the "created" or the shaped universe. Here in the physical, space-time world where we live there is a struggle between the universal Ideas that pull us toward the Good and the actual stuff out of which we are made that tends to pull us toward chaos and randomness.

Platonic philosophy was modified somewhat and further developed by Plotinus. According to Plotinus, evil is a cosmic necessity. It actually has no author or originator. In fact, Plotinus argued that evil is not actually something in itself. Rather evil is the lack of goodness. Just as someone could argue that cold is the lack of heat or that darkness is the lack of light, so for Plotinus evil was the lack of the good.

For Plotinus, God was a unity. All things that exist emanate from the ultimate One. In the One all goodness and perfection is found. As you move away from the One, you have various lessening degrees of perfection and unity until you get to the very edge of existence, the place where there is no being, no existence. As you move from the fullness of the One to the edge of nothingness, you move from ultimate perfection toward lack of perfection. So when you come to the edge of existence itself you have come to the ultimate evil which is nothingness. Evil then does not exist; rather evil is the lack of existence.

### Augustinian Idealism

In the early medieval church many Christian writers found the idealist tradition to be amenable to their biblical theology. According to Augustine, truth is rooted in eternal principles. It is God who illumines the mind. The Platonic ideas do not have an independent ontology, yet they do exist, said Augustine, for what Plato knew had to be "there" (if truth were ever to exist), actually was "there" in the mind of God. Plato's eternal, universal Ideas were in fact the eternal counsels and decrees of God.

There is no doubt that Augustine was influenced by Plato and Plotinus when he maintained that truth is rooted in universal principles. Nevertheless for Augustine our theory of knowledge must be centered in our theology. The key to knowledge is the human mind only insofar as God illuminates it. When people come truly to understand any fact in the real world it is because God has illuminated their minds. To know truth is to think God's thoughts after him. To understand a thing is to think about it the way God thinks about it. Correct thought processes could only come about as God illumines our minds and as he helps us to think as he thinks by giving us his ideas by revelation.

Everything that God does is good. God's thoughts are all pure and good. God has created everything that exists. Therefore, to think as God thinks is to think of reality as fundamentally good. In contrast to the Greeks who saw matter as inherently evil, Augustine believed that matter was created with purpose and order and inherent goodness.

In light of this theory it became clear to Augustine that evil must depend upon the good. There are degrees of evil; however, nothing is strictly evil in the sense that it ought not to exist at all. After all, if it exists it must have been created by God for some good purpose. Evil, then, must be the malfunctioning of something that in itself is a good thing. A well-worn but nevertheless useful illustration is that of a fire. Fire can cook your food and warm your house, or it can burn you and destroy your house. Fire is not evil in itself, but it can be misused and thus can produce evil results.

For Augustine all things that exist depend for their existence upon God and upon the ideas that are in God's mind. Therefore, nothing exists that does not have a purpose and that does not fit into some part of the total good. Even the smallest insect or the pebbles by the seashore have some purpose for their existence. Those things can be misused or they could malfunction and thus produce evil results. But they do not necessarily have to be misused, and when they are properly used they will fit together for the greater benefit of all things.

Thus evil for Augustine does not have its own existence, but its presence comes strictly from a misuse of something that is good. This, of course, led Augustine to affirm the ultimate source of evil as being in man's rebellious will. The greatest evil is sin, and because it touches reality sin will have an influence and an effect on all the things around it.

This effect and influence actually changes the way nature is put together. Where there is rebellion and where there is a challenge to God's will, there will also be consequences in the world. Thus evil entered into the world because of man's free choice.

### Idealist Theodicy

Philosophical idealists in the Christian tradition have argued that evil came into existence as a result of some form of rebellion against God. If God created matter, then matter must be good, just as Genesis claims. Thus evil comes about as a misuse of something that was originally good. As Augustine argued, "Where good is not, there evil is." But biblical Christianity is not dualistic in the sense that Platonic philosophy is. If we are convinced that evil does exist, the problem remains. How did evil ever appear in the first place if God made everything good?

## PHILOSOPHICAL AND RELIGIOUS ALTERNATIVES REGARDING EVIL

### Fatalism and Determinism

Another major philosophical option that has great implications for the problem of evil and suffering is that of fatalism. Fatalism is not exactly the same as determinism. If we spoke simply of a cause-and-effect situation in which the result of some chain of events was historically related to some original event, and if we assumed that relationship to be a necessary one, we would then be talking about philosophical determinism. Fatalism, however, usually refers to a belief that all things have been determined not by natural cause-and-effect or by historical events but by God himself.

Fatalism states that events are irrevocably fixed so that human effort cannot alter them. In other words, "whatever will be will be."

Things do appear to happen to us from the outside, and events over which we have no control do effect our lives. If the events are determined by God, then perhaps it would be possible to enter into a relationship with this God and thereby have some influence upon one's own destiny.

160

That was the basis of pagan Greek religion. Human life was seen in the context of nature and the various controlling forces of nature were thought of as gods. Each of these natural forces (or gods) have a rationale of their own. Fate is the overarching power, and people are essentially helpless before it. In Greek religion there is no free will for human beings. In fact the Stoics developed a concept of cycles in which life is periodically destroyed, and each new cycle begins in simplicity and innocence.

The intellectual problem of evil in Greek religion was tied up very much with the belief in the evilness of matter itself. But evil was faced psychologically simply by acknowledging that the things of life were beyond human control.

A similar idea shows up in Islamic thought. In the Qu'ran, individuals are powerless and totally dependent upon Allah. History is completely determined. Allah does neither wrong nor the impossible, but whatever Allah does is right even though to humans it may seem wrong. According to Islamic teaching, what Allah wills comes to pass, and what he does not will does not come to pass. Allah could torment believers and take unbelievers to heaven if he so chooses. He is the sovereign lord and can do whatever he wants with his creation. If Allah were to send all men to hell, that would not be an injustice, nor would it be wrong if he were to take them all to heaven. Whatever Allah does is right.

In this life, according to Islamic teaching, evil and suffering remain a mystery. But the Qu'ran constantly emphasizes the need to create a just society here and now. At the same time it emphasizes and looks forward to a day of judgment when evil will finally be overcome.

Fatalism, however, is not limited to ancient Greek religion, nor to modern Islamic faith. Frequently one will encounter those who teach that human destiny is something like a great wheel of fortune that turns arbitrarily. For example, one may recognize modern astrology as a strictly fatalistic interpretation of life. Astrology teaches that a person's destiny is in some way irrevocably linked to the time and place of his or her birth. Fatalism apart from belief in a loving, wise God leads to an overwhelming pessimism.

Many biblical critics have attempted to identify the

161

Christian doctrine of election and predestination with pagan fatalism. It is true that the doctrine of predestination does assume the absolute foreknowledge of God concerning future events. However, most Christian scholars differentiate doctrines of election and predestination from pagan fatalism, because Christian doctrine begins with an infinitely wise, holy, personal, and loving God. This righteous and infinitely caring God is seen as the source from which all things have their purpose. It would be unthinkable for the biblical God to punish all believers and take all unbelievers to heaven. So a belief in biblical predestination is not simply a belief in God's arbitrary power, but it is an affirmation of His purposive creation and his continued concern with human life.

When Christian theologians have overemphasized the true doctrine of God's sovereignty, they have run the risk of fatalism. Predestination rightly understood, however, is not fatalistic. Fatalism offers a solution to the problem of evil by emphasizing the reality of evil and the power of God. But it is precisely the element of God's perfect goodness that Christians cannot omit from their solution. Fatalism is not a Christian answer.

## Pessimism

Hinduism and Buddhism treat the problem of evil and suffering in a manner that most Christians would consider to be pessimistic. Evil and suffering for Hinduism and Buddhism is the very essence of existence itself. This world is inherently and essentially evil, and it is getting worse.

A number of scholarly studies have been made trying to determine the origin of the pessimism found in Hindu religion. Some argue that it results from environmental conditions. The geography and the economy of ancient (and modern) India may have been contributing factors. Others have suggested that by heredity the people could gain a melancholy temperament. Surely the metaphysical speculations of eastern philosophy have led to pessimistic views of the world.

In the Upanishads the question is frequently raised: "What is the reality which remains identical and persists through change?" In other words, what is the world rooted in? This ultimate Being or reality in which all other things are rooted is called *Brahman*. But Brahman is not thought of as an individual Being with personal characteristics such as Christians attribute to God.

*Atman* is the transcendental self or the inner man as opposed to the empirical or the psychological self. The atman is the real person within the physical body. The atman, like the Brahman, is non-sensory, and thus physical suffering is not a part of ultimate reality. Hindu philosophy considers the atman to be a part of Brahman. Thus, in essence, humans are a part of God.

However, there is a part of Brahman that is not human. *Maya* is the extension of Brahman that is not human. Maya is not a creation of Brahman, but it is the result of his nature. It can be thought of as evil in the sense that it is a by-product of Brahman.

If one considered maya as reality, that would be evil. One must come to perceive the true reality, the Brahman, and thus attain *nirvana* (the state in which all consciousness of self and surroundings is lost). To attain nirvana is to perceive and unite with Brahman. The physical world is not ultimate, nor is it final reality. Evil and suffering are clearly a part of physical reality, and thus are ultimately illusory and unreal.

However, there is a more serious problem in Hindu philosophy relating to *karma* and *samsara*. Karma is the moral law of cause and effect. One's faults, deeds, and words have an ethical consequence in fixing one's lot in a future existence. Samsara is the belief in successive reincarnation. By actions, thoughts, and words, one could burden his or her atman with karma. It is as if the soul were heavy and thus is caught in an endless cycle of life within an evil world of illusion. Salvation comes when someone is able to break out of this cycle by experiencing Brahman. By living a pure life of good works and proper devotion and proper knowledge, one could reduce the weight of karma on the atman and thus break out of the cycle of reincarnation. Thus the quest for salvation becomes a question of breaking this chain of rebirths, and at the same time it becomes a question of how to experience and know the truly real over against the deceptive or the partially real.

*Moksha* is salvation itself. Moksha is liberation and emancipation in the highest sense. Moksha can be obtained either by works or by devotion or by knowledge. The way of works is to follow ancient ritual. The way of devotion is to pay ardent and hopeful homage to a particular deity. The way of knowledge is to meditate and to achieve the certainty of right doctrine. It is the method rather than the content that is primary. So with "the way of devotion" Hindu philosophy is perfectly happy with devotion to Christ. Hindus believe someone can gain moksha by devoting oneself to the Christian God or to a Hindu deity such as Krishna. The content of "faith" simply does not matter.

Jesus said, "I am the way, the truth and the life." According to true biblical Christianity, salvation is not by works, devotion, or knowledge, but it comes by a personal, trusting relationship with Jesus Christ. That relationship will result in good works; it will produce devotion, and it will be based upon knowledge. Nevertheless, salvation for the Christian is defined as a unique personal relationship with Jesus.

Buddha also rejected the Hindu way of knowledge and the way of devotion. He taught that right feeling was the solution to evil. The source of evil is desire. Life in essence is suffering, and suffering comes from ignorant desires. That sounds simple. But salvation, according to Buddha, finally requires the dissolution of the self. Nirvana is the ending of all desire. One can achieve nirvana through right-mindedness and right speech and right effort and right concentration. All of these activities should result in the ending of desire.

For Buddha, human existence and evil are one and the same. Thus Buddha solves the problem of evil by leading us to the point where we cease to exist. There is no hope for a better life in Buddhist faith. There is only the hope of ceasing to exist. Salvation comes in the breaking of the chain of life and in the final dissolution of the individual self.

## Nihilism

In the western philosophical tradition, nihilism is a system of extreme pessimism that attempts to answer and explain the basic phenomena of life under the fundamental category or concept of nothingness. Philosophical nihilism is the denial of any objective reality. Epistemological nihilism is the denial of the possibility of any valid knowledge. Political nihilism is the denial of all standards and values.

Atheistic existentialism, as represented by someone like Sartre, concludes that the heart of the universe is not Being but rather nothingness. The world is ultimately absurd and meaningless.

Natural science in the modern day has apparently revealed a sinister and a meaningless world. The formation of the universe is thought to be coincidental and accidental. The ultimate destiny of the universe is nothing more than decay and disintegration. Many scientists believe that the universe will slowly run down and return to its nebulous state, and humankind will be totally swallowed up in the infinity of the universe.

From this perspective nature becomes a menace to human beings, and they must struggle alone against overwhelming odds. Still, resistance is vain. To solve the problem of evil and suffering nihilism argues that there is no meaning. Consequently, there cannot be any such thing as good or evil in the ultimate sense. There is nothing by which we can compare these ideas in order to define them. Nihilism says there is no good God, nor is there an all-powerful God, nor is there a definition by which we can understand evil. No meaning exists at all.

## THEISTIC FINITISM

Viewpoints that we have looked at so far have raised questions either about the existence of a good and powerful God, about God's goodness, or about the nature of evil.

Some philosophical idealists protect God's goodness by trying to redefine the existence of evil. As we saw earlier Augustine attempted to make evil simply the lack of the good. This makes evil "real" in our experience, but it does not make God directly accountable for it. God has done all things well, but some things God has not done. Some things are attributable to free will. Other things are evil in the sense that they are by-products of something that is essentially good. In other words, there is a strong tradition within

Christian philosophy to solve the problem of evil by changing the definition of evil so that it will be compatible with God's goodness and his power.

Fatalism affirms God's power to the exclusion of his goodness. Though many fatalists believe that God is good, they understand the term "good" to be by definition whatever God is. The dominant motif for understanding God is power. "Might makes right."

The other alternative we have reviewed so far was pessimism, the view that God either does not exist or is himself evil. (Nihilism is extreme pessimism.)

So our triangle has now been analyzed from at least two perspectives. Some have attempted to solve the problem of evil by changing the definition of C. Others have affirmed B so strongly that they were forced to reduce the impact of A. There is, however, another stream of philosophical thinking that attempts to solve the problem of evil by denying B itself. God is not all-powerful according to these thinkers. Because it is believed that God's power is somehow limited, this position is known as theistic finitism.

A theistic finitist is one who holds that the eternal will of God faces given conditions which God did not create. The idea that God could be finite and thus could be limited in some way is found throughout the history of philosophy. This viewpoint is not limited to any particular philosophical system, nor to any religious group, nor is it found only among non-Christians. There is in fact a broad range of thinkers throughout the Christian tradition who have taken positions which included some limitations upon God himself. It should be noted that these conditions are sometimes thought of as being self-imposed. At other times, these conditions are understood to be within God's own personality. Others have argued that the limiting conditions are external to God himself.

Looking back for a moment at Plato, we can see that his dualism imposed definite limitations upon God himself. Plato did not believe the God is the cause of all things. It is his affirmation only that God caused the good things. The creation account found in Plato's *Timaeus* represents God not as an omnipotent creator but simply as a good God who desires that all things should be good. God never intends for anything to be evil. God works then to accomplish his purpose with all of his strength and effort. But matter itself is as eternal as God is. In its natural state it is random and chaotic. The Demiurge (Plato's God) takes universal ideas and uses them to shape or form the things that we observe in the natural world. God always takes a perfect idea and uses it to shape material reality. Because the matter from which all things are made is to some extent recalcitrant, it does not take or hold its form perfectly. Thus it becomes evil in its lack of perfection. But God is doing the best he can.

Jesus surely wanted to heal everyone but he was unable to do so. It is not so much that he could not heal those with whom he came in contact but that he simply could not come in contact with everyone who was sick. There were many sick people in Israel who were never seen or healed by Jesus. One reason was the physical limitations involved in getting to everyone. So on a bigger scale some have believed that God is always working to heal us, and he is always working to produce good, but there are various limitations upon his ability to do everything he desires. Pierre Boyle suggested that God must be limited since more people are lost than are saved. Surely if we know anything about God at all it would be that God desires our salvation. The Bible teaches that it is not God's will for any to perish. And yet some do perish.

David Hume contended that a person simply cannot infer the reality of divine goodness in the face of evil unless one believes God is somehow limited or finite. Immanuel Kant suggested that none of the classical rational proofs for God concludes with an infinite God. The argument from design in the universe leads only to a great Designer but not to an infinitely powerful Designer. God would only need enough power to produce what has actually been produced. Perhaps God did not have enough power to produce a better world.

Some have suggested that evil may also be a part of God's surroundings. God was limited, perhaps, in that he could not create a world of free men that were free from evil at the same time. Or maybe God is limited in the sense that he is not everything. If God created the world, then God is not identical with the world. The world is different from God even though its source may be God. Some natural processes apparently lead to waste. There are some notable insufficiencies in the universe. Perhaps God is limited in that he cannot produce a perfectly efficient universe.

In another sense, God is sometimes said to be limited in his desire for goodness. Or from another perspective, evil is thought of as something that God must and will in the future overcome. Perhaps evil is in the world as a challenge to God. He will eventually overcome evil and thus prove himself to be superior, but perhaps he is limited in his ability to overcome evil instantly. As some scholars have tried to express it, God might be limited in physical strength but not in spiritual power. For example, B. H. Streeter suggested that God would prevent evil if he could. God's omnipotence according to Streeter is his infinite moral goodness. But omnipotence does not necessarily relate to an unlimited physical power on God's part.

The problem of evil's existence is so acute that some men have suggested that if God were all-powerful, then he must be the devil. If God has the power to overcome evil instantaneously but does not do it, then he must in some sense by his use of power maintain the evil in the world. This would traditionally be thought of as the work of Satan himself.

Process thinkers, of course, have suggested that God is the greatest possible power. But it may just be that the greatest possible power is not the greatest conceivable power. What is actually possible may not be the same thing as "all the power that exists" being united into one individual power. Omnipotence means power to the highest degree possible but not necessarily the totality of all power. In this interpretation God would be the most powerful Being, and he would have all possible power, but this would not mean that he had the absolute, unqualified ability to accomplish anything and everything he might desire.

One popular exponent of theistic finitism is E. S. Brightman. For Brightman human finitude explains some evil. Evil has a cosmic significance, however, and is therefore related to God. Why has God not destroyed evil if he can? Brightman could not find an answer to that question in traditional theodicies. Surely God is supremely conscious, supremely valuable, and supremely creative. Yet somehow

God seems to be limited by people's choices as well as by inner restrictions of his character. God's creation of persons entails a limitation upon God's power to rule the world. God is also somewhat limited in his knowledge of the future. God himself is affected by the free choice of persons. But Brightman goes even further to say that God faces conditions that he did not create or approve.

Christians who have suggested a theistic finitist approach usually argue that the concept of an absolutely infinite God is not authentically a biblical concept. They suggest that it is a Greek (in particular, an Aristotelian) position. The argument goes on to suggest that within the universe there is a residue of "absurd" evil which is so irrational and unbelievably cruel that it simply becomes impossible for it to have come from a good God. On the other hand, if we suppose that God's power is somehow and to some extent limited, and if we affirm that his will to do good is infinite, then we have a morally sufficient description of God and yet a reasonable explanation for evil. Goodness, according to this view, is more fundamental than power. Evil in the universe has been and is being overcome by God. It becomes the instrument of God's expression, while at the same time it is God's obstacle.

In response to all of this, many evangelicals have questioned whether we can ever be justified in limiting God's power simply because we cannot fully understand evil. Our problems with evil may not be God's problems with it. The ultimate philosophical question is not just why are things structured in the way that they are, but why does anything exist at all? To think of God's power as being limited to the extent that he cannot overcome evil in the world is not to solve the problem of contingency itself.

Theistic finitism may teach us something. It may force us to open our minds and thus think of new perspectives. But where and in what sense do the biblical writers ever suggest that God cannot accomplish his purpose in the world? Such a theory is ultimately alien to the biblical materials. We must look elsewhere if we are to find a biblical solution to the problem of evil.

# GLOSSARY

Allah
Atheism
Brahman
Buddha
Confucius
Demiurge
Determinism
Existentialism
Fatalism
Hinduism
Idealism
Islam
Karma

Maya
Mosque
Nihilism
Nirvana
Platonism
Reincarnation
Religion
Samsara
Shinto
Taoism
Theodicy
Yoga

# 9

# God and Evil: Part Two

*The Classical Formulation Reformulated*
*Eight Elements of a Biblical Theodicy*
    *Satan*
    *Eschatology*
    *Punishment and Retribution*
    *Discipline*
    *Probation*
    *Revelation*
    *Mystery*
    *Redemption*
*A Christian Response to the Problem of Evil and Suffering*
*Summation and Postscript*

In the previous chapter, the problem was defined. We do have evil to contend with in this world, and for biblical theists this is a problem, since essential attributes of God (namely his absolute goodness and his unlimited power) would seem logically to exclude the possible existence of evil. As we saw earlier, in Chapter 3, logic is necessary for clear thinking. Thus we will not really solve the problem of evil by denying the logic of the problematic triangle. Rather we must show that the triangle does not define the problem correctly. Since the logic of the triangle seems to be valid, the only recourse seems to be to reexamine the initial postulate that denies the compatibility of evil, goodness, and power. Statement (1) is the source of our misunderstanding. The basic structure of a successful biblical theodicy must show that premise (1) is in some way faulty and that in fact one can affirm A, B, and C without self-stultification.

It is from Scripture that we learn the true nature of God's goodness and God's power, and it is to Scripture that we must turn to find a viable solution to the problem of evil. In one sense, the Bible itself is a theodicy. The Bible consistently proclaims the goodness and the power of God, all the while acknowledging the harsh realities of evil's existence. Is the Bible contradictory after all, or is there yet another way to approach this matter? Is it correct to say (with no further qualifications) that God's desire to achieve the greatest good requires the immediate abolishment of evil? Is it possible to consider this as the "best of all possible worlds"? If not, does that mean that God is responsible for the evil of this world? Is there any good purpose that could justify creating a world like this one?

## THE CLASSICAL FORMULATION REFORMULATED

As we look back at our original formulation of the problem of evil as illustrated by our triangle, some things do seem to be inadequately stated by that illustration. The Bible surely would suggest that there are other relevant characteristics of God in addition to his goodness and his power. For example: God is righteous; God judges sin; God is holy; God is purposeful; God is sovereign; he is all-wise, unchanging, eternal, and aware of all that he has created. All of God's revealed nature should be considered if we are to use any part of it to study an intellectual problem such as this. We must not abstract God's goodness and power from other equally important aspects of his character.

Some additional work also needs to be done on the definition of evil itself. A breeze is refreshing; a tornado is not. Fire keeps us warm and cooks our food, but uncontrolled it can be most destructive. Plants are alive, but no one thinks it is evil for a cow to eat grass. Yet some may think it is evil for a lion to eat a cow. At what point, exactly, does something good become something bad?

Animals have many behavior patterns that are similar to human behavior patterns. Some live in family groups. They communicate. They have feelings of various kinds. Animals react to danger in order to survive, but they apparently do not have a consciousness or fear of their own future death. They apparently do not have the same kind of self-consciousness that has been given to mankind. The evolutionist believes that humans have accidentally been kicked upward in the natural processes of nature to the point where we have gained self-awareness. On the other hand a Christian believes that our self-conscious identity and capacity for understanding were given to us by God himself in a purposeful act of creation. We are made in God's image. Thus the human sense of evil is not to be equated directly with animal pain and suffering. This is a helpful clarification, though it is admittedly only a first step toward solving the problem of suffering in the animal kingdom.

Hurricanes would not necessarily be considered evil unless they destroyed human life or private property. It is the loss of life and the economic loss that leads people to consider hurricanes as evil. The Bible speaks of earthquakes as being a natural process somehow related to God's judgment upon the earth. But it is not clear whether every earthquake is to be given equal significance.

Paul says in Romans 8 that the creation itself groans and struggles, waiting for its redemption. Since the days of Noah there has been a promise from God that there would never again be a universal flood, but there have been many, many local floods with destructive power. Some have seen these natural processes as evil. They are related to the Genesis curse on the earth, and they are evil in one sense of the word. The Bible, however, teaches that those natural processes (such as flooding) are under God's control, and they have been limited in their scope. Apparently God does not consider earthquakes or hurricanes to be incompatible with his purposes in this world. They may well be dangerous from our viewpoint in that they may destroy our life and our property. But that is not the same thing as saying that they have no place or purpose in God's universe.

In other words, evil is a very complex problem. Natural evil may certainly be "evil" from one standpoint, but it may not be ultimately or inherently evil in the divine scheme of things. The Bible is unequivocally committed to the position that we are living under judgment as well as grace.

God created humanity in a state of perfect fellowship with God, but Adam sinned and the relationship was broken. The man and the woman were cast out of the garden; and thorns and thistles made it difficult for them to work and grow their food. The original situation in the Garden of Eden was one in which they were instructed to keep (guard and/or protect) and cultivate the garden, but there was always an abundance of food. After the judgment they were forced to get their food by hard work. They had to struggle against the forces of nature that were from then on characterized by decay, corruption, and conflict.

A more difficult aspect of the problem of evil is the question of disease and the deadly attack against human life from physical deterioration. Some disease, of course, is due to a lack of sanitation. If God's moral laws were kept, it would apparently be impossible for there to be widespread venereal disease or AIDS. Some disease bacteria and many viruses may perhaps be mutations of previously innocuous ones. Some are harmful only when they are out of place.

Perhaps there are other explanations for these things. It is clear, however, that not everything that can in some sense be called evil should be put in exactly the same category. Human cruelty to other human beings is not the same as a natural disaster nor is it the same as physical pain or suffering from disease.

Thus the problem of evil is no longer a simple three-sided dilemma. God is not only good and powerful, but he is also holy and just. These and other revealed traits of God's character are in no sense contradictory to one another, for they describe the one and only God. But holding all of them in balance will prevent improper interpretations of, for example, God's goodness. God is not "good" as a grand-father might be in the sense of giving in to every request of his grandchildren. That may be good for a grandfather, but not for a father. So it may be that our concept of goodness may not be the proper concept of goodness for God. We must keep his fully revealed character before us when we think of either his goodness or his power.

Nor can evil be just a single point in the triangle. Evil is a complex word that carries many implications. Evil is real, and the intellectual problem does exist, but its scope is not as massive as it might at first seem. Much suffering can be readily explained, and some evil is only evil from certain viewpoints. We will see this even more clearly as we look at the biblical materials. It is surprising how much of the Bible is in fact dealing with this very issue of the existence of evil and suffering.

# EIGHT ELEMENTS OF A BIBLICAL THEODICY

These biblical themes are indispensable, however, for any viable Christian answer to the problem of evil.[1]

## Satan

In looking at the biblical material we discover several motifs or principles for dealing with the problem of evil. One of the most obvious is the idea of an individual Satan, a personal being who once existed as a glorious angel but who seemingly deceived himself into believing that he could oppose God successfully. Belief in the Devil as a source of evil is one of the oldest ways of dealing with the problem. Both the Old and the New Testaments support the concept of a conscious entity known as Satan.

In the prologue of Job, Satan appears as an adversary in the heavenly court. He accuses the righteous before God. Again in Zechariah 3:1 Satan is pictured as an accuser. I Chronicles 21:1 pictures Satan as the one who led David to do wrong. Satan's function then, in the Old Testament, is to accuse people of wickedness or at least of a lack of righteousness. Sometimes Satan tempts a person so that he or she *will* do wrong, therefore giving Satan something definite to use for his accusations.

In the New Testament, Satan resists the children of God. He uses deceit in order to fulfill this function. Scripture seems to imply that Satan not only accuses human beings before God, but he also provokes human beings to accuse one another, thus leading them to conflict and war. Satan also causes an individual to be tormented by self-accusation arising from his or her own sin.

---

[1]My former professor and colleague, John P. Newport, in *Life's Ultimate Questions* (Word, 1989) summarizes eight biblical themes that speak to the issue of evil and suffering. His summary is based on insights from H. Wheeler Robinson's work and from at least two doctoral dissertations prepared at Southwestern Baptist Theological Seminary over the years. Thus I make no claim of originality here.

All of the synoptic gospels introduce Satan in a personal way. The first and most notable reference is in the accounts of the special temptation of Jesus following his baptism. Satan is assumed to be behind each instance of demon possession that Jesus confronts during his ministry. In the New Testament epistles the Christian life is sometimes described as a race or as a battle. The Christian life is one of resisting or overcoming or being victorious over Satan. He is called a deceiver, a tempter, an accuser, one to whom and from whom men are sometimes delivered. The book of Revelation pictures the final struggle with the forces of Satan and gives the Christian the assurance of a victory for the Lamb.

Nevertheless, the existence of Satan does not solve the philosophical problem of evil and suffering. It is always to be remembered that in Scripture Satan is never presented in any other way than as a created being. Satan is not the omnipotent creator. Satan may influence the creation, but Satan is not the source of reality. Humankind is held responsible by God for the willingness to give in to the temptations of Satan. Satan, in Genesis 3, is punished because of his work of temptation, but Satan is not able to force people to sin. Satan tempts and influences people to do wrong, but human beings are held responsible for their own sin. The Devil did not *make* Adam do it.

Satan does not have unlimited power. Christianity does not teach that there is a good force and an equivalent evil force existing in the universe. God is supreme and superior and before all things. Satan himself could have no existence apart from the creative will of God. In fact, the doctrine of Satan's existence raises the problem of evil in a very acute form. Why does God allow Satan to live? Why does God allow Satan to influence humankind? Why does not God simply destroy Satan immediately? To argue that one day God will destroy Satan is not to explain why God allows Satan to exist now. The existence of Satan is in fact the problem of evil in the universe. So this biblical principle does not solve the problem. Perhaps we can say it clarifies the nature of the problem somewhat.

## Eschatology

The Bible also promises that God will resolve the problem of suffering eschatologically. There will be a complete victory over evil in the end times. In fact, the Bible seemingly indicates that God will triumph at the moment of the greatest historical expression of evil. All of the prophets speak of a coming kingdom of righteousness. Chapters 24-27 of the Prophet Isaiah provide a classic example of the use of the eschatological motif. Isaiah praises God for his full deliverance from sin, death, and the grave.

The last six chapters of Daniel are another classic example. Daniel foresees the ultimate deliverance of God's people. At a moment of great persecution and in an hour of great darkness, God establishes his millennial kingdom. In the final verses of Daniel, the resurrection of the dead from the grave is described as a source of assurance that the wicked shall receive their just retribution and the righteous will ultimately be victorious. Evil is doomed. God will not be defeated, even by death.

Several of the Psalms speak of the ultimate destruction of the wicked and the prosperity of the righteous. Psalm 1 is, of course, the classic expression of the two ways. The apparent reversal of those roles in our present life does not alter the promise of God for a righteous judgment that will set things right at the end. Psalm 73, for example, considers the prosperity of the wicked but suggests that their end will be death. The righteous are assured of an unbroken fellowship with God, because death cannot separate the righteous man from God's love. The concluding chapters of the book of Job show that Job came to believe that while evil does exist in this present life, God in his own time and in his own way will ultimately vindicate the righteous and finally blot out the evil of the world.

The New Testament gospel centers around the promise of eternal, abundant life for the righteous. This eternal life is given to the believer within history upon his or her faith in Christ, but it is actually realized only when Christ raises us from the dead at the end of the age. Our spirit continues to consciously exist in an "intermediate state" between our death and our resurrection. New Testament eschatology is always resurrection eschatology.

The promise of eternal life is always that God will raise us up in the last day. Jesus taught that the sufferer in this life should rejoice because his or her reward will be great in heaven. Perhaps the best known New Testament story teaching this principle is found in Luke 16:19-24 (the story of the rich man and Lazarus). The beatitudes speak of inheriting the kingdom or of receiving a reward. Eschatological passages such as Matthew 24-25 are sometimes difficult to interpret, but they are clear enough to see that while Jesus spoke of great tribulation he also gave assurance of deliverance. The blessed hope of the New Testament is the personal coming of Christ at the end of the age.

Romans 8 or I Corinthians 15 cannot be correctly interpreted apart from an eschatological emphasis. The groaning of the creation is temporary. The decaying universe is awaiting a redemption in Christ, and our mortal bodies will put on immortality when he returns.

Peter says that if you suffer for what is right, you are blessed. Judgment will begin at the house of God, but then it will move to the world. If judgment begins with the family of God, what will the outcome be for those who do not obey the gospel of God? I Peter 4:19 concludes: "So then, those who suffer according to God's will should commit themselves to their faithful creator and continue to do good." It is Peter who reminds us that the Devil is like a lion looking for someone to devour, and Peter charges us to resist him, standing firm in the faith, because we know that our brothers throughout the world are undergoing the same kind of suffering that we are experiencing. "And the God of all grace, who called you to his eternal glory in Christ, after you have suffered a little while, will himself restore you and make you strong, firm and steadfast" (I Peter 5:10).

These eschatological promises frequently relate to suffering that comes for doing what is right. In other words, if we suffer because we are serving God, we will be ultimately vindicated. But not all suffering is of that type. Diseases or pain in our physical body is not necessarily the result of our good works. Thus, the eschatological motif is sometimes limited to a particular type of evil. Even if the motif is understood to be related to other types of evil, it must not be taken alone as a final solution. It is not all right for me to torture you just because I agree to compensate you adequately for the privilege. To say that it will be worth it all when we get to heaven may be true, but what of the starving child in India? He will die and may go to hell. We must look further for more information to help us understand the principles by which suffering and evil are dealt with in Scripture.

**Punishment and Retribution**

Eschatological vindication is a special case of the retributive or punitive principle. God is righteous. Therefore righteousness will be rewarded and unrighteousness will be punished. This is perhaps the most dominant biblical theme.

Genesis 3 tells us of God's judgment upon mankind because of Adam's disobedience to God's revealed will. Perhaps the classic Old Testament passage expressing the retributive principle is Deuteronomy 28. Many times the principle is illustrated in Old Testament history. The nation of Israel is punished because of the sin she is led by her king to commit. Or God will judge a king because of his own personal or political sins. The message of the prophet frequently is that God is judging Israel in the form of famine or pestilence or earthquake or defeat in battle as a penalty due to her sin. On the other hand there is just as frequently the promise of great blessing on the condition of the nation's repentance and the faithful keeping of God's law.

One of the most famous New Testament examples of the principle of retribution is the instance where Jesus curses and so withers a fig tree because of its barrenness. In Acts 5 there is a swift and awesome judgment that falls upon Ananias and Sapphira because of their deliberate deception of the Christian community. On the other hand, those who serve God faithfully in this life will receive God's blessings. In fact, the stereotype of one who thus serves God faithfully is one who endures physical suffering as well (cf. Lazarus in Luke 16). There is plainly an eschatological element built into the retributive principle itself. However, as usually described, the retributive principle emphasizes the fact of temporal blessing or punishment based upon a consistent response to God's revealed will.

God, of course, is holy, and his righteousness demands righteousness among his people. To the extent that sin is viewed in the Bible as a rebellion against God's nature and against his revealed will, any sinful act would seem to demand a righteous response from God. Sin must be judged, and righteousness must be visibly approved. However, it is obvious that piety does not invariably lead to prosperity, nor does impiety always lead to physical suffering in this life. If the retributive principle were the only biblical principle, the logical conclusion would be that physical and material prosperity are the incontrovertible evidences of God's approval of an individual. Yet it was the rich man, not Lazarus, who ended up in torment. "Lord, if this rich man cannot be saved, then who can be saved?" the disciples asked on another occasion.

An even more basic question concerns the suffering of innocent people. Sometimes even infants or young children starve to death or undergo excruciating pain or live in stark terror. Sometimes men are born blind, not because of their sin nor because of their parent's sin (John 9:23).

No doubt, the retributive principle is a basic biblical teaching that clearly offers itself as an explanation for the problem of evil. In fact, the other biblical solutions are sometimes seen as extensions or refinements of the retributive principle. We must not discount its legitimate value in pointing out that sin leads to suffering. But we must not turn that around to conclude that all suffering is the direct and immediate result of some specific sin (remember Job), nor is material prosperity an automatic sign of God's blessing.

### Discipline

Another biblical explanation that is very similar to the retributive principle is sometimes designated the disciplinary principle. God chastises his children in order to discipline them collectively and individually. His purpose is to bring them closer to himself, to warn them against establishing a sinful habit, or to lead them in the paths of righteousness. God sometimes needs to teach his children a lesson in order to bring them to maturity. He sometimes will accomplish that purpose through means that may include pain and suffering. A human father who truly loves his child will discipline the child. So some theologians argue that the discipline of suffering is God's greatest compliment.

Through some of our suffering God shows us that he loves us and that he wants us to be righteous.

There are many biblical examples of this principle. Perhaps the classic case is found in Jeremiah. The nation of Israel is pictured as a piece of clay with God as the potter. God shapes the nation and sometimes must crush the nation in order to produce the final and perfect result of his purposive will.

Proverbs 3:11–12 specifically reminds us that the chastening of God is similar to the discipline of a father for his beloved son. Abraham's faith was tested. He suffered mentally and physically in order to follow God's command. Abraham was obedient, even to the point of sacrificing his own son. By that he proved his great faith in God. Jonah's experience surely was an example of God's discipline for the prophet.

In the New Testament the book of Hebrews reminds us that Christ himself was made perfect through suffering. We think immediately of his suffering on the cross. But almost certainly the reference here is not to the cross alone but primarily to his experiences in life. In fact, the writer of Hebrews tells us that Jesus learned obedience by the things he suffered. Since Jesus lived a sinless life, his suffering could not be retributive, but it seems clear that it was positively disciplinary.

Paul speaks of a great joy that we should have in tribulation because that discipline of God will bring us to a steadfast maturity. James also describes the overwhelming joy that comes in the midst of trials, because these trials teach us patience.

God's purpose does not always suit us human beings. God desires spiritual growth, and that cannot always be accomplished by leading us down the easy road of life. Again, however, we see that this principle cannot be the total biblical answer. In the first place, it is clearly only a partial explanation of human suffering. In what way could an infant's suffering be disciplinary for the infant? Some suffer but do not learn. As they suffer they become even more embittered. If we suffer and thus learn to love God more, we may look back on that experience as one of great joy in the long run. But if suffering hardens a man and turns him away from God, then we are hard pressed to explain that suffering as a disciplinary action on the part of God. If it was intended to be disciplinary but failed in its purpose, we still have a problem concerning God's ability to accomplish his purpose. Some may correctly argue that there are self-limitations in God's character that prevent him from acting in certain ways, but the concept of God's omnipotence would be totally meaningless if he cannot accomplish his own purposes. The Bible never suggests that God might be unable to accomplish his purposes. The Bible never suggests that God might be unable to accomplish His creative and sovereign will. Thus, again we have found a legitimate biblical principle, and yet we are forced to recognize that it does not totally solve the problem of evil.

## Probation

A similar and yet somewhat different biblical principle is the probational or evidential principle. The idea here is that many aspects of the world are essentially evil, and often events are actually controlled by wicked men. The righteous must wait for God's final disposition of evil. Thus, we are living in a probationary period in which our faith is being tested. We are living under difficult circumstances. How we respond to the world around us will reveal (give evidence of) the true character of our faith. Thus the righteous life will inevitably be a struggle.

Some of the Old Testament prophets speak of pagan nations as being instruments of God to judge the people. But this punishment will only be temporary. Evil will ultimately be judged and the pagan nation will not forever remain in power. However, until the time of resolution even the righteous man will suffer under the rule of the pagan conquering nation. Psalm 37 reminds the righteous man not to be deceived by the prosperity of the wicked, for they are ultimately destined to destruction, while righteousness will result in an enduring happiness. Job surely believes that God will eventually vindicate him. Paul glories in the privilege of suffering for Christ. In fact, the New Testament suggests, in numerous places, that because Christ found it necessary to suffer, his disciples must also suffer for a while to fulfill God's purposes.

This also is a biblical solution, and it can provide a large measure of comfort for one who is suffering. Nevertheless, as with our other principles, this one also is not a total answer. What about someone whose faith is never visibly rewarded? There are men and women who go through intense struggles with pain, and they never overcome that pain. Terminal bone cancer, for example, is a form of suffering that must seek an eschatological resolution. But even with that, we wonder if such pain and hopeless suffering can ever be justified when the victim is a devout, lifelong saint. Some aspects of evil in the world literally destroy our lives completely, and it seems that the good and the bad are afflicted equally.

This probational or evidential approach to the question of evil is an important part of the biblical teaching about evil and suffering. This biblical teaching helps us to cope. But it will always be only a partial answer. It may be true that suffering is inevitable in this evil world, but it is not true that people should seek to suffer in order to fulfill God's purpose. Jesus surely admitted the reality of pain, but he did not urge it upon others. Suffering is not a goal to be sought. Martyrdom is not the greatest of all goods. Suffering may be necessary, but it is not in every case necessarily good. Our suffering may be due to evil circumstances, and that does give us a chance to demonstrate our faith. But that "opportunity" does not seem to be a sufficient reason to account for the existence of these circumstances.

### Revelation

Another basic biblical motif dealing with the problem of evil and suffering is the revelational principle. Scripture sometimes sees evil as a means of entry into a fuller knowledge of God. We all know instances where people have claimed to have achieved or developed a new relationship with God because of an experience of suffering in their own life. In fact, many people apparently have been introduced to a relationship with God through some experience of suffering. The classical biblical illustration is, of course, Hosea. Hosea gains a new insight into God's relationship with Israel through his tragic domestic situation.

Job also has an experience with God that comes because of and through the intensity of his suffering.

There is no doubt but that God *can* reveal himself in a new way through suffering. The New Testament book of Revelation was written out of an experience of persecution and great tribulation. Paul reminds us to rejoice in the hope of the glory of God, but he goes on to say:

> Not only so, but we also rejoice in our sufferings, because we know that suffering produces perseverance; perseverance, character; and character, hope. And hope does not disappoint us, because God has poured out his love into our hearts by the Holy Spirit, whom he has given us (Rom. 5:2–5).

Suffering can be a means by which we learn more about God. He can and does speak to us through our difficulties and trials. This principle is an important truth. But again it does not apply universally.

### Mystery

Not all suffering produces a new and better awareness of God. Not every instance of evil leads people to love God more. Not all evil is a punishment for individual sin. Not all evil seems to relate to Satan's work of immoral temptation. Not all suffering functions in a disciplinary way. The eschatological hope is comforting to believers, but it does not tell us why our suffering must be so intense and so seemingly arbitrary. It must be admitted that sometimes suffering simply remains a mystery to our minds.

Throughout most of the book of Job, his suffering remains a mystery to him. Job does not know the information given to the reader in the early verses about Satan. Job is accused by his friends of having committed some great sin. They pay him no attention at all when he claims innocence, because they are persuaded beyond doubt that no righteous man would suffer as Job suffered. In fact, a careful reading of this biblical drama will show that Job never actually gets an answer to his question, "Why?" He simply comes to a point of ultimate confidence in God. Surely God is doing what is best even if it does not seem best to the sufferer.

God does have a sovereign purpose that he pursues in history. Human beings cannot ultimately judge whether God is accomplishing his purpose or not. It is presumptuous for them to try to tell God how he ought to operate his universe. Therefore, we discover that at the heart of the whole matter, the biblical solution to the problem of evil is often more of a practical solution than an intellectual one.

Jesus does not explain why people are sick; he simply provides for their healing. Jesus does not explain the source of evil, but he provides a way for us to be victorious over it. The New Testament affirms that every good gift comes from God. But it is almost silent regarding the origin of evil. Rather than preach sermons explaining intellectually the features in God's character or the aspects of God's purpose that allows evil to exist, Jesus simply involves himself in the suffering of those around him. He is perfectly confident in his Father. He suggests that we humans can with equal confidence trust God in spite of the mystery of pain and suffering.

Jesus himself prayed in the garden of Gethsemane asking whether the "cup" might be removed from him. He suffered, and in agony on the cross he cried out in the words of the psalmist to ask why. No public answer was given to that cry of Jesus from the cross. No voice came from the sky on that day saying, "This is my beloved Son." But God demonstrated that there was an answer, and by the resurrection of Jesus from the dead, God proved to us that he is not unconcerned, and that he does have a purpose and the ability to bring good out of evil.

All of these solutions found in the Bible are legitimate approaches to the problem of evil. Each principle has a specific application, but none of them claims to be the total or final answer. There is always that element of mystery.

### Redemption

Before concluding this study of the biblical principles for dealing with evil and suffering, we must turn to one other. Suffering is sometimes redemptive. Suffering can be substitutionary. It can be on behalf of others.

Genesis chapters 37–50 tell the stories about Joseph. The sufferings of Joseph turn out to be redemptive. Because he suffered, he was able to save his family. The brothers meant what they did for evil, but God used it for good. Joseph did not always understand the suffering he endured, but looking back on it he was able to see how God had used those events to bring him to the place where he could serve his brothers. Thus we have a clear concept of victory through suffering.

The classic Old Testament passage would surely be Isaiah 40–55. There is apparently some reference here to the nation of Israel suffering on behalf of her heathen neighbors. But the ultimate fulfillment of the suffering servant theme is an individual who bears a burden of suffering himself on behalf of his own people. The final fulfillment of this motif is Jesus Christ himself. The prophet may at first have had in mind the nation, or he may have realized all along that God's revelation referred to an individual messiah. But surely the nation proved to be inadequate to fulfill the functions assigned to the servant. Whether Isaiah understood the servant individually or not, it was only Jesus who completely fulfilled God's purpose for the suffering servant. One can hardly read the New Testament without identifying Jesus with that messianic suffering servant. Not only is this taught in the latter half of Acts 8, but Jesus himself said that the Son of man did not come to be served, but to serve, and to give his life a ransom for many (Mark 10:45).

John describes himself as our brother and companion in the suffering and kingdom and patient endurance that are ours in Christ Jesus (Rev. 1:9). Peter reminds us that it was to suffering that we were called: "Because Christ suffered for you, leaving you an example, that you should follow in his steps" (1 Peter 2:21). One of the favorite verses in all the book of Romans is in the 8th chapter, the 28th verse: In all things God works for the good of those who love him, who have been called according to his purpose. Nothing, not even suffering, will be able to separate us from the love of God that is in Christ Jesus our Lord.

A frequent teaching in the New Testament regarding the death of Christ is that he conquered evil by his blood. The victory has been won on the cross. Christ was not the victim; he was the victor. He triumphed over all the forces of evil by his cross (Col. 2:15; Gal. 1:4). Many have suggested that victory is an overall theme in the New Testament. The child of God can be victorious over evil. By faith in Christ we can be victorious over sin. And finally by God's grace we can be

victorious over death. Nothing can separate us from the love
of God in Christ Jesus our Lord.

## A CHRISTIAN RESPONSE TO THE PROBLEM
## OF EVIL AND SUFFERING

This study may not have answered all of our intellectual
questions. Christians still do not know why God allows
every particular instance of evil. But we do believe that we
can show that the existence of evil does not constitute a
"logical proof" for atheism. Quite to the contrary, it is in the
context of evil that we can even more clearly see the
transforming power of God.

Evil is not ultimate in the universe. Even the greatest
evil, the crucifixion of the Son of God, has been transformed
into the greatest good by which full atonement is made for
our sin and by which sinners are reconciled to God. Because
of the cross, there is hope even for the struggle going on in
the natural universe. The decay and death that characterizes
all of life is not the final word. Jesus said, "Be of good cheer.
I have overcome the world" (John 16:33). Transformation is
the key word, and the primary example is the cross and the
resurrection. By God's set purpose and foreknowledge,
Christ won the victory over evil.

The cross appeared to be ultimate. Evil and suffering
had seemingly won the day. The Jews had expected the
Messiah to come in power and set up an earthly kingdom
immediately. God has all power. God is supposed to win.
Human thought constantly, if not inevitably, views power as
more significant than goodness.

But the biblical God is characterized by more than sheer
power and might. Goodness is not like a monolithic object
that is controlled and defined by power. Goodness is a
quality, an attribute, a loving relationship. Goodness stands
as an aspect of God's being. He is good. Power is something
God possesses. Goodness is something God expresses.

People tend to define goodness and love in terms of
indulgence. Love is supposed to be naive and uncritical and
passionate. That is why we are so often unable to think of
self-love without at the same time thinking of egotism. But
self-love, according to Jesus, was the model for our love for

our neighbor. Love in the biblical sense is not simply naive indulgence. Love is responsible action. From the human standpoint, love is obedience to the commands of Christ. "If anyone loves me, he will obey my teaching" (John 14:23). From the divine standpoint, love is the expression of God's grace (John 3:16).

God cares. His greatest power is seen in his grace. We do not have to climb Jacob's ladder in order to drag God down; rather God initiates the action, and he comes down to us. If the Christian God were nothing more than the Islamic Allah, we would never be able to find any answer to the question of evil. But in the Christian faith there is an added dimension. God himself has entered into history, and thus we are capable of having a personal relationship with him.

When we talk about salvation we frequently speak about a relationship with Jesus Christ, but when we come to an intellectual problem we seem to think that we must have all the answers in purely logical form. The most meaningful answers, however, will be found in the context of a personal relationship with the God of all truth. We may never be able to fully explain everything by reason alone. Yet in all things we believe God is working for good, because the God we know personally has assured us that this is true. It is the personal relationship with Christ that allows us to believe even more than we can prove by reason alone.

But what is the good toward which God is always working? Ultimately God's good purpose is to form a new people in the likeness of Christ. Jesus was the first-born among many brothers. God wants to produce a new community, a new relationship, a new people.

Not everything that happens is God's will. The Bible clearly states that it is not God's will that any should perish. And yet some do. God gave us the good gift of responsible choice, but it is not God's will for us to sin. And yet all do. God is not directly responsible for man's rebellion. But God works within that which exists (even in our sinfulness) to bring about his good purpose. The cross and the resurrection do not logically solve the problem of the origin of evil; they do, however, remove and destroy the power of evil.

The biblical solution to the problem of evil will ultimately arise from a real and authentic relationship with God

188

through Jesus Christ. The biblical principles outlined above may not adequately handle every conceivable aspect of the intellectual problem of evil as such. But they do give us insight into God's manner of handling the problem.

## SUMMATION AND POSTSCRIPT

We have considered the nature of the problem of evil from several angles. Evil does exist, and it is a problem both practically as we individually face it, and intellectually from the apologetic standpoint. We have looked at various historical and religious solutions finding that most of them denied the truth either of God's power, God's goodness, or the existence of real evil.

Each of the eight biblical principles gives answers to various parts of the problem. The total solution, then, turns out to be a complex answer. The simplistic atheistic use of the triangular dilemma does not even begin to be successful, though it does cause us to think seriously about many issues.

The problem of evil is real, but it is not unsolvable. There is a strong basis for believing that God is fully good and all-powerful and that there is a divinely understood reason for the existence of evil. The evidence supporting the truth of Christian faith does not depend upon our ability to resolve every problem.

We must remember that Jesus also faced this problem. He attacked evil at every level. He cast out demons. He resisted temptation. He healed the lame and the deaf and the blind. He raised Lazarus from the dead. He calmed a threatening storm.

Yet he endured a cruel mocking. He experienced the agony in Gethsemane. He wept. He felt the lashes. He suffered on the cross for sin he did not commit. He cried out to God and became submissive to his Father's will even unto death.

This is not the best of all possible worlds. Heaven will be better. As Norman Geisler has correctly reasoned, God must always do his best. Since this world is not itself the best, then it must be true that this world is the best way to accomplish God's best. God made Adam capable of committing sin. Whether we understand it all or not, we can with confidence

189

believe that God's creative choice was a better way to make a human being (and to make a world) than any other way. Had there been a better way, God would have done it that better way. Adam's ability to sin apparently made him a far more significant being than he could have been otherwise. God did not desire or encourage sin, but Adam sinned as God knew he would. Thus God from eternity provided the best possible solution. God's way of redemption does not compromise his nature nor Adam's nature, and yet it allows God to forgive sin and restore relationships. This is the authentic Christian answer. There is finally no other answer except one based upon the confidence we have in God that he will do, has done, and is doing right.

oOo

Evil, though it is a continuing problem intellectually as well as practically, does not refute nor destroy the massive evidence upon which a reasonable faith is built. Christianity stands or falls—no, it stands—on the truth of the resurrection of Christ. If Christ be not raised, our faith is vain. But he was raised, and he ascended to the right hand of the Father. Thus if you confess with your mouth, "Jesus is Lord," and believe in your heart that God raised him from the dead, then you will be saved, and you will enter into a new relationship with God that will provide a context for facing evil and suffering with dignity and confidence. Truly we can praise the Lord, Hallelujah!

# GLOSSARY

Atheism
Eschatology
Judgment
Millennium
Revelation

Salvation
Self-stultifying
*Summum Bonum*
Theodicy

# APPENDIX ONE

## THE AUTHORITY OF HOLY SCRIPTURE

Throughout the history of the church, Christian believers have assumed that Christ was the Son of God, that salvation was provided for us by Christ's death on the cross, and that the Bible was the authoritative Word of God. Today, all three of these assumptions have been challenged. Since the first two are not only crucial to the proclamation of the gospel but are based upon and known only by means of the third, much attention has been focused in recent years upon Scripture and the nature of its authority.

Many books and articles have been written concerning the authority of the Bible. The veracious character of the Bible is an essential element of its authority. But the epistemological issues, as always, are primary. Logically there are only two possible sources of knowledge about God: (1) Personal experience; and (2) the testimony of others.

Personal experience is at once the most and the least certain of sources of knowledge about God. Obviously if one actually does have a personal experience with God, then it must be true that God exists. Moses, having met with God on Sinai, had no doubt about God's existence, nor about God's authority. Paul assured us that he knew the one in whom he believed.

But one major problem with relying upon immediate perception is that the knowledge gained in this way is private knowledge. No one can challenge your experience, but neither can your experience belong to anyone else. Private experience is pure subjectivity. How do you know that you correctly understand your own experience? Experiences are easily and often misinterpreted. If experience alone is the final and absolute test for truth, then one is forced into relativism and irrationalism. Contradictory propositions end up being affirmed simultaneously. For example, one must believe that God truly does exist if one has experienced him (or if one thinks he or she has had such an experience). On the other hand, if one does not personally experience God, and if experience is the only test for truth, then one could not affirm God's existence. Moreover, someone may claim to have had an experience with Krishna or Zeus. If private experience is unchallengeable and not subject to objective criteria for evaluation, then Krishna and Zeus exist. Others may claim that supernatural beings have revealed to them that the biblical God does not exist.

Thus experience alone (or the lack of it) could lead two individuals to affirm opposite ideas, that God does and that God does not exist or that a pagan or a Hindu god exists. These are contradictory conclusions, and thus all of these claims cannot be true at the same time (if by "true" we mean corresponding with objective reality). Yet all could be justifiably affirmed if private experience alone is the final source and arbiter of truth.

If one believes that all experiences are equally valid, this results in having to believe that more than one religion is equally true and valid, because all religions have experiences that seem to support their reality and truth in the minds of their own followers. While it is theoretically possible that religion is a purely mystical "reality" and that all religions might be "true" for those who hold them, this position is not only plagued by the incoherence of relativism, but it is also an internally contradictory position in light of claims by biblical religion to be exclusively salvific. It is not possible to affirm that all religions are true if one religion includes an essential claim that the others are false.

Therefore, private experience (as a source for knowledge of God) is incapable of standing alone. The testimony of others seems to be a necessary supplement to personal experience. In fact it is an essential element in any adequate epistemology. The testimony of others can be compared and studied. It is objective testimony (external to the individual). Historical claims can at least potentially be evaluated by various means and by criteria that actually enable us to distinguish fact from fancy. Theological ideas in historical contexts can be compared for harmony and consistency. Both rational and empirical (evidential) testing can be done. That testimony which fits the most facts, and at the same time is the most coherent, and at the same time finds an experiential response in one's own mind and heart is that testimony which is most likely to be true.

It is the Christian's affirmation that the collected testimony found in the Holy Bible is true for those very reasons. What Moses learned from God on Sinai was not adopted by Israel on "blind faith." Moses asserted his claims in the public arena. He threw down his rod before Pharaoh, and that which had happened in private was confirmed in public. How much more public could the claims of Moses be than they were in Egypt or in the wilderness?

Public confirmation of the "private experiences" of Moses (and of other biblical prophets and apostles) occurred over and over. Their claims were tested and verified time and time again. Jesus was accredited by God through miracles, wonders, and signs, especially by his resurrection and his witnessed appearances. It is the "experience" and the verifying "testimony of others" that gives us so much confidence in the Bible as truly being the mediated Word of God.

Christians also believe that alternative claims, such as those made by naturalists or by pantheists or by people holding other worldviews, can be shown to be false either because they are self-defeating or because they do not fit the facts or both.

It is only in the modern day (primarily since the Enlightenment [eighteenth century]) that Christians themselves have raised questions about their own basis of authority. Non-believers had long questioned the authenticity of Scripture. But this was no issue among believers. In recent centuries, however, some Christians have tried to affirm Christian theology from a new base. No longer could Scripture be considered as the absolutely true basis for theology, they said. One may use Scripture as a primary source, they suggested, but not as the only source, for doctrine.

Modern philosophy has now filtered down to lay believers. Many Christians today have lost the biblical sense of divine authority. Preachers do not speak often of providence, nor do our people spend very much time seeking after God and trying to conform to his will. Many people today do not believe it is possible for an ancient book to be infallible or authoritative for modern life. Thus they no longer believe that the Bible is fully truthful even though they may believe that it has many good things to say.

But if one denies the truthfulness of an authentic biblical teaching, then one no longer accepts any of the biblical teachings simply because Scripture affirms them. What is believed is believed for "persuasive" reasons. Man's mind and man's reason becomes the final arbiter. But this is exactly the relativism that can never ground any truth.

Please notice that this is not at all to say that if Scripture has one error in it that it becomes automatically untrustworthy in every part. Such a conclusion would be manifestly false and totally unreasonable. But it is to say that the affirmation of Scriptural error does reflect a change in the epistemology of the theologian. Decisions are now made as to what we can believe and what we cannot (or should not) believe on some other basis than that God has spoken through Scripture. This willingness to affirm biblical error reflects the philosophical shift toward modern religious skepticism. Relativistic epistemology will never acknowledge the absolute authority of God. Can two walk together if they are without common ground?

If it can be shown (and it can) that Jesus spoke and taught as if every part of Scripture were true and if it can be shown (and it can) that the apostles everywhere assume the full authenticity and authority of Scripture; and if it can be shown (and it can) that the New Testament bears the same marks of authenticity as the Old, then it seems that veracious biblical authority is not an issue to be taken lightly, nor is it to be discussed superficially, nor is it to be denied by one who calls Christ Lord and Master (Teacher).

# GLOSSARY

Absolute
Authority
Bible
Christian
Contradiction
Evangelical

Hermeneutics
Inerrant
Inspiration
Propositional Revelation
Revelation

# APPENDIX TWO

## ELEMENTS OF THEISM AS A WORLDVIEW

Theism as a worldview would include at least these basic elements:

A. An Infinitely Complete Being Exists.
   1. This Being lacks nothing necessary for existence.
      a. This Being is not a physical substance.
      b. Physical substance is not an essential feature of that which exists. For example:
         (1) Mathematical formulas are thought-forms that exist both theoretically and in practice. Mathematical formulas express relationships, but they are not physical substances.
         (2) Scientific laws are forms of thought that exist to describe the activity of physical substance, but the laws themselves are not physical substances.
         (3) Mathematical formulas and scientific laws simply illustrate the principle that existence (in a commonly understood meaning of the term) is possible even when physical substance is not directly affirmed of the entity being described. By no means do these illustrations exhaust the possibilities for non-substance existence.

(4) If physical substance is universally contingent, as some evidence indicates is the case, then it would seem to be both logically and existentially necessary to affirm at least one non-contingent reality on which the contingency of universal physical substance depends. That non-dependent reality must be an actual Being if the contingent reality that depends on it is real, and that non-contingent reality could not itself be physical substance (since physical substance appears to be universally contingent).

(5) Thus it is certainly possible that something could exist that is not itself physical substance, and theists argue that it is essential that such a Being exist.

c. An infinitely complete Being does not inherently require physical substance in order to exist.

(1) Theists assert that personality, mind, and rational thought exist apart from and prior to physical substance. These are essential elements of the God theism affirms. This God is one Being.

(2) Human personality, mind, and rational thought have their source in the one infinitely complete Being that exists. This God is the creator of all things other than himself.

d. An infinitely complete Being would be absolute and in essence unchanging.

(1) Since this Being is infinitely complete, all aspects of essential being would be complete (mature, fulfilled, fully actualized). Thus there would be no need to change, nor would a change in essence be possible.

(a) There could be change in any non-essential aspect of his being.

(b) There could be change in relationships with created things.

(c) There could be change in the means by which this absolute Being would be known by the rationally conscious parts of contingent reality.

(d) This Being could choose to change anything except his own perfections.

(e) Thus changes in God's goodness, his love, his truthful character, or in any other essential aspect of his being would not be possible, if by "change" one is thinking of an event which adds to or takes away from those essential aspects of his perfect being.

(2) Since all aspects of essential being would be complete, there is no attribute possessed by this Being that is not possessed completely.

    (a) This Being is conscious, aware, and active.

    (b) This Being communicates, chooses, and achieves.

    (c) This Being examines, evaluates, and loves.

    (d) This Being originates, sustains, and directs.

    (e) This Being is good, just and holy.

(3) Therefore, this Being is in possession of and is the source of all knowledge, all goodness, and all power.

e. An infinitely complete Being may choose to relate directly or indirectly to physical substance.

f. An infinitely complete Being may choose to relate directly to physical substance by dwelling in a physical body.

(1) This would be a voluntary act that is possible but not necessary for an infinitely complete Being.

(2) To act in such a way would be to go beyond that which is necessary.

(3) Christian theism affirms that in space and time this Being has chosen to directly appear to men in a physical body (Jesus of Nazareth, the Christ).

(4) Other theists may affirm only an indirect relationship to physical substance.

(5) Therefore, theism is a necessary assumption of Christianity but not vice versa.

g. Should such a Being not exist, no explanation for the existence of contingent physical substance seems possible.

(1) It is not impossible to believe that an infinitely complete Being does not exist, but if that were true, all meaning, value, and purpose would also be lost.

   (2) Even "meaningful" arguments against Theism would be "meaningless."

2. This Being has no weakness.
  a. This Being is mentally perfect.
   (1) This Being has all knowledge.
   (2) This Being makes no mistakes.
  b. This Being is morally perfect.
   (1) This Being does not lie.
   (2) This Being always does what is best.
  c. The lack of physical substance is not a sign of weakness.
   (1) Power may be expressed through physical force, but this is not its only means of expression.
   (2) The power to create physical substance is greater than any power that might be expressed by that substance which had been created.
   (3) An infinitely complete Being would have the power to create.

3. This Being is uncaused.
  a. To be infinitely complete is to be eternally complete.
  b. To be eternally complete is never to be lacking in anything necessary for existence.
  c. To be eternally complete is never to be less than fully complete.
  d. To be eternally complete is to be uncreated.
  e. Thus there would never have been an occasion of need, nor could there have been a situation in which an infinitely complete Being would be caused (either to exist or to act) by anything outside of itself.
   (1) A self-cause is possible for actions.
   (2) A self-cause is not possible for existence.
   (3) No being can cause itself to begin to exist.
    (a) If it already existed it would not need to cause its own beginning, nor could it.
    (b) If it did not exist, it would not be able to cause anything to begin to exist since there would be nothing there to do the causing.

B. A Temporal, Finite, Contingent Reality Exixts.
 1. The universe does exist.

    a. The universe is a collection of related, physical substances that persist.

    b. The universe is observed to exist by human beings. This observation is confirmed by all known means of gathering and testing information.

    c. The universe is observed, protected, and influenced by the infinitely complete Being who originated and sustains it.

2. The universe is probably not an eternal reality.

    a. The Second Law of Thermodynamics describes the consistent loss of the availability of energy for useful work, and thus it points to the necessity for a beginning in time.

    b. The observed pattern of cause and effect points to the necessity of an original cause.

    c. The scientific evidence available today seems to imply the possibility, even the likelihood, that the universe is steadily expanding. Should this prove to be the case, this would also suggest the likelihood of a beginning of this expansion.

    d. Out of nothing, nothing comes. Therefore, if the universe had a beginning, then it seems necessary for the universe to have had a cause.

    e. If physical reality could begin without a cause, then all hope for a consistent, meaningful explanation of the universe (or for anything in the universe) would be lost.

3. The universe is seemingly finite.

    a. There is insufficient scientific evidence to accurately measure all aspects of the universe.

    b. Nevertheless, the available evidence points to a limited size and a definite mass for the universe.

    c. A finite universe is consistent with what a theistic principle of creation would predict and expect.

4. The existence (including the origin, the current moment, the past, and the future) of the universe is totally dependent upon its relationship to the source of its existence, the infinitely complete Being.

    a. The universe is orderly and regular, thus, to the extent that it is properly understood by some mind, it is predictable and meaningful.

    b. Exceptions to the order and regularity of the universe are possible since this order is dependent upon the sustaining desire of the infinitely complete Being.

       (1) Thus the occurrence of miracles is a possibility though not a necessity.

       (2) Claimed or supposed instances of miracle could and should be tested by gathering and evaluating the reliability of the historical evidence relating to the event.

       (3) Naturalistic bias in the interpretation of the evidence is, however, a serious instance of begging the question.

    c.  Pure evil (as opposed to the so-called "evil" which is due to the finite limitations of men and things) is directly related to the lack of a proper relationship with the infinitely complete Being.

5.  Mankind is a unique part of the temporal, finite, contingent reality that exists.

    a.  Human beings have bodies made of the same physical substance as the universe.

    b.  Human beings are also in some sense like the infinitely complete Being in that they have personality, mind, and rational thought in a unique way and to a high degree.

    c.  Human beings have many if not all of the characteristics of the infinitely complete Being except that each human characteristic is expressed in limited and incomplete ways.

    d.  It is incorrect to reason from psychological or sociological grounds that the infinitely complete Being is merely a projection of human characteristics to an infinite scale.

       (1) It is not logically impossible to reason this way, but actually this is not the normal reasoning of mankind. Many non-theists exist, and many limited "gods" are and have been worshipped.

       (2) Moreover, the evidences offered for God's existence may or may not be conclusive or even persuasive, but they can be and have been offered without reference to psychological or sociological factors, and these arguments must be evaluated on their own merits.

(3) It is to be noted, however, that God's existence does not depend upon successful formulations of theistic proofs. Existence is not caused by "proofs." Reason is a means of knowing, not a cause of existence. Moreover, reason is not the only tool available for knowing, though it is an essential part of cognitive communication and understanding.

C. Christian Theism Affirms:
 1. The infinitely complete Being is appropriately called the LORD God.
    a. God is that which is thought to be worthy of worship.
    b. An infinitely complete Being is worthy of worship.
       (1) There is nothing more ultimate than an infinitely complete Being.
       (2) An infinitely complete Being would be of infinite value.
       (3) That which is the source of all existence other than itself is that which is of the most value for that which exists.
       (4) Nothing is more worthy of worship than the uncaused cause of all else that exists.
    c. The God of Christian theism is uniquely worthy of worship.
       (1) He is the LORD God (the common translation of Yahweh-Jehovah Elohim).
       (2) Yahweh and Jehovah are alternate transliterations of the same revealed personal name of God.
       (3) This personal, biblical God has expressed his redemptive grace to men through the events of biblical history.
       (4) The appropriate response of mankind toward God is worship, obedience, and loyal allegiance.
 2. The LORD God is not known by rationally inescapable arguments.
    a. Rational arguments for the LORD God's existence have been proposed.
       (1) These arguments have stronger and weaker forms.

      (2) The stronger arguments are based on claims of existential necessity (how something has to be) rather than on strictly logical necessity (how something must be conceived).

  b. Reason itself depends upon the existence and the unchanging nature of the LORD God for its validity and possible correspondence with reality.

      (1) The mind of God is the ultimate source of all created reality.

      (2) God's rationality is the original source of all human rationality.

      (3) If God's mind were not rational (or if it did not exist) then there would be no basis for reason (and knowledge) except the random, thoughtless movements of an impersonal natural process.

  c. The existence of the LORD God does not depend upon human ability to find adequate rational support for belief, rather he is that which does eternally exist whether humans believe or not.

3. The LORD God is known personally as he takes the initiative to approach people.

  a. He is known to all humans by general revelation through nature, history, society, and family relationships.

  b. He has made himself known to many through special revelation.

      (1) The LORD God revealed himself and his will to men gradually and progressively.

      (2) The final and supreme manifestation of the LORD God's revelation of himself to men came in the historical incarnation when the LORD God became a human being and lived among his people.

        (a) Jesus of Nazareth, the Christ, is the LORD God in human flesh.

        (b) Jesus gave his life as a substitutionary sacrifice, thus paying the penalty for sin.

        (c) By the grace of the LORD God, upon the condition of repentance from sin and faith in Christ, individual humans may be forgiven for their sin and thus may be saved from the righteous judgment of the LORD God.

c.   The authoritative written account of divine
     revelation is the Old and New Testament
     Scriptures found in the Bible.

o◯o

According to this outline, theism has two main affirmations.
1. An infinitely complete Being exists; and
2. A temporal, finite, contingent reality exists.

The twofold structure suggested here might be challenged on
the technical grounds that theism as such demands only the first
assumption. If such a Being exists, this Being would appropriately
be called God. The affirmation of the existence of this God is the
essence of theism. Without the second affirmation, however, there
would be no one to make the first affirmation except God himself.
In that case, it would hardly be necessary for the affirmation to be
made, for there would be no one who doubted God's existence, nor
would there be anyone who needed telling.

Therefore, as a practical fact, the second affirmation is a part of
classical theism as a worldview. It is included specifically to
distinguish theism from pantheism (which considers God and the
world to be the same reality) and naturalism (which affirms the
second affirmation of theism while denying the first) and other
worldviews that make affirmations or denials about God and the
world. Theism affirms the real existence of both God and the
created world, but it never identifies God with the world, nor does
it assume the eternality of matter.

o◯o

The outline given above is not an exhaustive analysis of all true
statements that a theist may accept. For example, a theist may also
believe in the existence of a spiritual reality as well as the physical
universe, holding that both were created by God. This spiritual
reality may be divided into parts such as heaven or hell; it may be
populated according to its own independent set of laws that may or
may not differ from the scientific laws of the physical universe.
Beliefs such as these are not essential to theism as a worldview; thus
they are not included in the outline above. Such views are held by
many theists, however, and a full study of this worldview should
include information on these commonly included ideas.

As part C of this outline of theism shows, Christianity is a form
of theism. Christian theism does include the standard elements of
theism described above. Within Christianity, however, there are

several varieties: Catholic, Protestant, Orthodox, Cultic, etc. Within Protestant Christianity (and to a lesser extent within other major traditions) there are several varieties with indistinct boundaries: liberalism, neo-orthodoxy, existentialism, evangelicalism, etc. There are also denominational groupings: Baptists, Presbyterians, Lutherans, etc. Moreover, there are several kinds of Baptists, etc.

Any superficial description of evangelical Christianity will always be open to further analysis and clarification. However, as a working hypothesis, these elements seem to be essential to evangelical Christianity.

1. The existence of the God of the Bible.
2. The full truthfulness of the Bible.
3. The reality of the Incarnation.
4. The lordship of Christ.
5. The necessity of salvation on account of human sinfulness and the means of salvation being by God's grace through faith alone (as opposed to salvation by human works).
6. The efficacy of the substitutionary atonement of Christ.
7. The sovereignty of God in creation, in history, and in the consummation of all things.

# GLOSSARY

Argument
Being
Cause
Christian
Contingent
Essence
Existence
Finite
God
Infinite

Necessary
Proof
Reality
Reason
Substance
Theism
Thermodynamics
Transcendent
Worldview

# APPENDIX THREE

## THE IRENAEAN THEODICY

One of the most influential books in modern times that deals with the problem of evil is *Evil and the God of Love* by John Hick (New York: Harper & Row, 1966). The first two hundred pages of the book treat the Augustinian type of theodicy. Augustine suggested that evil is the privation of good stemming from misused freedom. Evil is the absence of good. The question: "Why is good absent?" is answered by the so-called "Free-Will Defence." Sin is the basic evil.

### CALVIN

Hick traces Augustinian ideas through Calvin and Barth. In Calvin, of course, the dominant solution is simply the doctrine of predestination. The point of prime concern is the doctrine of the fall. Why did the angels rebel? According to Calvin:

> Paul gives the name *elect* to the angels who maintained their integrity. If their steadfastness was owing to the good pleasure of God, the revolt of the others proves that they were abandoned. Of this no other cause can be adduced than reprobation, which is hidden in the secret counsel of God (*Institutes* III, xxiii, 4).

Why did Adam fall? Calvin says:

> Scripture proclaims that all were, in the person of one, made liable to eternal death. As this cannot be ascribed to nature, it is plain that it is owing to the wonderful counsel of God. It is very absurd in these worthy defenders of the justice of God to strain at a gnat and swallow a camel. I ask again how it is that the fall of Adam involves so many nations with their infant children in eternal death without remedy, unless that it so seemed meet to God? Here the most loquacious tongues must be dumb. The decree, I admit, is dreadful;

and yet it is impossible to deny that God foreknew what the end of man was to be before he made him, and foreknew because he had so ordained by his decree. Should anyone here inveigh against the prescience of God, he does it rashly and unadvisedly. For why, pray, should it be made a charge against the heavenly judge, that he was not ignorant of what was to happen? Thus if there is any just or plausible complaint, it must be directed against predestination. Nor ought it to seem absurd when I say that God not only foresaw the fall of the first man and in him the ruin of his posterity; but also at his own pleasure arranged it. For as it belongs to his wisdom to foreknow all future events, so it belongs to his power to rule and govern them by his hands (*Institutes* III, xxiii, 7).

Evil is present because of the fall. The dread consequences of sin are humanity's own fault. Adam sinned and thus brought death and decay to the world. But human freedom, according to Calvin, is not true freedom. Humanity freely chooses only that path that God has predestined for it. Adam's fall was foreordained. Evil thus was foreordained. If we should thereby challenge God's goodness, Calvin simply quotes Romans 9:19-23.

Hick understands all of this to be an emphasis that is abstracted from the total Christian conception of the divine nature. In fact, for Hick it calls into serious question the goodness and the love of God. Hick claims that the supreme insight of New Testament monotheism is that God loves all his human children with an infinite and an irrevocable love. The Calvinistic idea that God loves a special, chosen "in-group" and hates the alien "out-group" destroys that basic insight. Hick argues that it is our natural human pride that tries to affirm our salvation by setting up a contrast between us (who have it) and them (who do not have it). "We cannot be content to believe that God loves and accepts us unless we are assured that he hates and rejects someone else" (p. 131).

Hick believes that some other approach must be found. If the Calvinistic idea of God's sovereignty is correct, why does not God simply elect all men to salvation? Scripture explicitly teaches that it is not God's will that any should perish. God is pictured as patiently delaying his judgment so that others might come to repentance. Surely, according to Calvin, God could elect all to salvation if he so desired. But he apparently does not so desire. God simply is not perceived in fully agapeistic terms in Calvin's Augustinian theodicy. It makes no sense at all to say that God loves the reprobate. Hell is anything but an expression of God's love, if words have meaning.

## BARTH

Karl Barth is the most influential theologian of the modern day. He is generally thought of as the father of neo-orthodox theology, but he always claims to be solidly within the Reformed tradition. A characteristic emphasis of Barthian theology is the paradoxical nature of revealed truth. Hick is quick to point out this Barthian paradox relating to evil. Barth's term for evil (in the strongest possible sense) is *das Nichtige*. It has nothing in common with God, and yet it is not nothing. In Barth's words, "Das Nichtige ist nicht das Nichts." It is something. In fact the great paradox is that *das Nichtige* must be taken with utter seriousness as a mortal threat, even though (paradoxically) it has been completely overcome by the atoning death of Christ on the cross.

*Das Nichtige* is not simply metaphysical evil. That is, it is not finitude or temporalness. Those things Barth calls the "shadow-side" of creation. The sun (which is good) and a tree (which is good) will necessarily produce a shadow. That shadow does not stand in direct opposition to God's will. Evils of finitude do not constitute the real problem. But *das Nichtige* is true irreconcilable evil. *Das Nichtige* is that which crucified Christ, that which we know by faith to have been defeated by Christ's death, yet that which is still active and powerful in our world today.

Sin is the most concrete form in which we encounter *das Nichtige*, yet the concept cannot be exhausted by sin alone. Its origin is found in God's decision to create a good universe (not in man's rebellion). When God decided to create something good, he consciously chose not to create something else. That something to which God said "no" is not nothing. It exists only as God chooses to do the good, but it exists nevertheless. That which God rejects is *das Nichtige*.

Hick very quickly accuses Barth of falling into the old semantic problem of thinking of "Nothing" as if it were "Something" simply because it is grammatically parallel. Barth furthermore appears to be speculating, a practice that he himself criticizes in others. Barth, however, claims only to be affirming the apparently contradictory truths that are found in the Scripture itself. Evil is God's enemy, yet it is under his control. Barth chooses to leave these ideas in an unresolved dialectic with no hope of finding an intelligible unity.

Hick, on the other hand, points out that Barth is precisely inconsistent at that very point, because his speculation as to the origin of *das Nichtige* is nothing less than a speculation suggested to enable us to understand how and why evil has come into existence in the first place. An even more serious charge is leveled at Barth, however, relating to this theory of evil's origin. If God "creates" *das Nichtige* by creating something good, did he desire thus to create evil or did evil result because of some ontological necessity beyond his control? Is God really free? Could he have created the world without producing evil?

Barth stands on the conviction that God can defeat *das Nichtige*, but God cannot avoid having to defeat it. God is thus limited by something that opposes him. Yet Barth's theology supposedly affirms the absolute freedom of God in keeping with the better insights of the Calvinistic-Augustinian tradition. This internal contradiction in Barthian theology leaves it essentially unintelligible.

No doubt Barth could take the other possibility: that God deliberately created evil for a good purpose (supposedly the supreme good of redemption). But Barth never admits such a possibility. In fact he repudiates the very idea that God could ever positively decree *das Nichtige*.

Barth's account of the origin and the status of evil does not represent revealed truth. He does not begin to solve the real problems raised by his own discussions. To say that evil is that which God rejected in creating the universe is a blatant speculation of human reason that entails wholly unacceptable or outright contradictory consequences. In fact the real issues seem to get lost in the shuffle.

If we maintain the perfect goodness of God, we seem unavoidably drawn either to some denial of God's absolute power and freedom or we must find a place for evil *within* the overall good purpose of God. It is this second alternative that is designated as the Irenaean theodicy.

## HICK

On pages 262-66, Hick outlines the basic points of contrast and agreement between Augustinian and Irenaean types of theodicy. What follows is a very close paraphrase or digest of the points Hick gives. It is to be noted, of course, that Hick personally favors the Irenaean type.

First, Hick suggests that the primary motivation behind all Augustinian theodicies is the desire to relieve the Creator of responsibility for the existence of evil. This is done by making man responsible for his misuse of the good gift of freedom. Irenaean theodicies simply accept the fact that God is responsible for evil. He did not have to create. By choosing to create and by choosing to do that which brought evil, God acted freely. He knew evil would exist. Thus the Irenaean theodicy seeks to show what justifiable reason there is for God so to have acted. Knowing evil would appear, a good God must have a good reason for creating a universe in which evil would exist.

Second, Augustinian theodicies treat evil as "non-being." Evil is the lack of the good, or it is that which God chose not to create, or it is some other form of non-being. Evil lacks a substantial existence because a good God could only create that which is good. Hick claims that the Irenaean approach is not committed to this Platonic theory or any other for that matter. He says it is purely theological (whatever that means!).

Third, Hick interprets the Augustinian concept of God's relationship to his creation as being strictly or at least predominantly viewed in non-personal terms. As an alternative, Hick sees man as primarily created for fellowship with God. The universe is simply the proper environment for man, and whatever imperfections exist are in fact essential for the soul-making process.

Fourth, a major difference is seen in the contrasting theories regarding the historical point at which evil is to be explained. Augustinian theories always look back to the creation and the fall (of angels or men) as the central reference point. Irenaean theories center on eschatology claiming that the final justification of evil will be seen when God finally brings eternal good out of the temporal process.

In a closely related fifth point, Augustinian theodicies emphasize the Fall, whereas Irenaean theodicies do not necessarily deny the doctrine but deemphasize it.

Sixth, and most importantly, the Augustinian tradition points to a final, eternal division of mankind into the saved and the lost, the blessed and the damned, the elect and the reprobate. Irenaean thinkers, on the other hand, generally find the doctrine of an eternal hell to be the very doctrine that renders a Christian theodicy impossible. Could God ever be thought of as good if he sends millions to eternal torment simply because he sovereignly chose not to elect them? Unending and unresolved suffering; sin so great that it can never be paid for; everlasting torment for those who never even heard the gospel; can this be the nature of God's love? The doctrine of hell is no doubt the clearest statement of the problem of evil. How one treats that doctrine will say as much as any other thing about one's own approach to theodicy.

Several points should be made before we go any further. At the time of publication of the first edition of *Evil and the God of Love*, Hick had not yet made his radical shift toward eclectic theology and universalism, which is so evident in some of his more recent writings. He did hold out the hope that all might be saved. He never expected God to give up on man or to withdraw his offer of salvation. But he did not in this book dogmatically affirm that all would finally respond positively toward God.

There is no doubt, however, that Hick had already turned away from the Augustinian emphasis on the fall because he no longer believed it to be true. He clearly contends that the whole Genesis account is a myth. For documentation of the extent of his rejection of any supposed historicity at this point, see pages 180-81, and 281-89. He says it is simply "absurd" (p. 284) to attempt to draw historical conclusions from the story of the fall or from Paul's concept of heaven and hell. Biblical theology as outlined by Paul is simply a "product of religious imagination." Since we can no longer consider the fall to be a part of history, the theodicy built upon that belief must also be looked at critically if not discarded all together.

It may be, however, that even though Hick has built his theodicy on a non-evangelical view of biblical authority, we still may gain some valuable insights from his Irenaean approach. Hick is quite willing to agree that injustice, indignity, and inequity are results of human sin. However, much pain and suffering seem to come from sources independent of human will.

Sin is an inherent possibility if men were actually given the freedom necessary to produce moral responsibility. This world does give us real choices that are followed by real consequences. That is good. But drought, blight, flood, and storm are not easily traceable to human decision. Why has God made a world that leads to such a large bulk of apparently extra or unnecessary suffering? Our world seems to be structured in such a way as to produce this suffering.

Irenaeus, the early Hellenistic father of the church, did not regard Adam as having been created by God in a perfect and finished state. Rather Adam was in the image of God but not fully in the likeness of God as seen in Christ. Adam was not perfect but rather innocent. He was immature. He had the potential to grow in the likeness of Christ, but that was a future goal for Adam. Human beings are still in the process of creation. Our world was never a paradise from which all suffering was excluded. Humanity, so to speak, is the raw material from which God could produce true "children of God." The world is a fit environment for "soul-making."

This process of building up human goodness through the long history of human moral effort is perhaps seen by God to be of such value that it justifies the whole process and the environment necessary to achieve it. There would be no way to develop concern and care for others if there were no dangers or needs that they might encounter. If God so structured the world that no one could get hurt, there would be no need to learn discipline or caution. There would be no need to work since no harm could come to one who did not work. Ethical concepts could not develop at all if no consequences followed from choices. Courage would never develop. Generosity would be unnecessary or irrelevant.

No! The world of natural law and regularity will produce the possibility of suffering and pain, but it is so important to produce the moral qualities of the human personality that God permits, even directly produces, the environment that is best suited for soul-making. Death and separation and sorrow are evil, but they in fact may be the very things necessary to produce the good that God is seeking to produce.

But how could we ever know if this theodicy is in fact true? Hick says it can only be verified eschatologically. When we get to the end, God either will have brought the greatest good out of history or he will have failed. Only then will we know for sure what the answers are. Good seemingly does not result from all things in this life. Every person does not experience the good resolution of Romans 8:28. Thus this "soul-making" process must continue even after death if it is to be more than just a partial success. The Christian answer, says Hick, is that the future good achieved will more than adequately justify all that has happened along the way.

## AN EVALUATION

Several points in all of this seem to be real answers to the problem. The Bible teaches that Adam was in perfect fellowship with God but not that he was complete and mature in every respect. He was intelligent and fully capable of following God's will. The fall was from a perfect relationship, a state of perfect fellowship with God, a life in the very center of God's will. Sin instantly destroyed that relationship, and Adam hid from God. This original state had social implications. The sin broke the perfect relationship between man and woman, and they clothed themselves, hiding themselves from each other. Such an understanding of the fall is perfectly biblical, and this was the insight of Irenaeus.

But Hick then proceeds to claim Irenaeus as his source when the fall is de-emphasized as a part of the biblical solution to the problem of evil. Hick says that a soul would not fall unless there were some flaw in it that would lead to sin. This "flaw" turns out to be the absolute authority of God to which a free will chose not to submit. By definition and by its nature, free will is the ability to choose. Inherent in free will is the possibility of disliking God's authority.

Eden was not a hedonistic paradise in which pleasure was the supreme good. Adam had work to do. He was commanded to have dominion. Where does the Bible imply that such a task was to be easy?

So the Irenaean theodicy correctly emphasizes the good value of the "soul-making" process of some hard work and perhaps even struggle. But death and devastation of life and property are seen in Scripture to be a curse under which man must live because of the fall. When Hick ignores the fall he ignores the biblical answer. Evolutionary philosophy overrules biblical theology in Hick's thinking, and this gives us another example of its destructive power in the minds of men.

Hick wants to insist on the special character of human beings as personal creatures in the image of God, but that simply cannot be done apart from the historicity of Genesis 1-3. Evolution ties human beings to the animals, not to God. Theistic evolution ties God into the process and claims to see God's very work of creation in the process of mutation and the struggle for survival in nature. That fits well with a theory of salvation by works, but it is hard to reconcile with the actual teaching of Scripture on grace.

Hick is wrong in making his analogy between God and human parents. According to Hick God brings hardship upon man in order to produce moral qualities. But no good parent deliberately harms a child in order to teach him a lesson if the child has done nothing to deserve it. Work is not evil, and discipline is not evil. God may lead us through struggles, but God himself views death as an enemy to be defeated.

In fact this is the essential truth of the whole Irenaean theodicy. God's decision to create the existing universe was the precondition for the actual occurrence of evil. He is responsible for evil. But God believed it to be better to create than not to create. How is that possible? He made his decision with full awareness of the consequences. It was better to do what he did than to do any alternative thing. We know that because we know God through his self-revelation. We know him to be completely good.

God has also given us a clue to the dilemma that is apparently posed by our conclusion. God acted with full knowledge of the consequences. He knew evil would result. Therefore, before God even began to create, he accepted the responsibility and provided a way to redeem the world that would fall. That redemption was good enough and great enough to justify, indeed even necessitate, his creative activity.

> All inhabitants of the earth will worship the beast—all
> whose names have not been recorded in the book of life

belonging to the Lamb that was slain from the creation of the world (Rev. 13:8).

For you know that it was not with perishable things such as silver or gold that you were redeemed from the empty way of life handed down to you from your forefathers, but with the precious blood of Christ, a lamb without blemish or defect. He was chosen before the creation of the world, but was revealed in these last times for your sake (1 Pet. 1:18–20).

# GLOSSARY

Being
Eschatology
Neo-orthodoxy

Paradox
Theodicy

# GLOSSARY

**AAC** - An abbreviation for the Latin *anno ante Christum*: in the year before Christ.

*AB ABSURDO* - Latin for "from absurdity." Used to describe an argument or a position as false because the argument is based on absurd premises or leads to absurd conclusions, or because the statement of the position itself is an absurdity. If the necessary implications of a statement lead to the conclusion that "advocacy of the statement involves the denial of the statement" the advocate's position is meaningless and the argument absurd. Absurdity also results from obvious inconsistencies and utter improbabilities. (See **ABSURD** and *REDUCTIO AD ABSURDUM.*)

**ABSOLUTE** - The exact opposite of relative. The context is very important for understanding the meaning of this term. As a noun it is sometimes used with reference to God. More often the noun refers to a concept (in particular, a moral value) that is not modified by cultural circumstances; a concept that is universal and unchanging. An absolute is not limited by anything outside itself. As an adjective it describes that which is unconditional, uncaused, or totally independent.

In Hegel's philosophy the "Absolute" is a term that conveys Hegel's idea of the greatest, most complete concept of ultimate reality. Hegel's "Absolute" can and does grow, but it cannot diminish. It is the impersonal sum of all thought and being.

Biblical philosophy is built upon the affirmation that all truth is God's truth. God is (and his Word reveals) the absolute standard for truth and for morals. God's knowledge is complete, exhaustive, infallible, and perfectly true. God's knowledge is the standard by which a Christian defines truth. Therefore truth itself cannot change. Truth is always and forever the same. Thus truth is an absolute.

What God has revealed is to be believed because it is God's truth. The fact that "God has spoken and thereby revealed some of his knowledge" is a central affirmation of all Christian theology. The Bible as God's Word may be said to have truth without mixture of error for its matter. In other words, God's revealed character and his eternal purpose has not and will not change. The cultural situation, however, is constantly changing. The culture of the biblical world is very different from the culture of the modern world. Truth speaks of the universal and the unchanging. We must be careful that we do not hastily identify our ever-changing cultural opinions and interpretations with God's absolutes. God has spoken to particular people at particular times in particular places. Recognition of God's truth, which is eternally valid at all times and in all places, is the primary hermeneutical task of the biblical expositor. We must seek to discover God's absolutes and to apply them to our changing cultural situations. (See **RELATIVE**.)

**ABSTRACT (ABSTRACTION)** - A property, quality, attribute, or relation that is considered in isolation from any particular object or specific instance; a concept viewed separately and apart from other characteristics inhering in an object. For example, "honesty" and "whiteness" are abstract concepts. We understand these concepts even if no specific example is mentioned. Those words refer to characteristics of actions or things which can be considered apart from the particular instances.

Often the term "abstract" describes a theory considered apart from any concrete application. Abstract truth would be purely logical or conceptual truth not directly or necessarily related to factual reality. It is often an accusation of weakness to characterize a theory or an idea as being abstract.

**ABSURD** - Marked by an obviously ridiculous or unreasonable state of affairs; something that is self-contradictory or foolish; for example: a "two-sided triangle" or "forced love." Both of these phrases are normal grammatical constructions, but they are self-contradictory and are, by definition, clearly impossible in reality.

When Kierkegaardian existentialism pleads for belief in the Incarnation, one reason given is that we should believe because it is absurd. Some interpreters suggest that Kierkegaard possibly meant only that no man would ever think up the idea of this doctrine of the Incarnation on his own, that from the human perspective the idea of a God-Man is an impossible combination (foolishness to the Greeks). This may have been Kierkegaard's way of affirming the reality of the Incarnation. But many followers of Kierkegaard believe that he was suggesting that the Incarnation is a logically self-contradictory affirmation. Christian doctrines based on that central affirmation would thus be false or at least unknowable in their factual teachings. Nevertheless the gospel is to be believed, they say, in spite of the lack of factual truthfulness. Faith then becomes a "leap" in the dark, belief in spite of the evidence.

In scripture, faith is never absurd in this sense. We may not (we surely do not) know all truth. We may not be able to "prove" our faith with absolute logical certainty. Nevertheless biblical faith is always a step in the light. Faith has its basis in God's clear revelation in deed and word. (See **EXISTENTIALISM** and **FAITH**.)

**ACCIDENT** - An adventitious characteristic; a property that is non-essential and could, therefore, be destroyed without changing the essence of the object to which it belonged. Example: the color of a book. It may be red or blue, but that does not really change the book itself (the words and meaning).

This term is used especially in descriptive studies of Aristotle's philosophy and thus also in studies of the philosophical theology of Thomas Aquinas. The Roman Catholic doctrine of transubstantiation, for example, is that the essence of the bread and wine change into the body and blood of Jesus while the accidents (the outward appearances) of the bread and wine remain unchanged. To most evangelicals today, such supposed theories of transformation seem artificial, but they often do maintain distinctions between categories such as form and matter. Form may change while matter remains. Various biblical translations, for example, exhibit various forms but the teachings and affirmations (the matter) of Scripture remain. (See **SUBSTANCE**.)

**A.D.** - A calendar abbreviation. Latin *anno domini*: in the year of our Lord. Used to designate the number of years since the estimated year of Jesus' birth.

*AD ABSURDUM* - Latin: "to the point of absurdity." (See *REDUCTIO AD ABSURDUM*.)

*AD HOC HYPOTHESIS* - Applies only to a specific case and has no reference to any wider application. Such a feature is a mark of weakness if it is used to support a worldview. (See **HYPOTHESIS**.)

*AD HOMINEM* - A type of argument that appeals to personal feelings or prejudice rather than to intellect or reason. Such arguments often attack the opponent's character rather than the reasonableness of the position. Frequently a person will use "to the person" statements out of desperation; that is, when someone's position is shown to be unfounded or irrational, he or she often will respond emotionally by directing remarks at the opponents themselves rather than at the opponent's position. This, to say the least, is poor methodology. Truth is not related to our approval or disapproval of individual personality traits. Accusing individual Christians of hypocrisy or claiming that some Christians have poor attitudes, etc; has little to do with whether or not Christian doctrine is true.

*AD INFINITUM* - To infinity; without end or limit. A line of reasoning that can reach no conclusion; or a series of ideas, each one pointing to some other idea; thus a never-ending succession is begun. Circular arguments or pointless arguments can continue *ad infinitum.*

**ADVANCEMENT, THE** - A generic term, coined by the author of this handbook, to label the twentieth century. During the late nineteenth century, a blend of ideas began to emerge that have come to dominate the modern mind. The ideas characteristic of the Advancement include belief in (1) inevitable progress and (2) rapid historical development and change. Modern people seem to believe that technological improvements actually reflect an improvement in people themselves. Despite wars, crime, disease, and crises of all kinds, the modern mind persists in believing that the past was inferior to the present and that the future will inevitably be superior to the present. Evolution is the unchallengeable assumption of Advancement thought. Naturalism is the most characteristic worldview of Advancement thinkers. (See **EVOLUTION, NATURALISM, HUMANISM, ENLIGHTENMENT, SECULAR,** and **NEW AGE.**)

**ADVENT** - From the Latin for arrival. Refers to the coming of Christ (the incarnation, the birth of Christ). The second coming of Christ is called the second Advent, and some Christians who especially emphasize this doctrine are called Adventists. The calendar period beginning four Sundays before Christmas is referred to as Advent.

**AESTHETICS** - That aspect of the philosophy of art that asks the question, "What is the beautiful?" Though it appears to be a plural noun, it is commonly used with a singular verb. As an academic discipline it includes the philosophical study of the history, sociology, psychology, etc. of all forms of art. The study would include painting, music, architecture, literature, photography, etc. Its focus is on the nature of beauty and the beautiful and the analytical judgment of artistic taste, as it seeks to discover the ontological status of artistic merit. Aesthetic truth refers to normative truth. Aestheticism is the doctrine that the principles of beauty are basic and that other principles such as goodness or rightness are derived from beauty.

*AFORTIORI* - All the more: with even more convincing force. An idea or statement taken to be more certain than some other accepted conclusion or recognized fact. If Jesus himself was known to be truly resurrected from the dead, then *afortiori* (even more surely do we know that) the tomb in which the Lord's body had been placed was empty. *Afortiori* arguments are by definition quite strong because, while the initial premise is usually already strongly supported, their conclusion is even more so. (See **LOGIC.**)

**AGNOSTIC** - One who maintains continuous doubt about the

possibility of knowing God (or any ultimate) with any degree of assurance. No one could be a totally consistent agnostic about everything because he would have to be agnostic about agnosticism itself. This would be self-contradictory. If we cannot know for sure that we cannot know, then we might be able to know, and we are no longer totally agnostic. Usually agnostics are selective about what they doubt. (See **ATHEISM**.)

**AGNOSTICISM** - An intellectual position that takes neither an affirmative nor a negative position with reference to the existence of God. In broad philosophical usage it refers to the questioning of human ability to know anything; yet it leaves open the possibility that future evidence may clarify issues. (See **SKEPTICISM**.)

**ALLAH** - In the religion of Islam, Allah is the name of God.

**AMBIGUITY** - The condition of having more than one possible meaning, hence a factor that leads to uncertainty or lack of clarity. This is a weakness of a theory or a system of ideas. Language analysis makes its greatest contribution when it helps us to clarify our thought.

**AMILLENNIALISM** - This term technically tells only what a person does not believe. The "a" is negative and is used just like the "a" in atheism. Therefore by definition, amillennialism is a system of biblical interpretation that does not believe in an earthly, material manifestation of the millennium described in Revelation 20. Because this term only tells what is not believed, the term "amillennialism" is frequently repudiated by those to whom it is usually applied. However, no alternate designation has gained wide acceptance. A wide variety of theological ideas can be found within amillennial ranks, but as a summary of this interpretive system as it is used by evangelicals the following points should be noted: (1) The millennial kingdom is not understood to be an era of earthly prosperity and peace, but rather it is a spiritual reign of Christ in the hearts of believers. Some restrict the millennial blessings to the intermediate state; that is, Christ reigns in heaven over the souls of believers who have died (some restrict this to the martyrs only). The church is the only visible form of the kingdom on the earth. (2) Christ will visibly and personally return at the end of the millennium (that is, at the end of the church age). (3) The return of Christ will coincide with a general resurrection of both saved and lost, followed by a general judgment to determine each one's final destiny (heaven or hell). (4) Old Testament prophecies of earthly prosperity and peace during the messianic reign are taken to be completely figurative and are properly applied only to the internal spiritual condition of the church or to the heavenly state. (5) There is a distinct continuity between, or even a simple identification of the New Testament church and Old Testament Israel. (6) The world is gradually moving toward a climax that will be characterized by increased lawlessness. Many believe that a personal antichrist will oppose the church in the very last days, but the return of Christ will destroy the antichrist and establish the eternal kingdom of God. (7) The millennium of Revelation 20 is a biblical symbol that figuratively designates the period between the cross (the binding of Satan) and the end of the age. The first resurrection is the spiritual new birth of the true believer. The key hermeneutical principle for dealing with eschatological passages in the Bible, according to amillennialism, is to take them as symbols of real events. Thus Christ personally returns, but the events surrounding his return are said to be figuratively described by the biblical writers. The return of Christ may be at any moment, according to some amillennialists, but there will be no secret rapture and no historically manifested kingdom other than the manifestation through the existence of the church. (See **MILLENNIUM.**)

**ANALOGY** - A comparison based on a similarity between things otherwise unalike. Medieval scholasticism tried to draw on this concept as a way of talking about the supernatural. Aquinas suggested that we could not know God directly because God was different from created things which we know. But he thought that human minds could conceive divine things by analogy. For example: to say God is "good" is to mean something different from, yet in some way similar to, the idea that a person is "good." God's love is understood by the analogy of a human father's love for his children, but of course the human love is in many important ways different from God's love. Aquinas, then, believed that we could know God analogically but not directly or univocally. Only an infinite mind could know an infinite God in any direct way. (See **UNIVOCAL.**)

**ANALYSIS** - Detailed examination in order to clarify or explain more fully. The process of breaking down some idea into its most basic and essential aspects. A careful study of the implications or component parts of some presentation. To analyze someone's theology is to study it carefully and try to find out exactly what the person believes about basic issues and why.

**ANCIENT NEAR EAST** - A descriptive classification of the Old Testament world. The term is very broad and is sometimes used to refer to anything in the cultural history of the Bible lands prior to the rise of the Greek empire. In other words, some use this term to refer to the entire Mesopotamian region as well as Egypt during the Old Testament period. Thus studies of Canaanite culture, Egyptian, Assyrian, Babylonian, and Persian civilizations, Sumerian, Hittite, Philistine, and Israelite cultures, and more are all a part of Ancient Near Eastern studies.

This field of study is especially relevant to Old Testament exegesis and interpretation, because it provides insight into the origins of the Hebrew language, the historical setting, and the cultural, political, and religious context in which ancient Israel lived. There are some elements that might generally describe the period, but the ancient Near East is an era of such diversity that it is not especially helpful to try to list unifying features.

Many literary parallels have been claimed between the Old Testament and the national literature of other peoples. Studies of this kind require special attention on a case-by-case basis. Evangelicals generally argue, however, for the uniqueness of the biblical revelation, though some do find evidence of stylistic similarities between biblical and non-biblical materials. Some have suggested that these stylistic similarities demonstrate the unity of the biblical narratives and actually help to date the documents.

Literary (source) criticism (such as the JEDP theory of Pentateuchal composition) was developed before the ancient Near East was extensively studied, and many of the literary criteria used to identify the hypothetical sources have been found to be to some extent common to narratives from the era to which the biblical documents have been traditionally assigned. The most helpful information, however, has been the linguistic data and the historical materials discovered by scholars of Ancient Near Eastern studies that help us to contextualize the biblical narratives properly. (See **CLASSICAL PERIOD**.)

**ANIMISM** - the belief that natural objects (trees, rivers, mountains, stones, etc.) have conscious life and power. This is characteristic of tribal, primal religions within paganism.

**ANTECEDENT** - That which goes before. Normally a cause is understood to be antecedent to an effect. In logic, however, the antecedent is the condition on which truth depends. Theism is antecedent to Christianity: one must first believe in the existence of God, then it is possible to believe that Jesus is the Son of God.

**ANTHROPOMORPHISM** - A description of a non-human being using human attributes or characteristics. The Bible frequently uses anthropomorphic language to describe God. This is not an error (since it is intentionally done), and it is not a weakness of biblical language. It is a means of communication, a semantic technique, that is based on the doctrine of man's creation in the image and likeness of God. Thus God has "ears" and "hands" and he "walks" and "sits." We must also recognize the accommodation of God to human senses in divine revelation. God appears to Abraham, and Jacob and other biblical characters using a human form. Ultimately God chose the human body as the vehicle by which to express himself fully and supremely in Christ Jesus. Thus anthropomorphic language is natural in divine revelation, but it is still important to realize that in his essential being God is not a human being. This kind of language points beyond itself, but it presents God to us in an understandable way.

**ANTINOMIANISM** - From the Greek *nomos* "law." The theological doctrine that the gift of God's grace in the gospel dispensation frees the believer from any responsibility under any and/or all forms of biblical law (in particular, the moral law). Antinomianism stands in opposition to the law. Paul makes it clear that the Christian is under grace, not under Old Testament law. But his reference is to the change from an old covenant to a new one as the means of salvation. He does not suggest that God's moral expectations have been dismissed. Thus antinomianism is a misunderstanding of grace and tends toward moral license. Orthodoxy does not embrace antinomianism.

**ANTINOMY** - A seeming contradiction between two (or more) principles or conclusions that are each rationally valid and equally necessary. If reason were our only basis for determining truth, then an antinomy would appear to be a contradiction (see **CONTRADICTION**). In a true contradiction, however, one or the other of the principles involved must be false. In an antinomy, each principle seems to be necessarily and reasonably true, and yet a rational conflict is immediately apparent. In non-technical usage, an antinomy is often thought of as a contradiction (though they are not exactly the same thing).

Nor is an antinomy the same as a paradox (see **PARADOX**). A paradox arises when two ideas conflict, but one or both of the ideas is thought to be true on some basis other than strict logical necessity.

Although these terms are very similar, one should use "antinomy" when the conflict arises from logical deduction alone and the rules that govern contradictions do not directly apply; "paradox" when the conflict arises between reason and experience or between two experiences. A paradox (such as the mystery of human freedom and divine sovereignty—a conflict between revelation and experience) may be resolved by further information or by agreement on an objective basis of authority, such as Scripture or tradition. An antinomy, on the other hand, appears to be rationally irreconcilable and is not resolved by a simple appeal to authority. Since the principles are not strictly contradictory, however, they may both be true (and if so would be ultimately reconciled in the infinite wisdom of God). Our reason is not absolute and unfailing.

An early example of the antinomy is seen in arguments over the rational necessity to recognize change in the universe (Heraclitus) and the rational necessity to deny change (Parmenides). Kant

222

set forth rational antinomies (such as the necessity that the universe have a beginning and the necessity that the universe not have a beginning), a procedure that had a significant influence on Hegel, leading him to advocate the notion of dialectical synthesis and rational relativism.

**ANTITHESIS** - Direct opposition or contrast. The antithesis of "joy" is "sorrow"; of "love"-"hate". In Kant's thought, the antinomies of reason were always expressed by a positive thesis contrasted with a negative antithesis. Hegel picked up this feature of Kantianism and devised his famous dialectic. The Hegelian antithesis is the negative aspect of the triadic movement of thought that results in a synthesis which transcends the antinomy. For example, Hegel thought that the universe was essentially an expression of a rational mind. Being itself apparently exists. That thesis may be contrasted with its antithesis: Being does not exist. Those two ideas form an antinomy that seems to be a contradiction but actually can be overcome. Hegel believed that this thesis/antithesis could be rationally brought together in an ultimate synthesis: that reality is ultimately neither fully existing nor non-existent but both existing and not yet existing. Reality was rationally evolving. Reality is "becoming." This evolutionary worldview came to dominate the 19th century. The use of an antithesis was the rational key that allowed Hegel's theory to work. (See **DIALECTIC**.)

**APOLOGY (APOLOGETICS)** - Something spoken or written in defense of an intellectual position. "Christian Apologetics," therefore, is that branch of Christian theology which is devoted to defending the rational content of Christian faith with special reference to criticism of that content from outside the faith. Apologetics is concerned with reasons, evidences, and arguments in behalf of true Christian faith. (NOTE: this meaning in modern English has been corrupted. "Apology" is now used to mean an excuse offered to escape blame or punishment. The philosophical usage, however, is related to a very positive, aggressive, and dynamic defense of a position.) In ancient Greece, a charge formally and legally lodged against someone would be answered by an "apology," a defense against the accusations. Plato's famous account of the defense Socrates made at his trial is known as the "Apology." Paul, in Romans 1, says that the evidence for God is so strong and convincing that those who do not believe are "without excuse" (literally "without an apology"). Peter tells us always to be ready to give an answer (make a defense) when someone asks us why we have hope. Thus Christian apologetics has always had an important place in a well-rounded Christian theology.

*APOSTERIORI* - Argument based on knowledge acquired

empirically; i.e., based on sense experiences. Any conclusions that come after the observation and evaluation of facts and that depend on those observations would be *aposteriori* conclusions. To be contrasted with *apriori*.

**APRIORI** - Argument based on knowledge acquired by reason alone apart from and prior to sense experience; whatever is independent of experience. An *apriori* truth is one that is universally and necessarily true independent of and apart from any particular, factual state of affairs. Usually *apriori* claims are arrived at by deductive reasoning from accepted definitions, axioms, or commonly assumed principles.

**ARCHETYPE** - The original, the ideal, or the most extreme example. In Platonism it refers to a truly real, eternal, universal, spiritual "idea" of which temporal, existent, material things are mere copies. The psychologist, C. G. Jung, uses the term to refer to an inherited "pattern of instinctual behavior" derived from the total experience of the race and present in the individual's unconscious mind. Specifically, Jung refers to dream symbols that have continually appeared throughout history.

**ARGUMENT** - An explanation; a series of reasons or facts supposedly supporting or establishing a belief. The term may refer to a reason or statement intended to persuade either positively or negatively with regard to a matter under discussion. Not generally used by philosophers in the sense of a domestic quarrel, the term has no necessary connotation of emotional outbursts. The "argument" is the set of related ideas that leads to a conclusion. A theistic argument, for example, is a suggested "proof" or a collection of evidences that are used in rational attempts to justify belief in God. (See **LOGIC**.)

**ARISTOTLE** - Greek philosopher (384-322 *BC), Plato's most famous student, the tutor of Alexander the Great. He wrote on politics, literary criticism, and science (especially marine biology). He placed particular emphasis on the direct perception of the world as a means of gaining knowledge. Thomas Aquinas referred to Aristotle as "the philosopher."

**ARISTOTELIANISM** - The view (and the development within the tradition) of the philosophy taught by Aristotle. Essentially an empirical tradition; an emphasis on the particular embodiment of universal ideas; emphasizes material things and sensory perception as the epistemological starting point. Aristotle also spelled out the formal rules for syllogistic logic.

**ASCETICISM** - Devotion to the life of rigorous abstention from self-indulgence. Withdrawal from the world and from worldly, materialistic concerns. Opposition to physical pleasures and expensive life-styles.

224

**ASSUMPTION** - That which is taken for granted or that which is supposed as true; a presupposition, postulate, preconception, or axiom. Also, the term is used technically as the designation of the second (or minor) premise in a categorical syllogism. (See **SYLLOGISM.**)

**ATHEISM** - The belief that there is no God; the negation of theism. "Positive atheism" actively argues against the idea of God existing. This is militant atheism of the type represented by political activists who seek to remove all acknowledgment of God from public life. "Negative atheism" contends that there is no positive, valid, or conclusive evidence for God's existence; it claims therefore that we are unjustified in believing in theism at this time. But negative atheism finds no need to attack or resist theistic belief except when it becomes aggressively evangelistic. Antony Flew, a British philosopher of the twentieth century, has argued that atheism is like "innocence" in English law. It is to be presumed until "guilt" (theism) is proven beyond reasonable doubt. (See **THEISM.**)

**AUTHORITY** - Derived from the Latin *auctor* which means author or originator. Thus there are two main usages of the term. First, it refers to citations or references that document one's beliefs or opinions. When a student writes a term paper, the professor will look to see what kind of authority is used. The footnotes give the documentation to show where the ideas in the paper come from, and the authority behind each idea may be strong or weak. A similar usage is found in sentences like this one: "He set forth his beliefs by quoting from the Bible, which is his sole authority for matters of religious faith." This means (whether it is true or not) that he claims to have no other source for his beliefs than the teachings of the Bible. A second but related usage is found in sentences where "authority" refers to the right and/or the power to coerce belief or action, the right to expect or require obedience. The king has this kind of authority. In theology, some use the phrase "the authority of the Bible" with this second meaning as well as with the first. This usage is proper if one understands that God is the source of the Bible's authority (in this second sense). It is not the Book but the Author of the Book that has the right to expect obedience. The Book, however, is rightly understood to be God's Word, and thus conveys God's authority. (See **REVELATION, INSPIRATION.**)

**AXIOLOGY** - The theory or study of value: seeks to answer questions such as "What is value?" "Why do men value certain things?" "How can values be classified?" "What is the ontological status of value?" "Are values subjective or objective?" The Greek word *axios* means "worth." The primary focus is on intrinsic values such as those in religion, ethics, and aesthetics, but axiological questions may also be addressed to instrumental values such as those employed by politicians or economists.

**AXIOM** - A statement assumed to be true as the starting point of a formal proof. A statement or principle that is worthy of acceptance due to its intrinsic merit. In mathematics or logic, an axiom is a statement of a self-evident truth, such as the law of contradiction (See **CONTRADICTION.**)

**BAPTISM** - The religious ceremony by which persons are initiated into the Christian faith. Baptism by total immersion in water represents the new believer's identification with Christ in his death, burial, and resurrection. Some Christians practice baptism by sprinkling water on the head of the new convert (or in some cases of the infant of believing parents). In this latter case the water in the ceremony signifies the forgiveness of sins and thus the cleansing of the human soul.

**BAR MITZVAH** - Jewish religious ceremony for thirteen-year-old boys marking the point at which the boy takes on the religious and social responsibilities of an adult.

**BAT MITZVAH** - Some Reformed Jews hold this ceremony for thirteen-years-old girls in their transition to adult responsibilities.

**B.C.** - Before Christ: A calendar abbreviation designating the number of years before the estimated date of Jesus' birth.

**B.C.E.** - Before the Common Era: A calendar abbreviation used by Jews and others to avoid reference to Christ.

**BEHAVIORISM** - The American school of psychology which limits the data concerning the mind and consciousness exclusively to the observable evidence of the performance and functions of a defined organism (or a group under defined conditions). It limits the investigation of the mind to a study of behavior. By definition it rules out causative factors not explainable in terms of action and response to stimulation in the context of (and in interaction with) the material environment. Behaviorism interprets everything in terms of natural cause and effect. Man's mind or soul is viewed as having no existence apart from purely natural explanations of psychological phenomena. When accepted as the total explanation of reality, it becomes a serious challenge to Christian faith.

**BEING** - Something that exists is said to be existing. That which is existing is a being. To think of "being" itself is to contemplate the most basic concept of existence. If used with a capital B it is thought of as referring to the ultimate reality (God). Most often in philosophical writing "being" refers to that which is existing but is not subject to change or flux; that is to say, it is not "becoming." It is something contrasted with "non-being" (a term for those concepts which may be spoken about but do not exist).

"Being" may also refer to that complex of physical and spiritual qualities that make up an individual. We call ourselves human beings.

**BIBLE** - Holy Scripture for Christianity. Thirty-nine Hebrew books are accepted as Sacred Literature by Judaism. New Testament writings, originally in Greek, are included in the Christian Bible. Roman Catholics accept additional Greek documents (known among Protestants as the Apocrypha) as legitimate additions to canonical Scripture. Evangelical Christians believe the sixty-six book canon is the infallible Word of God.

**BIG BANG COSMOLOGY** - The observable spectral shift in the light from distant galaxies led some early 20th century astronomers to propose that these objects were moving away from the earth at great speeds (and thus from the Milky Way galaxy). If so, by reverse extrapolation, the conclusion was that in the past the universe was smaller in size and ultimately that it had all been in the beginning at one "central" location. Thus the rapid expansion from that original compressed state is described as a "Big Bang," an explosive expansion of the entire universe.

In 1965 a supposedly uniform microwave radiation was detected coming from all directions in the universe. This was taken as convincing evidence that the Big Bang was a "hot" explosion of which this radiation was the lingering trace.

Problems with the theory include: models for a "Big Bang" do not show that elements heavier than hydrogen would be common in the universe, and yet they are. Thus astrophysicists must postulate that hydrogen at first predominated, that stars eventually formed and over their stellar lifetimes "created" heavy atoms in their nuclear furnace cores, that these stars finally went to nova stage and spewed out heavy atoms in all directions. The particular combination and configuration of elements found on earth, then, is (according to "Big Bang" cosmology) the result of fortuitous circumstances. Though other planets exist in this solar system, there is at present only indirect evidence that planets exist elsewhere, and even if they do, it seems most unlikely that an earthlike combination of elements would occur more than once in the time span usually calculated as a maximum for the current configuration of the universe. Earth has liquid water in vast quantities (compared to other solar planets, which have almost none) and a nitrogen/oxygen atmosphere, a complex organic chemistry, and many other features that favor life. This collection of molecules (on naturalistic premises) cannot have been designed, and thus must be the result of random processes. Yet if these molecules were a little closer to the sun, or a little further from the sun, or if the earth were tilted differently, or if it did not have a moon of the proper size and mass and orbit distance, or if the ozone layer were absent, or if the sun were a little hotter or cooler or bigger or smaller, or if any of a vast number of other "ecologically balanced" factors were significantly different, life could not exist on this planet. Creationists believe that the statistical improbabilities that arise from this naturalistic "Big Bang" cosmology are sufficient to render it not only unlikely but false as an explanation of the universe that actually exists (which, of course, does contain our earth).

More recently the tell-tale isotropic microwave radiation (that has been so influential in leading scientists to adopt the "Big Bang" cosmology as a viable explanation of things) has been found to be "smooth" and thus to show no evidence of the "lumpiness" or the "instability" that one might expect to be necessary to get those first stars and galaxies to form. Moreover, galaxies are not evenly spread throughout the universe (as they should be if the "Big Bang" theory is correct). They exist in a variety of grouped patterns, some even appearing to be linked into great "wall-like" configurations. Many are "bunched up" into "clumps" of light even in our best photographs. Such existing features in the universe do not easily harmonize with current models for "Big Bang" cosmology. What is now known about quasars is not readily explained by the "Big Bang," nor can a "Big Bang" easily account for the "hidden mass" proposed as an explanation for some astronomical observations. Other proposals that explain the spectral shift with nonmotion-related causes are gaining some plausibility among astronomers and physicists. So in several significant ways, Big Bang cosmology does not seem to be finding the appropriate confirming evidence, and it may or may not be sustained by future scientific research. (Evidence from the Hubble telescope will be critical.)

Of great concern to many theologians is the fact that not a few Christians seem to have readily assumed that the hypothetical Big Bang was the event of Genesis 1:1 creation itself. Such links between theological doctrine and scientific theory have in the past always been problematic. Scientific theories that prove to be worthless tend to drag "linked doctrines" along with them in the popular mind. (See **CREATION.**)

**BRAHMAN** - Ultimate reality in Hindu thought. The Brahman is ultimately unknowable since it is beyond all intellectual categories. Brahman is formless, inexpressible, infinitely there. Brahman is all, and all is Brahman. (See **PANTHEISM.**)

**BUDDHA, BUDDHISM** - About 600 *BC a young Hindu prince set out to discover the meaning of life. He believed that Hinduism's polytheistic superstition among the common people needed to be reformed, and through a process of meditation he claimed to have been enlightened. Buddha (the Enlightened One) then set forth basic principles for self-denial, mystical meditation, and spiritual discipline known today as Buddhism. Salvation from the evil of existence is found in moderation and self-denial ultimately leading to mystical union with the impersonal reality of the universe.

**CATEGORICAL** - Used as an adjective to describe that which is absolute and unqualified, it refers to a clear, certain positive statement without reservations or obscuring factors. The **"Categorical Imperative"** in the philosophy of Kant is that ethical statement which he felt expressed the unconditional moral law for all rational beings: "Act only according to a maxim by which you can at the same time will that it shall become a universal law."

**CATEGORY** - A fundamental classification; one of the basic conceptions to which other ideas may be reduced. For example: "space" is a category of material substance because it is a basic and necessary assumption for the existence of matter. "Time" is a common category to express the continuing existence or duration of matter. It has been argued that "faith" is a basic category of all human existence because all human beings apparently live by the conviction (that ultimately rests on assumptions) that their own system of thought is satisfactory and coherent (in other words, it makes sense to them). If a man loses his "faith," that is, if he begins to question and doubt the basic categories (presuppositions) of his own thinking, he must either revise his basic conviction and establish a new pattern of thought or else face the possibility of nervous or mental collapse.

A category, however, is essentially a type or a kind. We group things or ideas together into categories in order to organize them by some aspect of their nature. It is debatable whether categories actually exist in fact or if they are only mental classifications (and if mental, whether they are universal and/or necessary).

**CATHOLIC** - From the Greek *katholikos* meaning general or universal. Something is catholic if it applies generally to human affairs (a catholic legal system). The term is especially used to describe the ancient, undivided Christian church (for example, in the Apostle's Creed). Groups of Christian churches claiming historical continuity with that ancient, undivided church have often used the term as a self-designation. Thus we have Roman Catholics, Greek Catholics (members of the Greek Orthodox Church), and Anglo-Catholics (members of Anglican or Episcopal churches). Evangelicals claim to be members of Christ's united body, but some of them reject the term catholic because of its association with certain doctrines that to Protestants seem to be clearly contrary to biblical teachings. *Catholicism* usually refers specifically to the doctrines and practices of the Roman Catholic Church.

**CAUSALITY** - The principle that physical reality needs a cause for its existence. (See **CAUSE** and **CONTINGENT**.)

**CAUSE** - The necessary antecedent of a given effect or event. That which determines any motion, change, or action, or produces or calls forth any phenomenon or resultant state. A cause may be some object, some event, or it may be a mental process. Some contend that "cause" is a necessary category for both thought and reality. Such a belief in the necessity of causality is an essential part of any cosmological argument for God's existence. David Hume attempted to show that the category "cause" has no necessary existence. Thus he claimed to have refuted all possible cosmological arguments for God. Hume was a skeptic. He did not deny God's existence, but he did claim that no one could prove God's existence because he believed that no one could prove that cause and effect were anything more than a habit of mind produced by the repetitious sequence of events in our experience. The concept of "cause" is therefore of some significance for philosophical theology.

**C.E.** - Common Era: A calendar abbreviation used by Jews and others to avoid reference to Christ.

**CHAIN OF BEING** - A reference to a supposed hierarchical structure by which all created entities are related to one another according to the level of perfection realized by each entity. The "chain" extends from God to nothingness. All things are thought to be linked together so as to fill every level of reality between the two. This has been an important cosmological theory in the history of the church, but it is more a product of Greek philosophy than an explicit teaching of Scripture.

**CHAOS** - The state of things when ruled by chance. A confused and unorganized state of affairs in which unpredictability is the main characteristic. (Contrast with **COSMOS**.) One interesting development in modern science is the discovery of true order even in the midst of processes and forces that in the past have been classified as examples of chaos.

**CHRISTIAN** - One who by God's grace and through true faith in Jesus Christ has been restored to a right relationship with God through the blood atonement of Christ on the cross. The term is often used philosophically to refer to those beliefs that are truly based on the worldview of the Bible. For example: Christian art or Christian philosophy or Christian literature is that which is consistent with biblical principles. To describe anything as Christian means that it is consistent with and based on the biblical worldview.

Frequently the term has no specific content, and serves as an adjective for traditional western ideas or western moral notions as

230

opposed to the philosophical worldview of eastern religions. Because of this we must seriously reevaluate our use of the term. Christian originally meant "little Christ" or "Christ follower." Due to the loss of definiteness because of the many mistaken and contradictory views of Christ, it is probably necessary in our day further to define the term by using additional adjectives, such as "evangelical" Christian or "nominal" Christian or some other descriptive term. Some who do not like labels say they just want to be known as Christians. They want no denominational titles. But to call ourselves "Christian" without any further descriptive qualifications may be interpreted by many today as if we were only claiming to be "patriotic" or "morally good" or "happy" or a thousand other things. New Testament believers must not fail to clearly identify themselves in whatever linguistic culture they find themselves. *Christianity* is the religion based upon the person and teachings of Jesus.

**CLASSICAL PERIOD** - Most students identify this label as applying to the time from the rise of the Athenian empire to the sack of Rome. Thus the classical period encompasses the devoloped civilizations of ancient Greece and Rome. Greek civilization actually began earlier, but the key period was the fifth and fourth centuries before Christ. Socrates and Plato were leading figures in Athens during the late fifth and early fourth century B.C. (Socrates goes on trial for his life in 399 B.C.). Plato remained as the leading idealist teacher in Athens, and along with his student, Aristotle, is studied with profit to this day. Aristotle later becomes the personal tutor of Alexander, who conquered the eastern Mediterranean world and beyond, spreading Greek ideals, Greek language, and Greek culture during the late fourth century B.C. Eventually, the Roman Caesars come to power, and Rome rules the world during New Testament days. The period is an age of law, philosophy, and pagan religion. Studies in Greco-Roman culture provide the essential context (along with knowledge of the Old Testament, of course) for understanding the New Testament. Augustine, the Christian bishop from northern Africa, marks the turning point in the church, but it was the sack of Rome by invading barbarians that technically marks the end of the classical era. (See **MIDDLE AGES.**)

**COGNITION** - The act or process of knowing. Specifically it refers to the intellectual process of gaining knowledge as opposed to "intuition" or other methods based on feeling or emotion. It also refers to the product of the knowledge process. The adjective "cognitive" refers most often to that which is capable of being reduced to empirical factual knowledge. (See **INTUITION.**)

**COHERENCE** - Ideas that relate to each other in a consistent, necessary, and non-contradictory pattern are said to be coherent.

Such ideas are thus "understandable." The term "coherence" also refers to a theory of truth built on the criterion of systematic consistency. A system of concepts and ideas in which the postulates are horizontally self-consistent and which vertically "fit the facts" is said to be coherent. Truth (according to the "coherence model") is not viewed as the property of any individual statement or particular proposition, but as a property of the system as a whole; that is, all the separate parts fit together naturally and consistently with one another and with experience.

The coherence theory can lead only to "probability" (not logical certainty) because coherence presupposes the existence of a body of truth (the very thing modern relativism denies). In the final analysis "coherence" as a model for discovering truth means that something can be believed if and only if it is consistent with what is already accepted or believed. We still have the unanswered question, "How does one justify the very first set of presuppositions? Is there any absolute truth?"

Therefore, the coherence of a set of ideas cannot alone finally determine the truth or falsity of those ideas or of the worldview presupposed by that particular configuration of ideas. But Christianity (for example) could not claim to be true unless it could also claim that its doctrines were coherent. The internal harmony of biblical truth with extra-biblical factual reality gives Christianity a very high level of coherence. An apologist using the epistemology of coherency might, after a careful and detailed study of the whole field, argue the case for Christianity as follows:

> The fact that the authentic biblical teachings (when properly interpreted) do provide a consistent, coherent worldview, combined with the fact that this biblical worldview provides meaningful answers to the great philosophical questions, along with the demonstrable fact that all major current and historical alternative worldviews fail to provide those answers, leaves us with two choices. Either there are no answers, and all is ultimately chaos, or biblical Christianity is finally and completely true. The first choice is self-defeating. If we do not believe that true and final answers are possible, then that statement itself (that answers are not available) may be and likely is in error. So it can be concluded that Christianity is the only real *answer*, and thus we can be fully convinced of its truth. The only real alternative to biblical Christianity is to deny that any final truth exists, which is to take a self-defeating position. [To deny that consistency is necessary is also

no answer, because that renders the objections to Christianity worthless. The critic surely assumes that his or her criticisms (taken as a coherent set of reasons) can be understood and should be accepted. How could one argue that Christianity is wrong if one does not accept the necessity of coherence? Thus we can know that Christianity is true, but not in a purely rationalistic sense. It is true because it alone seems to fit together with and make sense of all the data that we can observe. The Christian worldview is consistent with actual reality at every point. What more could one ask? (Compare **CORRESPONDENCE.**)

**COMMON GROUND** - In Christian apologetics this refers to the elements of understanding that believers and unbelievers both have and hold together.

Some apologists follow Tertullian's lead and ask "What has Athens to do with Jerusalem?" This view supposes that believers and nonbelievers have no common ground. They have inconsistent, non-overlapping worldviews. They hold no facts in common for they interpret all supposed facts differently. The unregenerate mind sees all things from an unregenerate perspective, and thus on no matter could a Christian actually agree with the unbeliever. They would so differently view every fact that they would not hold any set of facts in common (except superficially).

Other apologists believe that all people have reason (the laws of logic), and (still others add) the facts of experience in common. These Christians do not believe that the human fall of Genesis 3 destroyed our ability to reason correctly. It affected the will, making us unable to live above moral failure, but not the mind. Thus Christians may assume that a lost person is unwilling to believe but not that they are incapable of believing.

Generally a Calvinistic thinker tends to believe that the fall so affected the human mind that people cannot know God without the aid of the Spirit of God in regeneration. Thus there is no natural common ground, and we must present the claims of Christ directly, leaving all persuasion to the Holy Spirit. We command rather than plead with people: You must be born again. The evidentialist approach, on the other hand, believes that the "evidence demands a verdict." Other apologists believe that we can assume reason and the facts of experience as valid common ground between all people while at the same time affirming that our efforts to persuade must have a concurrent persuasion by the Spirit in order to convince the lost of the truth of the gospel. Virtually all apologists acknowledge the sovereignty of the Spirit in moving the unbeliever from the point where gospel truth is seen as truth to the point of "conversion" where the gospel truth is adopted, trusted, and acted upon in salvation.

**COMMON SENSE REALISM** - A theory of knowledge set forth initially by Thomas Reid (1710-96). In essence those who hold this view believe that true knowledge arises from ordinary awareness. (See **NAIVE REALISM**.) Supposedly, this theory describes how ordinary people gain ordinary knowledge. The view peesents itself as an alternative to the skeptical implications of strict empiricism (as developed by David Hume). Some basic tenets of "common sense" epistemology are as follows:

(1) God would not deceive us by creating us or the world in such a way that the use of our minds or senses would generally and consistently fool us so that we could not know reality.

(2) All normal people have a common internal "sense" that combines and makes proper associations from ordinary sensory information.

(3) The human mind has certain basic "built-in" categories or rules given to it by God for correct thinking.

**CONCEPT** - The meaning of a word or a phrase; an idea or a notion. The term usually refers to an abstract or universal idea, one that comprehends all that is normally or characteristically associated with a given term or thought. For example: there are many different books, many different kinds, shapes, sizes, styles, etc. But the concept of "bookness" is a universal idea that covers them all.

People have more or less clearly defined concepts about many things. Some have false concepts, such as the idea of God as being an old grandfather. Many times a person's concept of a thing will actually affect his or her perception of reality. Each person should try to let the facts determine his or her concepts rather than the other way around (See **PRECEPT** and **PROPOSITION**.)

**CONCRETE** - That which exists externally in the world outside of the mind. The term refers to that which is not "general" or "abstract." Something concrete is something particular and definite, something actual rather than hypothetical. (See **OBJECTIVE**.)

**CONDITIONAL STATEMENT** - Any "if-then" statement. For example: "If one believes in God, then one is not an atheist," or "If God says it, then I will believe it." The conclusion of a conditional statement always depends on the truth-status and the proper understanding of the "if" clause (the condition).

**CONFUCIUS, CONFUCIANISM** - The Chinese sage and

ethicist, Confucius (551-479 B.C.), set forth a philosophy urging a harmonious social order that is still practiced with devotion resembling traditional religious commitment. The *Analects* (attributed to him) have been influential in China and other Asian communities. The emphasis of Confucianism is respect for traditional wisdom, filial and ceremonial piety.

**CONNOTATION** - A meaning that is suggested by a word or phrase; the ideas or images associated with a particular term but not explicitly stated by that term. For example, the word "home" basically refers to the house and/or land where a person habitually lives (or where one's parents live, or the place where one grew up as a child). But the word usually has the "connotation" of security and comfort, or it may connote the focus of one's sympathies and interest, as in "Heaven is my home."

The student of Christian philosophy should especially be aware of these suggested meanings. Some modern writers speak of "God" (a word which connotes love and personality and all the many other ideas suggested by the Bible), but these thinkers may not actually mean to be making a reference to the biblical God as such; they may simply be referring to a universal principle or process with no connotation of definite personality.

When reading any theological or philosophical work, one must seek to understand the true intention of the author. We must never read theology only at the connotative level. To truly understand and make valid evaluations, the student must grapple with the "denotation" of the author's words; that is, the direct and specific meaning of each term according to the author's definition. (See **DENOTATION**.)

**CONSERVATIVE** - Any view that seeks to conserve, preserve, or keep that which is already considered to be good.

In political realms conservatives try to sustain the system of government according to traditional principles. Thus the term has very different content depending on the situation. In a democracy like the United States, conservatives fight for individual freedom, less governmental control, and gradual change by the will of the people. In a dictatorship, these ideas would be considered "liberal" and as ideas that could lead to an overthrow of the dictator. So a conservative under a communist dictatorship (a supporter of the system) would hold views quite the opposite of conservatives in the USA.

In Christian theology a conservative is one who believes and defends orthodoxy. Conservatives want to keep the elements of full biblical faith intact. Conservatives affirm the deity of Christ, the infallibility of Scripture, and the substitutionary death of Christ for their sin. (See **LIBERALISM**.)

**CONTEXTUALIZATION** - Any attempt to relate ideas, practices, or norms from one cultural environment specifically to another different and/or alien environment. For example, in biblical theology contextualization would be a descriptive term for all efforts to discover the essential truths of the biblical revelation in terms of the original environment and then to transfer those ideas and teachings into a different cultural environment. This involves principles of linguistic translation (often discussed under the rubric of "dynamic equivalence") as well as issues such as mindsets, motives, scientific awareness, economic understandings, educational philosophies, and sociological aspects of civilized human life.

The biblical teachings on offerings and sacrifice arise from within an agricultural society, one heavily dominated by farmers and sheep raising people in the ancient Near East. In a cattle raising area, or in an urban setting, the theologian sometimes has a problem trying to get this "alien" society to understand the biblical message.

One view is to simply teach the "aliens" (us) what the biblical culture was like so that they (we) can understand biblical teachings as the first readers would have understood them. This is traditional exposition.

Contextualists, however, often try to retell the biblical materials using modern (alien) images. Thus they try to contextualize the Scripture, that is, they "change" its literal form trying to make it readily and naturally understandable to those who live in the new culture.

Biblical culture spoke of the "bowels" as being the center of deep emotion. "Bowels" as modern Americans understand the word, does not convey that meaning. Thus some translators have tried to use a different image. They do not translate by standards of formal correspondence but aim for dynamic equivalence in order to contextualize the meaning.

Most evangelicals do not oppose paraphrase when idioms and figures of speech are involved. The problem arises in more substantive areas. Paul spoke of blood atonement, of substitution, of propitiation, of sacrifice. Were these ideas figures of speech? In a modern urban society in which these concepts are neither part of daily life nor even in the normal vocabulary of people, should the concepts be revised? On the mission field where sheep are not valuable but where pigs are highly valued, should we teach that Jesus is the pig of God? The greater issue, however, is whether we should maintain judicial images of atonement and forgiveness in a society that tends to think more in personal and relational images. Should we speak of God as Judge to a society where judges are corrupt political appointees, and should God still be Father to a victim of child abuse? Does contextualization allow us to explain away Paul's restrictions on women?

These matters are frequently debated in theological circles. Bible translators especially face such issues, but so do expository preachers. Topical preaching is by definition committed to a form of contextualization. (See **INTERPRETATION**.)

**CONTINGENT** - Not necessary; dependent on something else; capable of being proven either true or false only by experience or empirical testing. The term may also refer to a chance happening (an accident). A contingency is, therefore, a state of affairs which may or may not occur because it depends upon something else. Contingencies may be logical or physical.

This concept of dependence is important in cosmological arguments for God's existence. The world is said to be contingent. It is created by God and would have no existence at all apart from God. The existence of the world totally depends upon the non-contingent (necessary) existence of God. The world "occurs" only because God acts to make it so. This is a feature of existence that can perhaps be detected by scientific study though science alone cannot discern what the ultimate cause is. We can discern that things which have a beginning must have a cause, and modern science seems to be compiling massive amounts of evidence that the universe as we know it did have a beginning. (See **BIG BANG COSMOLOGY, NECESSARY,** and **COSMOLOGICAL ARGUMENT**.)

**CONTRADICTION** - A logical incongruity. The logical relationship between two statements which cannot both be true or false; if one is true the other must be false and if one is false the other must be true. A contradiction is an exact logical and/or factual negative of another term. For example, it is a contradiction to say that something both "is" and "is not" in the same sense at the same time. If you claim that only "A" is the case, it is a contradiction to say also that "non-A" is the case. If you state that all "A" is "B" then it is a contradiction to say some "A" is not "B." The rational law of non-contradiction includes the contextual qualifications that meaningful statements cannot be both true and not true in the same sense at the same time. (See **CONTRARY**.)

One Gospel writer says that there were two angels at the empty tomb and another mentions one angel. This bothers some readers, but the two accounts are not contradictory. A contradiction would exist only if the second evangelist were to say that there was *only* one angel (and if it clearly is a reference to the same time-and-place event). A real contradiction must fulfill all the conditions stated above. Such differences between various biblical passages may be difficulties for the interpreter but theoretically they can both be true if they are not contradictory.

Differences in parallel biblical accounts are not always easily explained, but it is a wise course for the interpreter of God's word to search for all relevant facts, to study the context, to seek the author's intent, and even then hesitate to affirm that biblical narratives contradict themselves or each other. If one does affirm that the authentic text of the Bible teaches contradictory ideas or doctrines, one either denies that God inspired the writer's affirmations or one denies that God's revealed Word is completely true.

A doctrine of progressive or cumulative revelation will allow for many differences to be expressed within the fully truthful pages of Scripture. Differences in the reporting of details by no means lead to contradictory teachings. Some seemingly opposite teachings are quite easily explained by the legitimate idea of fulfillment over time. Commands under the Old Testament Law, for example, are not contradictions of New Testament principles of Grace, because both are true at the time and place for which they were intended.

Evangelical Christianity believes that no real contradictions exist in the authentic text of Scripture. It is much more important, of course, to believe and live according to the clear teachings that are unquestionably found in the Bible than it is merely to deny that contradictions are found there. Nevertheless total trust requires total truth; thus the concern about seeming contradictions.

**CONTRARY** - The logical relationship of two statements, both of which may be false, but they cannot both be true. Two universal propositions, one denying what the other affirms. For example: "Every horse is black"—"No horse is black." (NOTE: These two statements are not contradictory because they do not meet all the necessary conditions. Both of these statements are false. See **CONTRADICTION.**)

**CORPOREAL MONISM** - Naturalistic theory of the Greek Milesian school (Thales, Anaximander, and Anaximenes) setting forth the doctrine that one physical substance ultimately underlies all things in the universe. Thales believed this one substance was water. In any case, the idea was to find the one unifying reality within nature itself. The existence of a "supernatural" reality was not considered.

**CORRESPONDENCE THEORY** - A theory of truth depending upon a state or condition of agreement between two things. This theory states that truth consists in the agreement between a statement and the fact it designates. The fact with which the statement is in agreement is an independently existing reality. If an idea is directly related to, correctly describes, and does not deviate from the actual state of affairs, then the idea is true (according to the correspondence theory of truth).

The problem with this theory comes in determining when actual correspondence exists. How does one compare an idea or a concept with "reality out there?" In actual practice we "know" only our ideas or our perception of reality. Correspondence as a theory does not solve the epistemological problem: it simply states what is involved in a truth situation. Statements that do not correspond to that which is the case are false.

Christianity claims to correspond with reality. Archaeological documentation and historical confirmation support this claim with extensive evidence. Of course, not every detail in Scripture is capable of direct documentation. Thus one could never prove that everything in the Bible is true if correspondence were the only acceptable epistemology. At the same time to affirm total truthfulness is to assert that the Bible does at every point correspond with reality. (Compare **COHERENCE**.)

**COSMOGONY** - A theory or account (whether scientific or mythological) concerning the origin or the creation of the universe. There are several competing scientific accounts of the formation of our present universe. There are also many creation accounts in ancient literature. Each civilization seems to have had its own theories. Christians believe, however, that the Hebrews based their ideas not on speculation but on divine revelation. A significant confirmation of their views came from God at Sinai (in the commandment regarding the Sabbath) and also through the prophets and inspired poets. One of the most amazing evidences of divine inspiration is that the biblical creation account (unlike other ancient accounts) cannot be demonstrated to be false even in light of modern scientific knowledge. The biblical account remains a realistic option for many scientists as well as for theologians.

**COSMOLOGICAL ARGUMENT** - An attempt to prove the existence of God (a Necessary Being) from the empirical fact that some contingent things exist. Since the universe is composed of individual contingent things, the universe as a whole must also be contingent. Therefore it requires a non-contingent source of existence, that is, God. In other words, all things appear to be related to or to be a result of some cause; therefore, the universe that exists is not self-explanatory or self-existent. There must be a first or an uncaused cause to account for the actual universe that exists.

Critics frequently challenge the assumption of contingency. They say that the universe may be self-explanatory. But this would require the contingent elements of the universe to be dependent upon themselves in a purely circular manner. Even if this were

239

possible, it would only account for the continuation (not the origin) of the universe that exists.

According to biblical philosophy, the universe is not self-explanatory. The universe needs a Creator. Yet the cosmological argument seems to have a serious weakness in that there is no immediately obvious or clearly necessary link between some "First or Uncaused Cause" and the transcendent, infinite-personal, holy God of Scripture.

The cosmological argument as it has been classically formulated may not "prove" God's existence in a rationally inescapable way. However, a carefully stated argument of this type can provide a compelling and persuasive set of reasons for believing in the theistic position. If properly constructed, a cosmological argument can leave us with a clear choice: either theism or else ultimate chaos (either God or no explanation at all). To argue that a dependent or contingent universe is its own source of existence is to give up all hope for any rational answer to the question of why things exist and to affirm a strictly irrational answer.

A consistent naturalist will choose to believe in ultimate chaos (he affirms that "no ultimate explanation" is the correct "explanation") and will challenge us to be "honest and courageous and face the reality of chaos." But chaos is no answer. Chaos is by definition undefined and unknowable.

Thus while it is surely intellectually possible to hold the logical position that "there is no answer," one is still left with God as the only explanation which can be affirmed. However, it is not clear that this "existential undeniability" is the same thing as proof of reality. Thus no absolute "proof" of God's existence has yet come from a cosmological argument though it is still an important study in the history of Christian apologetics. An "absolute proof" eludes the human mind in every quest for knowledge, however. It is not a weakness of theistic philosophy to find that it lacks an absolute proof in this strong sense. Existential undeniability would be considered as a very persuasive reason for believing anything other than theism, which is often resisted for spiritual and not strictly intellectual reasons.

For many theists, the cosmological argument is the essential rational element in theistic faith. If the cosmological argument does not describe reality or if it is essentially false, reason itself is rendered meaningless and all rational thinking fails.

It should be noted that there are three forms of the cosmological argument. One is based on existentially recognized contingency. This may be the strongest form of the argument; it is the version presented in the description above. A version based on the "principle of sufficient reason" still has some proponents and may have some merit. It does, however, appear to fail to meet certain technical objections and therefore is not presented here.

Another rather strong version is based on the intuitively known principle that things that have a beginning must have a cause. This is discussed under **KALAM**.

Students should realize that the cosmological argument is the philosophical counterpart to the theological doctrine of creation. Moreover, an argument may be true even if, for some technical reason, we cannot show it to be true. Many believe that the cosmological argument is logically compelling; others find it rationally escapable yet persuasive; still others are unpersuaded and remain in their state of unbelief (for which Paul says there is no acceptable excuse). Christian apologists, however, must remember that an argument is not the reality. Philosophical reasoning is a means of understanding, a means accessible to people who are aware of the world around them, even (perhaps especially) those without access to or knowledge of the written Scripture. (See **CREATION, KALAM,** and **NATURAL THEOLOGY**.)

**COSMOLOGY** - The systematic philosophical study of the formation and structure of the universe. A study of the processes and principles and relationships within the universe. A special interest of astronomers and cosmologists is the issue of ultimate origins. How did this particular universe arise? What are the structures and space-time relationships of the elements of the universe? (See **COSMOS**.)

**COSMOS** - The Greek word *kosmos* refers to order and in particular to the universe as an example of an orderly system. (Contrast with **CHAOS**.)

**CREATION** - Usually "creation" refers to the things that God has made. "The world is God's creation." In this sentence "creation" refers to all space-time, finite reality; it is a synonym for the existing universe.

But creation also is a series of divine actions by which he produced the space-time, finite reality. "God's creation of the world is reported in Genesis." In this sentence "creation" sums up a series of actions and events.

Creation also names an explanatory theoretical model of origins. This model assumes the existence of an eternally living Source of all matter, energy, life, order, and organized complexity (information) in the current universe. Traditionally creationists have held that God created a complete and functional universe during a unique week of creative activity, and that on the seventh day God ceased all of his work of creation (so that the unique processes of creation are no longer operating).

**CRISIS THEOLOGY** - Neo-orthodoxy: one characteristic of

early neo-orthodoxy was its pessimistic view of human nature and human institutions. So sinful and hopeless is mankind, and so internally contradictory are its institutions such as government, that the crises all people must ultimately face in their despair is the only means by which people might be persuaded to consider and accept help from the "outside," from divine revelation. (See **NEO-OR-THODOXY**.)

**CRITERION** (pl. **CRITERIA**) - A standard by which something is judged. A basis for identification. A mark or a trait that characterizes something in such a way that it can be distinguished from other things. An acceptable means of recognition or evaluation.

**CRITIC** - One who expresses a reasoned opinion on a matter. One who engages in analysis and evaluation in order to interpret or explain the meaning and/or the value of a thing. For example, an art critic is one who loves and studies art so as to evaluate and interpret it for others. The term biblical critic has a similar meaning. The word "critic" is not necessarily a negative term. Any analytical scholar may be properly called a critic even if he or she never expresses harsh or censorious judgments. It is not uncommon, however, to use the term "critic" to refer to one who opposes a position on the basis of analysis and evaluation. Context must help the reader decide whether a negative connotation is attached to the word.

**CRITICAL** - In philosophical terminology this does not refer to harsh or severe and unfavorable attitudes on the part of people who are given to the habit of noticing minor imperfections of someone's character, etc. In biblical studies the term "critical" describing a certain edition of the Greek New Testament, for example, simply refers to one which includes major variant textual readings and scholarly notes and evaluations. The so-called "critical text" is a product of painstaking study and is an attempt to produce objective evaluations as to what is the authentic (original) text. To do "critical" work means to engage in analytical examination seeking valid criteria for evaluation. Critical philosophy of history, for example, is an analysis of basic methodological questions rather than a study of major systems or patterns of history. To ask critical questions is to analyze the primary issues and ask those questions which are most basic and important. To make a critical study is to make a careful, analytical study. Linguistically the Greek root behind this term is related to the same term that gave rise to "criterion" and "critic."

**CYNIC; CYNICAL; CYNICISM** - The Greek philosopher Antisthenes of Athens (born about 444 B.C.) taught that virtue was the only good and that self-control was the only effective way of acquiring virtue. His followers formed a sect that developed this principle into a full scale philosophical system of thought. They emphasized the suppression of desire in their quest for virtue. (This school was not strong in New Testament times and had little impact on biblical writers.)

In an interesting turn of meaning, a cynic today is one who believes that all people are motivated by selfishness. Thus the modern cynic is not likely to trust someone else's motives. A cynic mocks or sneers at the supposed virtues of others. Cynicism, then, when it is not used to describe the doctrine of the ancient Greek Cynics, refers to an attitude that is scornful of virtue and bitter or sarcastic toward motives.

**DATUM** (pl. **DATA**, sometimes used as a collective noun with a singular verb) - The basic fact or assumption on which an argument is based, or the given starting point from which an intellectual system is constructed. Even the specification of the data is usually a product of certain assumptions and methodological decisions, so one should never presuppose that the "data" is neutral and objective.

**DEDUCTION** - A method of logical thought or reasoning which passes from the general to the particular. In deductive reasoning the conclusion follows necessarily from the premises. Deductive logic is a helpful analytical tool. For example: In the deductive syllogism:

1. Every human being is mortal.

2. Socrates is a human being.

3. Therefore, Socrates is mortal:

the conclusion (3) is a particular case that is logically necessary if the universal premise (1) and the specific assertion (2) are both true. But one must already have "truth" (1 & 2) to get "truth" (3) in a purely deductive system.

Some Christians have argued that divine revelation provides the true starting point and thus they build their theology deductively. Critics say that such theological methods are inherently weak because they assume (among other things) that the theologian can infallibly interpret divine revelation and can properly state its content in the form of universal premises.

The most obvious value of deduction is that by carefully following accepted rules of logic, we can come to see what implications various suggested premises have, and thus we can often use this method to test the coherence of a suggested theological system or formulation. One must admit, however, that the text of Scripture is not a collection of universal premises;

therefore, deduction alone could not produce a fully biblical theology.

We can see by deductive reasoning, however, that humankind needs revelation from some absolute source of truth if we are ever to gain logical certainty for our conclusions. One may or may not ever be able to demonstrate conclusively that infallible revelation has been given to humankind, but if it has not been given, then we have been left with a pluralistic source of knowledge and all truth must be relative. To show that humankind needs infallible revelation is not the same as proving that we actually have it. But it is a first step toward a comprehensive apologetic. (See **INDUCTION**.)

**DEISM** - Theism comes from the Greek word for god (*theos*) and deism comes from the Latin word for god (*deus*). Both terms affirm a belief in the existence of God. In modern usage, however, the terms are not synonymous. Theism often carries the connotation of orthodoxy (correct opinions about biblical doctrine), while deism generally refers to the concept of an "absentee God." God started it all by creating the world but he has left everything to run by itself. Natural law is divinely ordained, and God never interferes with his established order. Thus a deist characteristically denies the miraculous and affirms the sufficiency of man's natural reason for explaining religion. It is also characteristic of deistic thought to attack the Hebrew-Christian Scriptures in particular and the necessity of revelation in general.

Deism was a large and powerful movement during the seventeenth and eighteenth centuries. It no longer exists as a major worldview, but its influence is not limited to that historical period.

Matthew Tindal (1656-1733) is a typical English deist. God is perfect, he argued, and thus the true religion must be perfect (not capable of being improved). The Bible certainly did not fit that criterion, according to Tindal, but the Creation itself did. No later "revelation" could improve upon God's original natural revelation given through the Creation itself. After all, Tindal continued, God does not change, so he could not change the religion he gave in the first place. God is impartial, and he would not give a special revelation to a single group of people. The Bible is not a proper candidate for being a revelation from God anyway, he said, since it is full of errors. Tindal's book *Christianity as Old as the Creation* (known as the "deistic bible") was answered by Bishop Butler's famous *Analogy of Religion* (1736).

Today it is apparent that deism's attack on the reliability of the Bible is definitely out of date. Archeology alone has overwhelmingly confirmed the general reliability of the Bible. But even more to the point, deism's view of God is self-contradictory. Creation itself is a miracle, and the laws of nature are contingent upon God's nature. A God who cares and who chooses to create human beings is a God who is able to speak to them. He may even choose to act on their behalf. Deism has a valid emphasis upon God's revelation of himself in nature, but it is not an adequate worldview. (See **THEISM.**)

**DEMIURGE** - Plato's term for the "divine" creator, who formed the world out of pre-existing matter (creation *ex materia*). An aloof being who is like a weak craftsman. According to the *Timaeus*, the Demiurge fashioned and shaped the material universe by using transcendent ideas (the "Platonic Ideals") as models. The Demiurge was impersonal, an abstract force that ordered the universe. Possibly Plato used the term as a figure of speech, a symbol of reason itself that operates and structures the universe. (Compare **CREATION.**)

**DENOTATION** - A semantic concept referring to the strict and actual definition of a word or phrase. Because words may carry layers of meanings that go beyond this basic meaning (See **CONNOTATION.**), it is important to know how a word or phrase is being used.

**DETERMINISM** - The theory that all actions are entirely and directly a function of their formal cause; that is, all events are conclusively fixed before they occur. Theologically this shows up as belief in a fatalistic predestination of all things (Islamic belief). Atheistically, the theory would teach that all human action results from a person's chemical and psychological make-up interacting with one's environment, so that any thought of freewill is simply an illusion. Determinism as a corollary of naturalism applies to all events, not just to human actions, but the theological consequences show up most clearly in the denial of any significant freedom for the human mind or for the human will. The challenge specifically comes at the point of denying that human beings have a will which is independent of purely natural cause and effect (or stimulus and response) mechanisms. (See **FATALISM** and **NATURALISM.**)

**DIALECTIC** - A theory and a practice of attempting to arrive at truth through rational discussions and debate.

> (1) In *pre-Socratic philosophy,* the "dialectic" refers to that kind of rational dialogue in which a conclusion was reached by critically evaluating the logical consequences of a statement. For example, Thales might suggest that the basic substance of all reality is water. His critics would try to show that such a claim had specific implications which could not be sustained in light of such realities as fire or earth. Many believe that Zeno's Paradoxes were actually intended to show the absurdity

of the position on ultimate Being that was taught by Parmenides.

(2) In *Socrates*, it is the method of inquiry by use of questions and answers in dialogue. The Socratic method was to draw out the implications of someone's views by asking relevant questions. But due to his epistemology (that our minds or souls are simply a part of the universal mind and thus that all knowledge is possible through meditative recall and self-reflection), Socrates did not directly teach a constructive system of theoretical knowledge. He believed that truth existed, but that it could only be approximated by continual dialogue and constructive debate.

(3) *Aristotle's dialectic* was a method of arguing with probability on any given problem. For Aristotle, this was an art half-way between strict demonstration and pure rhetoric.

(4) In *Stoicism*, the dialectic is simply formal logic as contrasted with rhetoric and grammar.

(5) In *later Kantian thought*, the dialectic is the critical treatment of paradoxes and logical fallacies. (A *paradox* is an argument that draws seemingly contradictory conclusions by valid deduction from acceptable premises.) In Kantianism, the dialectic may also refer to the use of principles which are only applicable to empirical data in the attempt to determine or gain knowledge of transcendental objects (such as the soul or God).

(6) In *Hegel*, dialectic refers to the logical process of constructing more comprehensive levels of thought by resolving apparent contradictions; that is, the dialectic is a triadic principle of rational change involving a thesis and an antithesis that is inevitably resolved into a synthesis. This synthesis then becomes a new thesis calling forth a new antithesis and thus a new synthesis (which in turn becomes another thesis). Pure dialectical thought could never maintain any thesis (except the "final" one) as an absolute. Hegel not only saw this dialectic in the realm of human thought, but also asserted this methodological concept as the explanation of the process of history and even the development of the universe, which for him was a product of a Divine Mind thinking. In Hegelian thought the dialectic ultimately culminates in an ever-expanding Absolute Spirit

246

or Idea. Hegel is therefore categorized as a dialectical idealist.

(7) *Marx* views the process of history as a dialectic (like Hegel) but denies anything other than a materialistic conclusion. The movement in history is determined not by thought but by economic and natural forces. Thus Marx is classified as a dialectical materialist.

(8) *By its nature,* dialectical thought demands repeated critical inquiry with regard to one's own presuppositions. This is one of its most important values for evangelical theology. But in principle it denies any ability (even theoretically) to state absolute truth propositionally. Dialectical "truth" is always in tension with some other "truth" and would never be considered as final. Truth is evolving and may over time change significantly. One could never say that some doctrine or moral principle is true now and forever. It is at this point of apparent relativism that many evangelicals disagree with dialectical methodology.

**DIONYSIAN ORPHISM** - Dionysius was the god of vegetation, often associated with Orpheus. Dionysian Orphism taught the doctrine of the transmigration of the soul. Dionysian rites were emotional and passionate, a threat to rational religion, a stark contrast to Olympian religion as set forth by Homer and Hesiod. The Dionysian orgies and ecstatic frenzies (music, dancing, sexual license, night meetings, even live animal sacrifices) offered the worshiper the chance to experience "unity" with the gods. Dionysian religion continues (in more or less dramatic forms throughout history) as a type of worship.

**DISPENSATIONALISM** - A system of biblical interpretation held by many conservative, evangelical theologians. Dispensationalism views the world (and, in particular, human history) as a household run by God. In the process of time God administers his household in various ways according to his sovereign will and his overall plan of redemption. Each of the various stages of divine revelation can be marked off by recognizing the distinguishably different economies in his plan. These various stages of God's administration are known as dispensations.

The clearest example of the necessity for recognizing dispensations is the biblical distinction between the Old Covenant of the law and the New Covenant of grace. In the days of Moses, God instituted a covenant of law by which he administered the world from Moses to Christ. Then God initiated a new covenant of grace through the blood of Jesus. The world is now redemptively governed by the New Covenant.

Dispensationalism as a systematic interpretation of the Bible usually finds seven distinct periods of time in which distinct principles of God's administration are recognized. From Creation to the Fall is the dispensation of freedom (that is, Adam was not created as a slave to sin). The dispensation of self-determination describes the relationship of man to sin between the Fall and the Flood. After the Flood, civil government is imposed, though it too leads to disaster. The people fail to govern successfully, righteously, or obediently, so the judgment at Babel results. The dispensation of promise describes the way God dealt with Abraham and his descendants until Moses and the establishment of the law. A final dispensation is usually predicted as beginning at the second coming of Christ and extending until the Great White Throne Judgment. This is the dispensation of the kingdom (the millennium) and is sharply distinguished from the present age of grace. The essential dispensations, however, are three: the Mosaic Law, the present age of grace and the church, and the future kingdom age.

Most but not all dispensationalists believe that there will be a pre-tribulational rapture of the church. There are a growing number of post-tribulational rapturists who nevertheless hold to the three essential dispensations.

Generally dispensationalism is built upon the literal interpretation of Old Testament prophecy. Dispensationalists oppose those who spiritualize prophecy and apply it to the church directly. They do not believe that the Old Testament prophecies about Israel apply to the church. Thus, they will always hermeneutically distinguish between Israel, the Gentiles, and the church. God, they believe, administers a plan for each group throughout history.

Although dispensationalism has been the object of many "straw-man" refutations, there are also serious questions about some of the positions defended by its scholarly advocates. The *Scofield Reference Bible* and the *Ryrie Study Bible* are representative sources for learning more about this type of biblical theology.

**DUALISM** - In metaphysics: any theory which teaches that basic reality can be reduced ultimately to two substances (usually opposing substances or forces: such as good and evil, mind and matter). In epistemology: the theory that the "idea" in the mind is not to be equated with the "object" of that idea in the act of knowing, but that they are to be seen as distinct, with knowledge being inferential (not immediate).

**EMANATION** - That which necessarily "flows" out of something (like light rays from the sun). Plotinus believed that the world emanated from God (without conscious or intentional effort on

God's part). This is sometimes an element of pantheistic philosophy. (See **PANTHEISM.**)

**EMPIRICAL** - That which relies on experience, observation, and testing alone (without regard to a particular theory or system). It refers to factual information and observation rather than theoretical knowledge. In modern times it is usually considered a strong point in favor of some conclusion if it can be said to have an empirical base. Such usage refers to the presence of factual or experimental evidence supporting the conclusion. "Empirical" carries the idea of possible verification by testing. Thus when one speaks, for example, of theology, a scientist may ask if the speaker is speaking empirically. In other words, the scientist wants to know what factual testable evidence supports the theology. (See **VERIFICATION PRINCIPLE** and **LOGICAL POSITIVISM.**)

**EMPIRICISM** - An epistemological theory stating that we are born with a blank mind (*tabula rasa*) and that no knowledge is innate or *apriori*: all knowledge comes from sense experience. In other words, empiricism is a method of coming to know the truth which strictly relies on induction rather than on other means of gaining knowledge such as intuition, speculation, deduction, or dialectics, etc. (Compare **RATIONALISM.**) A typical advocate of empiricism was John Locke (1632–1704). (See **EPISTEMOLOGY.**).

**ENLIGHTENMENT** - The true beginning of modern thought, usually dated as centering in the 17th and 18th centuries. Key figures: John Locke, Voltaire, Rousseau, David Hume, Immanuel Kant. In the post-Reformation era the growth of individual political and social freedom was slow but intellectual freedom came rapidly. The 17th century saw great political and cultural changes. Kant came to believe that his generation had finally surpassed the cultural and intellectual level of the classical world. Thus the past was disparaged. The "Middle Ages" became, for "Enlightenment" thinkers, a time of intellectual darkness (the "Dark Ages"). The Middle Ages, however, were clearly an age of religious faith. The "Enlightenment," on the other hand, is a speculative era of intellectual pride. Agnosticism was on the rise (though it was clearly a minority view until after Kant). Under the influence of the Enlightenment, science made great technical progress. This was the era of Francis Bacon (1561-1626), Blaise Pascal (1623-1662), and Isaac Newton (1642-1727). (See **SECULARIZATION.**)

**ENTROPY** - A measure of disorder or randomness in a system. Entropy is a measure of the potential for a system to experience some type of degenerative change that would appear to the ordinary observer to be spontaneous. As energy is used, the disorder of the system increases. Gasoline, for example, is a highly structured organic molecule that when rapidly oxidized produces heat and gaseous by-products. This process is not, however, reversible. Once the energy is released, it dissipates into the atmosphere in a less ordered, less usable form. Thus the available energy in any closed system will ultimately be exhausted and entropy will be at a maximum and no further work can be done. According to some proponents of naturalism, the destiny of the universe is death by entropy maximization. One day the sun will burn out, and every star will die, and all work and movement and energy exchange will come to a halt. This is the ultimate meaninglessness of life for the atheist and the naturalist. The laws of nature give no hope for the furture. Energy systems always tend toward a state of equilibrium where no more work can be done. This universal tendency toward disorder is a problem for evolutionary theories since they require an increase rather than a decrease in the order of a system. Evolutionists counter special creationist arguments at this point by noting that evolutionary theories only require localized increases in order (decreases in entropy) not universal ones. But this clarification is only helpful if the mechanism for capturing energy and channeling it to do useful work is already in place. Thus entropy remains a problem for naturalistic philosophy. (See **THERMODYNAMICS.**)

**EPICUREANISM** - The school of philosophy founded by Epicurus (341-270 B.C.) who assumed that many gods existed, but believed they had little if anything to do with human affairs. Reality is essentially atoms and empty space. It functions mechanistically. Individuals, therefore, are of central importance. The greatest good is pleasure. Suffering and pain are the greatest evils. The mind has control over human life. All people have free will (in contrast to Stoicism). Thus we are free to follow the self-centered pleasure principle, because upon death our atoms disperse, and we cease to exist.

**EPISTEMOLOGY** - The study of knowledge: what it is, and how one gets it. From the Greek *episteme*, the term has special reference to a study of the limits and validity of knowledge. To discover someone's epistemology is to learn a great deal about his philosophical perspective. The epistemological question is: "How do you know what you know?" (See **AUTHORITY; COMMON SENSE REALISM; CORRESPONDENCE; DEDUCTION; DIALECTIC; DUALISM; EMPIRICISM; EXISTENTIALISM; FAITH; FIDEISM; IDEALISM; INDUCTION; INTUITION; KNOWLEDGE; LOGIC; LOGICAL POSITIVISM; MYSTICISM; NAÏVE REALISM; NATURALISM; NATURAL THEOLOGY; NIHILISM; PARTICULAR; PLATONISM; POSITIVISM; PRAGMATISM; RATIONALISM; *RATIONES AETERNAE*; REALISM; REVELA-**

TION; SCHOLASTICISM; SCIENTISM; SKEPTICISM; SOLIP-SISM; *TABULA RASA*; TRUTH; UNIVERSAL; VERIFICATION.)

**EQUIVOCAL** - An adjective referring to a term, phrase, claim, or proposition of any kind that is ambiguous, inclusive, or decptive because it has two or more meanings. One may equivocate if in an argument one uses the same word with two different meanings. Sometimes one may make a deliberate play on words (either for humor or at times for raising the level of conscious attention within the audience) without losing the clarity of the message. Biblical prophets will often use words this way.

Normally, however, we apply the concept of equivocation to those instances where the speaker or writer is deliberately attempting to create uncertainly or ambiguity or to cases in which the speaker or writer is unnecessarily ambiguous.

Careful philosophical analysis will always point out and correct equivocation. God-talk is a serious issue discussed by philosophers of religion. The language used to describe God is based on human speech patterns. We say God hears our prayers, but we do not mean that God has auditory sensations. In fact, some philosophical theologians have asked whether it is possible to speak descriptively about God without equivocating. Is God living in the same sense that we use the term "living" to speak about humans? Is God good? Does he love? Is he powerful? What do these words mean when applied to God? What does it mean to speak of an "infinite being"? This is one of the important questions addressed by theologians interested in the philosophy of religious language. (See **AMBIGUITY; ANALOGY; LANGUAGE ANALYSIS; UNIVOCAL**.)

**ESCHATOLOGY** - A study of the "last things," including questions about death, the intermediate state, immortality, judgment, heaven and hell, and the ultimate destiny of humanity and the universe. The study of "last things" for Christians will also include a survey and an interpretation of biblical references to the final advent of Christ, usually called the "second (visible and personal) coming."

Eschatology is a part of any complete philosophy of history. One perennial question is, "Where is history going?" Is there an overall cause or purpose which can explain the flow of human events? Does history fit recognizable patterns? Is there a necessary goal or a predictable conclusion for history?

Eschatology may be a secular or a theological study, and it is by no means limited to Christian studies. However, the future can only be known with certainty by revelation from a nontemporal, history-controlling source. Such revelation is claimed by Christianity, and examples of predictive biblical prophecy which have been previously fulfilled serve as a model and as a persuasive argument for

believing that yet-unfulfilled biblical prophecy will be truly historical as well. History is moving toward a goal. Christ is coming back.
How then should we live? (Biblical eschatology always has ethical
implications.)

**ESSENCE** - That which is necessary for a thing to be whatever
it is. The essence of something is the characteristic property (or the
sum total of properties or attributes) that are necessary to the nature
of something. If the essence of a thing were taken away or
destroyed, it would so alter that thing that it would no longer exist
or would at least be radically changed. Carbon, for example, is an
essential element of coal. If there were no carbon, there would be no
coal. Removing the carbon (by using heat to oxidize it) will result in
the destruction of the coal leaving only ashes.

God is not limited by our definitions, but as an example we
might say that "love" is a part of God's essence. Without love, God
would not be God as traditionally defined by classical theism.
Wisdom and power and righteousness are also aspects of the
essence of God.

In a similar but slightly different sense, "essence" refers to the
most important ingredient or the crucial element of some com-
pound.

In philosophy, however, the term "essence" is most often used
to name the unchanging universal aspects of a class of things as
opposed to the "existence" of a thing or a class of things which is
always changing. Human beings live, grow, work, change, move,
and ultimately die, but the idea of being human seems to transcend
these temporal changes. This universal notion of what it means to
be human is the essence of our being. (Compare **PLATONISM** and
**EXISTENTIALISM**.)

**ETHICS** - The study of moral values and moral practices. A
system setting forth not only what is right or wrong but an
explanation of why one should act or not act (think or not think) in
certain ways. Biblical ethics are statements of the moral principles
set forth in the Bible. Applied ethics would be a study of issues not
addressed directly by a specific teaching in one's moral code but
nevertheless involving questions requiring a moral decision.

**EVANGELICAL** - That which relates to and is in agreement
with the New Testament worldview as understood by Protestant
orthodoxy. Specifically the term refers to the theological viewpoint
that emphasizes the necessity of salvation by grace through faith in
the atoning death and resurrection of Jesus. A strong view of the
authority of Scripture, the priority of preaching over ritual, and an
emphasis on personal conversion are characteristics of evangelical
theology. Evangelical Christians are also characterized by mission-
ary zeal and concern for correct doctrine. A doctrine of the full

inspiration of Scripture is perhaps the key to understanding evangelical theology because all other Christian doctrines believed and taught by evangelicals flow from and are based on the teachings of Scripture. Though evangelicals are orthodox in theology, they do not have the separatist emphasis common to Fundamentalism and usually have a more favorable attitude toward scholarship. The term "evangelical" is from the Greek *euangélion* (the good news).

**EVIDENCE** - That which is used to demonstrate the truth or the falsity of something. "Evidence" is an outward indication or a publicly demonstrable item that serves as the basis for knowing something.

In popular speech it is a synonym for proof. "I have proof that this is true" usually means "I have substantial or conclusive evidence that this is true." Technically, however, evidence should be distinguished from proof. There may be more than one possible interpretation of the evidence. One has proof only when there is only one viable interpretation of the evidence.

Design, for example, is an evidence of purpose and order. A mind is responsible for design. The fact that the universe shows some evidence of design makes it reasonable to suppose that a divine Mind is responsible for that fact, and thus for the existence of the universe. But the design argument for the existence of God is not proof of God's existence, because there are other possible ways to explain the same evidence. Yet these other interpretations only block "design" as an absolute proof. Design is still an evidence. Non-theists call the evidence for design a fortunate circumstance, or an unusual collection of events, or a coincidence, or the result of natural selection.

Evidence is not always proof. But if certain facts do support a particular conclusion (such as theism), then these facts can be viewed as evidence for that conclusion. Christian evidence is that collection of facts which supports the truth of the Christian faith. (See **PROOF**.)

**EVOLUTION** - Frequently used to designate any sort of simple variation or change. The Theory of Evolution, however, is a philosophical model that refers technically to the specific hypothesis that higher and more complex life-forms originated in and developed from lower and less complex forms. In its most common usage among western secularists, evolution is the hypothesis that all life originated spontaneously from inorganic matter, and that life developed over a period of millions of years by "natural selection" from single-cell creatures into the great variety and complexity of the biological world today.

Though originally the theory of evolution applied only to

biological systems, it soon became accepted in the secular scientific community as a general explanation of all reality. Thus astronomers propound theories of stellar evolution; chemists suggest patterns of evolutionary development for the periodic chart; sociologists develop theories of social evolution; philosophers explain historical and cultural changes in terms of overall evolutionary criteria.

The biological theory of evolution faces a serious challenge today from known facts and experimental data relating to the second law of thermodynamics, the law of biogenesis, and the laws of genetics. The evidences supporting the theory are open to alternative explanations and thus are circumstantial. (See **CREATION and THEISTIC EVOLUTION.**)

*EX DEO* - "out of God." A theory of creation that claims that the universe originated out of the being of God. Often leads to pantheism. (See **CREATION** and **PANTHEISM)**

*EX MATERIA* - "out of matter." A theory of creation that holds that the material substance and energy of the universe is eternal and that the present universe is merely the current shape of that matter.

*EX NIHILO* - Latin phrase correctly translated "out of nothing." A theory of creation by a God who had the ability to originate new matter and energy (as well as form) by his conscious will without it being transferred from any source. God literally brought new reality into existence for the first time. The most common usage of the phrase is to contrast the concept of absolute creation (as taught in Genesis) with the idea of creation as the creative organization of external matter (as taught by Plato and other philosophical dualists). *Ex nihilo* creation is also set against all ideas that matter might simply be an emanation from God's eternal being (as taught by Plotinus and others).

When God created, he did not simply take a part of his essence and make it become visible and substantial. God actually produced a new reality that previously had no existence in any form. It is understood that God already had the idea of matter before he produced it, but creation means that God actually brought matter into existence out of absolutely nothing. In other words, there are two and only two kinds of reality. Nothing exists except God and that which God has originated. All things depend upon God for their existence. All of reality, including such universal ideas as "truth" or "knowledge," have a dependent existence. Everything (personal and impersonal) is contingent and depends upon the necessary being of God for its existence. *Ex nihilo* creation at least carries all of these stated implications. (See **CONTINGENT, COSMOLOGICAL ARGUMENT, CREATION,** and **NECESSARY.**)

**EXISTENCE** - That status of being that occurs and that interacts with other things. That which lives. That which can be properly described as being. That which is either materially or spiritually real. It is not a property of a thing. A thing does not possess existence. A thing must exist in order to possess or lack any attribute. Thus existence is an affirmative description that permits the possession of attributes. That which does not exist may be discussed only in the realm of speculation. (See **BEING** and **ESSENCE.**)

**EXISTENTIALISM** - The philosophical viewpoint that existence (the state or fact of "being") precedes essence and must be clearly and consistently distinguished as having that order. A pure existentialist would believe that human existence is not explainable by any scientific theory nor is it describable in rational terms.

Existentialism is pure empiricism without reference to any covering hypothesis or theory. It relies upon a phenomenological approach to knowledge (and morals) by stressing subjectivity (usually in terms of anxiety, despair, suffering, guilt feelings, etc.) in order to show the need for people to make vital choices by using their supposed freedom in this uncertain, contingent and apparently purposeless universe.

A Christian existentialist would stress the responsibility of each person for fashioning his or her own "self." The Christian form of existentialism will emphasize the natural desire of a creature to seek his or her creator (cf. Augustine, Pascal, Berdyaev, Marcel), or it will emphasize the great chasm between sinful humanity and the holy God (cf. Kierkegaard or Karl Barth). In existential theology (cf. Bultmann) the emphasis is on humanity's absolute dependence on God and on the complete subjectivity of all religious experience.

In non-Christian philosophy, existentialism has a strong atheistic, pessimistic, and nihilistic emphasis (cf. Sartre or Heidegger). Existentialism has had a great influence on modern art and on contemporary "popular culture." (See **BEING, EMPIRICISM, ESSENCE,** and **EXISTENCE.**)

**EXPLICIT** - That which is clearly and fully defined and openly stated with precision or boldness. Graphic depiction. (Compare **IMPLICIT.**)

**FAITH** - Some define faith as belief in things that cannot be known to be true. Others, more biblically, see faith as a very strong form of knowledge going beyond intellectual assent and expressing submissive commitment to things that are known to be true. Biblical faith is contrasted with sight but not with knowledge. Authentic faith is based upon propositional revelation from God. Existential faith that is not based upon divine revelation is not adequately protected from relativism and subjectivism.

**FALLACY** - An argument that may seem logical but is in fact invalid because of a mistake in reasoning. The term may also refer to the particular deceptive idea itself. Philosophical training should enable students to recognize fallacies in their own reasoning as well as in the arguments of other people. It goes without saying that Christians should try not to present the truth of the gospel with arguments that contain logical fallacies.

A logical argument is fallacious if the premises do not have the proper relationship to the conclusion. A false premise does not make an argument fallacious. On the other hand an argument may be fallacious even if all of the premises and the conclusion are true. Thus it is important to know the rules of logical analysis if fallacies are to be avoided. (See **LOGIC** and *PETITIO PRINCIPII*.)

**FALLACY OF IRRELEVANCE** - Actually this is not one simple fallacy. There are many ways to make irrelevant points in logical argument.

One has been dubbed "Chronological Snobbery": when something is considered to be false because the idea can be dated. To call an idea medieval or primitive or prescientific is not thereby to prove it false. A Victorian moral standard is not necessarily wrong. Ideas are not true or false because of age. Modern thought is not necessarily true just because it is modern. Old ideas are not necessarily false just because they are old. The argument from age is generally irrelevant as a criterion for truth.

Another form of the fallacy of irrelevance is the *ad hominem* argument in which the truth value of a idea is supposedly discredited because of the character of the person proposing it. But hypocrites do not prove anything negative about the truth of the ideas they supposedly profess.

Testimonials are also often logically fallacious, however persuasive they may be to some. To hear a football star tell how fine some product is does not settle many questions about the product. He may say "I like it, and you will too," but in fact you may not like it.

This same fallacy shows up when a researcher cites an authority on an issue that is outside the authority's range of competency. The opinion of a chemist would not necessarily be especially valuable on a non-chemistry-related question of foreign diplomacy. For a Nobel prize winner to say that "God does not exist" does not make it so.

Emotional qualifiers are not arguments. To call an idea "stupid" or "foolish" may express your viewpoint or your feelings, but it does not refute the idea. Discrediting the source is not the same as refuting the idea being proposed.

Many non-Christians use these irrelevant techniques in their attempt to discredit Christian doctrine. The history of the church is

256

not always pretty, but the wickedness of some Christian leaders does not prove Christianity false with regard to its actual teachings.

To make a point that really does not relate to what a person sets out to prove is to commit the fallacy of irrelevance.

**FATALISM** - Belief in the inevitability of events. The basis for this belief (as distinguished from strict "determinism") is not that events flow from strict, natural cause-and-effect processes. Rather, the sense of inevitability comes from a belief in the omnipotence of the Deity or deities. If God rules all things absolutely, then human thoughts and actions have no ultimate bearing on things. Many interpret Islam's view of Allah as leading to fatalism. (Compare **DETERMINISM**.) Greek religion saw the action of the gods as arbitrary and beyond human control. Astrology is a fatalistic "religion" with impersonal "gods."

**FIAT** - A Latin word transposed into English. *Fiat* is the third person singular present subjunctive of *fieri* (which means "to become"). Thus "fiat" is properly translated "let it be done." The term is often applied in the sense of "permission" as when someone acts with the official sanction or endorsement of the king. This is naturally tied to a conscious decision and a verbal command by the king. If the command alone is capable of producing a state of affairs without further effort, this is an act of will by fiat. In politics, fiat refers to a government decree that establishes an arbitrary value (e.g. on paper currency) or an arbitrary law. In theology, a special usage has developed that is not always noted in standard English dictionaries. When God created the universe, he did so (according to Genesis) by speaking, "Let there be. . . ," and it was done. Thus theologians have referred to this as creation by fiat, or simply as fiat creation. God said, and it was so. No factors were involved other than the will and command of God. (See **CREATION**.)

**FIDEISM** - The theory that knowledge (particularly religious knowledge) is based strictly and ultimately on faith alone. [Latin *fides* means "faith."] This is contrasted with theories of knowledge based upon reason or upon evidence (whether the evidence is objective or experiential).

There are many forms of fideism. One may fideistically assert biblical infallibility (Cornelius Van Til). This affirmation is not defended by evidence, however, because Van Til believed that to offer evidence was to assume that "belief" was a matter of human decision. He taught that an appeal to the human mind was in effect to move the initiation of faith away from God's sovereignty and to make "faith" a human "work." We must believe not because we have satisfactory evidence but because God commands us to repent and believe. We are to act on pure faith alone because and only because the Spirit of God gives us the faith we need.

Blaise Pascal argued that the universe was much too complex to understand with reasoned assurance. We should not wait until all the evidence is in. We should go ahead and choose (without full evidence) based on a simple "wager." If we "gamble" that there is a God, we cannot lose whether right or wrong. But if we gamble that there is no God, we can lose, since if we are wrong we would die and face his judgment. So simply on the basis of potential consequences, we should choose to believe in God. This belief will benefit us if it turns out to be right. If wrong, the consequences would be the same.

Søren Kierkegaard is often thought of as an extreme fideist in that he seems to have believed that truth and reality were found in the realm of individual choice. Neo-orthodoxy is influenced by this Kierkegaardianism and is thought by some to be essentially fideistic. Karl Barth, for example, opposed all appeals to evidence and/or to natural theology. Barth argued that man had no natural capacity for receiving God's revelation. Knowledge of God must come about by pure faith as a result of the Holy Spirit's work.

Thus a strict and rigid fideism rejects the idea of "common ground" between believers and non-believers. However, it appears that fideists confuse what is to be known with how we come to know it. To believe that God exists is to believe correctly. But fideism does not see the need for an adequate basis or warrant for belief. In fact it is hard to see what basis a fideist has for truth claims at all. Of course, the dedicated fideist is not threatened by this criticism since he or she is likely to be convinced of the impossibility of making such a claim in human terms anyway and may claim that truth can be grounded nowhere else but in God and in his initiative toward us. (See **COMMON GROUND**.)

**FINAL CAUSE** - The end or purpose for which something is done; such as the purpose God had in mind when he created the universe. The term comes from Aristotelian philosophy. Final cause must be distinguished from first cause. A first cause would refer to the original source for some effect. Final cause is not a chronological term. In fact, God's purpose (final cause) was determined chronologically prior to his initial act (first cause) of creation.

**FINITE** - That which has specific, definite and definable boundaries or limits. Usually the term includes the idea of being by nature limited, as opposed to being absolute, infinite, or infinitesimal. The world is finite. God is infinite.

Some modern theologians have emphasized human creature-hood (implying finitude) in stark contrast to God's nature. They usually imply that finitude is to be equated with imperfection. On this basis they believe that any human document (including Scripture) is inherently fallible. All finite (human) language is necessarily errant when it refers to God, they say, because God cannot be described truthfully since the very use of language would limit God to a finite description.

No doubt there is an element of truth in such a position, and we must not try to limit God through the use of human words. But the New Testament does not seem to have adopted that theory of language and finitude when dealing with the Old Testament. The words of Old Testament Scripture are assumed to be truthful. They are quoted as having full authority and as being the very words of God.

Thus some evangelicals have tried to develop a biblical concept of finitude and then relate that to biblical language. God is not limited to or by finite concepts and descriptions; nevertheless, the words of Scripture can and do truly express the self-revealed nature of God, because God himself created human language partly for that purpose and explicitly with that capability. He caused the revelatory events that are recorded in the Bible. In many different ways God actually spoke through his servants who wrote the Scripture.

Sin and imperfection are moral categories which are not inherent in finitude. Adam was no less finite before he sinned than he was after. God created finite reality and said it was "good." Thus a human document is not necessarily fallible. Scripture is believed to have been prompted by a special supernatural work of God's Spirit. The same Spirit guarded and kept it free from error. Though finite, it is—properly interpreted—nevertheless true. Scripture does not contain all the truth there is, but what it does contain is no less true. While each individual truth may be finite, the totality of truth is lost in the infinite reality of God. (See **INFINITE**.)

**FLUX** - Refers to inevitable change or becoming. An analogy could be a flowing river and its constant movement. To say that a system is in flux is to say that it lacks stability, that it is always changing, that it has no definite and permanent commitments or beliefs. It may have some "banks," and there may be a general "direction" or "cause." But the system as a whole is always changing.

A philosophical theory that changed constantly would lack persuasive force. It is possible to argue that reality itself is in constant flux (as Heraclitus did), but the outcome of such a theory would seem to be skepticism (if one held such a theory consistently within a materialistic universe and pressed the theory to its logical conclusion).

**FORM** - That which defines the shape of a thing. In Plato's philosophy the "Forms" are the universal Ideas that define reality. Sometimes "form" refers to the outward appearance as opposed to

259

the "matter" or the inner substance of a thing. (See **IDEA, MATTER,** and **SUBSTANCE.**)

**GENETIC FALLACY** - This is a special form of the reductive fallacy. It is committed when some idea or thing is reduced to nothing more than its origin.

To say of a great national leader that he is nothing more than a "country-boy farmer" is to reduce him to his origins and thus to demean or belittle him because of his humble beginnings. For a naturalistic psychologist to point out that "moral behavior is learned" is frequently an attempt by the psychologist to deny the value or the truth of one's moral code. When someone claims that God does not exist because children must be taught to believe in him, they commit the genetic fallacy. The truth or meaningfulness of an idea does not depend on how or when it is learned.

Evolutionary naturalists frequently commit a classic example of the genetic fallacy. According to the evolutionist, moral and theological ideas are merely highly developed animal instincts. Thus the evolutionist claims to have destroyed the truth value and the binding quality of these beliefs. But the same argument would destroy the validity of evolutionary theory as well since it must also have arisen by reason and thought which in turn must be nothing but developed animal instincts. If we cannot trust our minds to provide truths in the moral and theological realm, then why trust our minds to provide truth regarding evolutionary theory. Thus evolutionary philosophy tends to invalidate itself.

Freud's attempt to explain belief in God in terms of people's psychological projection of their fears onto the universe is another form of the genetic fallacy. Whatever psychological mechanism may be involved in coming to belief in God, the truth of that belief cannot be determined by its origin alone. God could use the child's experience within the family to bring about the correct idea of God's nature. It is never valid to reduce an idea to "nothing but" its physical or social origin. (See **REDUCTIVE FALLACY.**)

**GOD** - The word designates that which is worshiped or that which is thought to be divine.

In a real sense, God is the ultimate. People must come to terms with whatever they consider ultimate. If nature is regarded as the final reality, Nature becomes a god for that person. Many ancient and contemporary philosophers use the term to mean the Religious Object or the Religious Idea whether understood in personal, impersonal, pantheistic, or even imaginative terms.

In Christian theology, God is the transcendent, infinite-personal, holy, and righteous Absolute; the supreme Authority; the Creator and Sustainer of all existence; the Necessary Being on which all contingent, limited, finite, space-time reality depends. He is the personal being who provides meaning and purpose for existence, the alternative to chaos. God's essence is revealed in Scripture to be trinitarian. He is the source of all love, goodness, truth, and righteousness in the New Testament and is primarily identified as the Father of our Lord Jesus Christ.

**HEDONISM** - An ethical theory first formally stated by the Greek philosophers known as Epicureans. Essentially hedonism asserts that the highest good in life is pleasure or happiness. Thus whatever furthers that purpose is moral, and whatever ultimately retards pleasure is to be avoided.

Hedonism is also a psychological theory stating that all human behavior is motivated at the most basic level by the pursuit of pleasure and the avoidance of pain.

**HEDONISTIC PARADOX** - This phrase is commonly used to refer to the apparent inconsistency found in hedonistic ethics. According to the theory of hedonism, actions are right in so far as they contribute to happiness or pleasure, and actions are wrong if they contribute to unhappiness or suffering. But while pleasure is the sole good, it should not be the sole object of desire. When pleasure alone is sought, it cannot be found.

**HELLENISM** - From Greek *hellenismos*: to imitate things Greek or to use the Greek language. The influence of Greek culture, Greek ideas, Greek language, and Greek attitudes and styles following the death of Alexander the Great. Roman culture was deeply affected, especially in Palestine and in the Mediterranean world. The Septuagint (a Greek language translation of the Hebrew Bible) is an example of Hellenistic influence among the Jews in New Testament times.

**HERMENEUTICS** - The science and art of interpretation. In Christian theology the term refers to the development and study of the guiding principles for biblical interpretation. The "hermeneutical task" is to correctly understand the implied and intended meaning of a communication, whether written or oral or visual.

Principles of hermeneutics for written material such as the Bible would include all the inductively discovered grammatical rules of the original languages. This would include comparative studies in cognate languages and extra-biblical writings to produce accurate lexicons and to aid in syntactical analysis. Studies of the cultural context, the geographical situation, the historical background, and the relevant personal values involved must be developed according to careful guidelines and procedures.

The question of the legitimacy of finding "hidden" meanings or "fuller" meanings that are not clearly a part of or go beyond the literal meaning of the text must be carefully handled. This leads into studies of various figures of speech and symbols. Spiritual or theological meanings must not be arbitrarily assigned to a passage but must be legitimately drawn from the text.

Special hermeneutical principles will guide doctrinal studies, typological considerations, and ethical pronouncements. Different literary genres such as poetry, apocalyptic, drama, proverbial sayings, prophecy, or narrative must be recognized and interpreted properly.

Hermeneutics as an academic discipline will include studies in the history of interpretation. To some extent it covers the field of study relating to the communication of ideas not only from the text to the exegete but also from the exegete to (one or more) other people.

**HINDUISM** - The ancient religion of India. Commonly practiced as polytheism. In theory all the gods are manifestations of the one Brahman. Hindus believe in reincarnation. Salvation is release from the cycle of reincarnation. Sacred books include the *Upanishads* and the *Bhagavad-Gita*.

**HISTORIOGRAPHY** - The "writing of history" is one sense of the word historiography, and "written history" itself is another meaning. The study of historiography is the study of the methods, presuppositions, and results of writing history. To study the methods of research and writing, to study the philosophy of evidence, the logic of inductive research, the nature of historical objectivity, the nature of historical explanation, or to study the various systems or suggested patterns for history is the work of the philosopher of history. The term historiography, however, is broad enough to include all of these studies.

A historian studies historical events, but a historiographer studies the historian's product. He or she will classify it as to type and will analyze it for evaluation. Of course, sometimes the historian is also called a historiographer since he or she is a writer of history. This is the case especially if the historian is a chronicler of some events related to a group or a public institution by which he or she is employed.

The philosophical meaning of broad, secondary study of historical writing is the more common usage in academic studies, however. (See **HISTORY**.)

**HISTORY** - No single definition has ever been fully accepted by the scholars. Two levels of meaning are readily distinguished: 1) History names the actual events of the past; and 2) history is the record of past events (usually written, but in modern times a variety of visual and auditory records are available). Though many definitions have been offered, most of them seem to be too narrow or too broad or too ambiguous, etc. Nevertheless, history may be defined as that portion of the past space-time reality which for whatever reason is of present interest to a human mind. There is room here for trivia. The definition does not rule out supernatural causes. All the past is potentially included, yet there are definable limits. (See **HISTORIOGRAPHY**.)

*HOMO MENSURA* - "man is the measure of all things." The motto of Enlightenment thinkers who with unrestrained confidence believed that humanity needed no reference to God in order to judge things or properly understand them. The originator of the phrase reportedly was the ancient Greek philosopher Protagoras, a leading Sophist of the pre-Socratic era.

**HUMANISM** - Any view or system in which interest in human welfare is central. As such it would seem compatible with or even essential to Christianity. However, in philosophical usage the term refers specifically to a doctrine or life-style that centers upon human values rather than upon God. "Secular" (as opposed to "Christian") humanism rejects all forms of supernaturalism and attempts to establish the dignity of man on a naturalistic base through reason and the scientific method alone. Humanity replaces God as the supreme fact of reality.

Humanism properly describes any system that tries to find coherent and unified meaning to life by starting with humanity alone. Humanism is usually optimistic and hopeful in its outlook because man is thought to be basically good.

**HYPOSTATIZE** - To speak of an abstract idea as if it actually existed in substance; to mentally convert an abstract idea into substance as an ontological entity or category. To hypostatize is to attribute concrete or personal characteristics to abstractions. For example: one non-biblical theory is that "God" is merely a hypostatization of "society." Such a view supposedly explains why most people define evil in terms of what destroys their ideal way of life or their society. To talk of evolution as if it were an actual entity, or to describe a scientific principle as if the "law" were a thing is hypostatization. Though this is commonly done, hypostatization adds no strength to any proposal.

**HYPOTHESIS** - A judgment or an assumption or a proposed solution which is tentatively accepted by the mind in order to examine whether or not by adopting this hypothesis one can explain or interpret some aspect of reality in a more adequate manner. A hypothesis generally is a supposition stated in such a manner as to enable a person to study the logical or empirical consequences directly implied by the hypothesis. The study of the hypothesis is for the purpose of determining its relationship to the knowable data and to evaluate its interpretation of that data. A hypothesis is not necessarily false or inadequate and should not carry that connotation, but it does connote "preliminary" and "not yet settled." An idea remains a hypothesis only as long as its implications are not fully known. Once tested and proven to be adequate, the hypothesis would become a "theory" or a generally accepted "law." It is sometimes debated, for example, whether biological evolution is a theory or a hypothesis. One should not downplay the significance of a hypothesis, however. Hypotheses are often well conceived and powerful even when they are not yet firmly proved.

**IDEA** - Commonly defined as the result or object of mental activity; a formulated thought or a particular opinion. However, this word is a key term with special meanings in the history of thought.

(1) *In the philosophy of Plato,* "Idea" is synonymous with "Form" and refers to a universal archetype of things, an eternal essence, a universal and eternally real object. Plato believed that eternal Forms existed and were related in a hierarchial system to the Idea of the Good which was supreme. Other ideas which Plato thought of as actually existing were, for example, Justice, Truth, Duty, Beauty, etc. The physical world and material things are only copies (shadows) of the real world of Ideas. This dualism is the key for understanding Platonic philosophy. Mind (thought) is the fundamental reality. The Ideas are believed to exist separately from all matter, and the Ideas cannot be known directly by empirical investigation of the material world. Plato also taught the eternality of chaotic matter. His doctrine of creation does not relate to the formation of matter but to the origin of the present state (form) of existence. Physical things come into being when this chaotic "material-stuff" takes on Form or Idea. Matter is imperfect and is not suited for expressing eternal Ideas. Thus the Ideal "Tree" as it expresses itself in the material world is imperfect. It is found in many shapes and with various individual characteristics, even though all particular trees partake of the same universal Idea. The Ideas are real and unchanging. In fact they are the only permanent and thus truly real beings. Physical things are real only to the extent that they are accurately patterned after the Ideas. Matter is constantly changing and temporary and thus is not capable of being known with certainty. In that sense matter is unreal, because whatever is real can be an object of knowledge, according to Plato. Matter without Idea is chaos and thus unknowable and unreal. For Plato, human values are

264

but copies of eternal essences which exist in the supra-temporal world of Ideas. All values are related to the Good. The Ideas can be grasped only by rational intuition. But the fact of their existence is a central affirmation of Plato's thought.

(2) *For Aristotle,* matter never exists apart from some Form. Matter is conceived as always in process but nevertheless structured by the formative "Idea" that makes a particular thing what it is. The Platonic Ideas were always "within" matter (not outside or separate) actualizing its potentialities. Aristotle did believe that Pure Idea existed—the Unmoved Mover (Aristotle's God). In fact this Pure Form was guiding the process of all things to definite final goals. For example, the oak tree is potential in the acorn and a house or a chair is potential in the wood of the tree. The Pure Idea is not a personal being, however. It is an unconscious force acting by nature rather than being prompted by concern or interest. Perhaps a magnet could serve as a physical analogy.

(3) *For John Locke,* an idea is the object of sensation or reflection. This object is at first strictly of a plain, unanalyzable character and is thus a simple idea. A complex idea is a product of the mind as it combines and relates simple ideas.

(4) *For David Hume,* an idea is a memory copy or a faint image of sense impressions, not the impression itself.

An English dictionary will also define "idea" as a plan or a method for doing something or getting somewhere. The term, so used, carries the important connotation of "purpose." Our ideas (our formulated thoughts rather than our flow of consciousness) are what give meaning to our lives.

   **IDEAL** - A model or a standard, generally a perfect standard, a high standard, one that is fully complete so that people should seek to imitate it or try to achieve it. An ideal is a worthy goal, an objective that is desirable. "Ideal" may also be used as an adjective to mean perfect or nearly perfect, having all desirable elements (e.g. my ideal vacation). When used as an adjective, the term often has the connotation of "imaginary" or "impossible."

   **IDEALISM** - Though in common speech idealism is the practice of seeing things optimistically as they ought to be rather than as they actually are, in philosophical studies idealism is a metaphysical theory of ontology based originally on the theories of

Plato. There are many types of idealism; for example: Platonism, Absolutism, Subjectivism, Panpsychism, Personalism. Modern idealists usually do not agree with Plato in details. Nevertheless the central doctrine of all idealism is found in his affirmation that ultimate reality is ideal, mental, and rational. Unity is more fundamental than diversity. Mind is prior to matter.

*Absolutist pantheism* is a form of idealism in that it views all reality as eternally existing as one mental being. According to Hegel, reality is one rational Mind (the Absolute) eternally in dialectical development. According to Berkeley's *subjectivism*, only minds (persons, spirits) and their ideas exist because one could never know (and thus one could not affirm the existence of) anything other than the ideas or sensations of which he was conscious. *Panpsychism* sees reality as made up of active, living mentalities of infinite number and of various organization levels. *Personalism* teaches that nature is an expression of the eternal consciousness of God, yet it is physically real. Reality is a system of persons. God, the eternal Person, is the center of the system. Therefore, reality is entirely Ideal or mental in character.

In summary, idealism is a philosophical system which begins with mind as the most fundamental reality. It often involves a dualism between mind and matter. This is probably the most important philosophical viewpoint in the history of western thought.

**IMMANENT** - Contrasted with "transcendent," the term carries the meaning of nearness, being part of, within, or indwelling. In contemplating the world, Hegelian idealism considers "mind" to be immanent, that is to be inherent and intrinsic. Used theologically, the term refers to God's presence in the universe. The term refers especially to the nearness and indwelling of God. (See **IDEALISM** and **TRANSCENDENT**.)

**IMMORTAL; IMMORTALITY** - That which is not subject to death or cessation of existence. That which has always been and will always be. In this sense, Scripture speaks of God only as having immortality. By the gift of eternal life, God grants immortality to human souls (i.e. "life everlasting"). Many Christians believe that God gave immortality (the eternal survival of the soul in the future) to all humans at creation. Thus both heaven and hell are endless for those who are there. Christianity does not teach the immortality of the soul in the Greek sense of inherent everlastingness (from all eternity past to all eternity future).

**IMPLICATION** - The relationship of logical inevitability or necessary consequence. The logical status of the second of two propositions related in such a way that if the first is true the second cannot be false. Used in another less technical sense, an implication is a suggestion or an impression intended but not stated. Sometimes what is said "by implication" is more important than what is said by our words taken at face value. (See **INFERENCE**.)

**IMPLICIT** - Something is said to be implicit if it is capable of being understood or developed from something else, even though it is not specifically expressed. For example: a philosopher may not directly and "explicitly" define his understanding of God, but the fact that he is pantheistic may be implicit in his published works. The oak is implicit in the acorn. (Contrast with **EXPLICIT**.)

**INDUCTION** - Reasoning from the particular to the general, from a part to the whole, from the individual characteristics to the universal qualities. The logical methodology on which empiricism is built.

Usually induction leads to inference of a general principle which is drawn from a large number of particular instances. This is a characteristic of modern scientific methodology.

Inductively we can discover what claims the Bible makes for its own authority. This is a necessary study because it would not be theologically sound to defend any view of biblical authority which is more or less than that view which the Bible claims for itself. The best and most biblical theology or theological system is one drawn from an inductive study of Scripture itself. (See **DEDUCTION** and **LOGIC**.)

**INERRANT, INERRANCY** - Not errant, without errors. In Christian theology, a special usage of this word appears in the phrase "biblical inerrancy." The reference is to the truthfulness of the Bible. One who believes the doctrine of biblical inerrancy believes that the Bible is completely truthful in all of its actual affirmations and contextual teachings. Properly understood, the doctrine of inerrancy does not deny the value of textual criticism. Comparative textual study is essential since inerrancy applies only to the authentic text. Any accurate copy or any accurate translation of the original text is considered to be authentic. Inerrancy does not imply that biblical language has no ambiguities or figures of speech, nor does it imply that all who affirm biblical inerrancy will always agree on the interpretation of every passage or text. The term does set forth one's belief that the Bible is divinely inspired, the authentic Word of a fully truthful God. It also indicates that one denies the foundational premise of modern biblical criticism (i.e., that Scripture is strictly an evolving human witness to special "religious" experiences). Biblical inerrantists believe that God by supernatural means conveyed and secured his Word to his people. Scripture, then, is only secondarily a human witness. It is first of all a contentful divine revelation and thus is unlike all other books. Biblical inerrancy is an interdenominational affirmation of evangeli-

267

cal Christianity that distinguishes much of conservative theology from liberalism, neo-orthodoxy, existentialism, process theology, and other non-evangelical theological options. (See **REVELATION** and **INSPIRATION.**)

**INFERENCE** - The reasoning process which arrives at a conclusion: the act of passing from one set of propositions to another by valid reasoning either deductively or inductively. "Implication" is a logical relationship; "inference" is a form of rational activity. (See **LOGIC** and **IMPLICATION.**)

**INFINITE** - Without limits of any kind; having no end or boundaries. Most frequently the term designates something indefinitely large though it may also be used to describe something so small as to be immeasurable ("infinitesimal"). The term literally means "not finite." Thus it is a negative term and does not properly convey any positive content. To say God is infinite is to tell us what he is not, but it does not tell us what he is. This is, however, an important distinction to make. God has revealed himself to us as being without limits in any essential aspect of his nature. God is all in all. He is absolutely complete. Nothing controls God. He does not depend on anything. He is self-sufficient. God is that on which all else depends. Thus he possesses all of his attributes in an infinite capacity. (See **FINITE.**)

**INFINITE REGRESS** - The teaching that there is no original or first cause but that the chain of cause and effect extends infinitely into the past. (See **COSMOLOGICAL ARGUMENT.**)

**INNATE** - Inborn, inherited; arising from the mind rather than from experience. Animals as well as people may have innate characteristics. Birds seem to "know" how and when to migrate without being taught. Most commonly, though, the term is used by rationalists to describe ideas which they believe a person does not learn but which belong to a person's mind from birth.

There has been much discussion as to whether the idea of God is innate or is derived from experience and conditioning by others. Descartes believed that the idea of God was innate to the human mind. Empiricists, such as Locke, deny that there are any innate ideas at all. The mind, he said, is a *tabula rasa* (a blank tablet) at birth. Knowledge of God is a product of reason. Others, such as Kant, argue that ideas *per se* are not innate (they all arise from experience) but that there are innate categories in the mind by which all experiences are interpreted and organized.

**INSPIRATION** - As a technical theological term, inspiration refers to the special work of the Holy Spirit through which the revelation of God comes to us in reliable human language.

God sometimes spoke directly in human language to a prophet. (That is divine revelation, not inspiration.) For example,

God's Ten Commandments were given to Moses in written form. The Commandments, then, were not "inspired." They were revealed directly in verbal (in this special case even in written) form.

But sometimes (perhaps most often) God revealed himself through miracles and/or through mighty acts without speaking in human language directly. When the human authors of Scripture described these mighty acts of God, when they worshiped God with Psalms, or when they recorded God's revelation in whatever form it came to them (including their narrative accounts of God's providential guidance of his covenant people), the Holy Spirit moved them to write (in the first place) and then so influenced them through his spiritual relationship with them that they did in fact correctly record the contentful revelation of God. (This is the work properly called inspiration.) The Spirit's work enabled the prophets or the apostles to understand God's revelation correctly and then to record that revelation in human language without introducing erroneous ideas. The result of this spiritual work of God was to produce the Scriptures which have God for their ultimate author, salvation for their theme and purpose, and truth, without any mixture of error, for their matter (their content).

Inspiration may not always be used in this technical theological sense in philosophical literature. The most common usage perhaps is to describe an idea as being especially creative or useful. A person who concentrates on a project and does exceptional work may be said to be inspired. People who overcome hardships and go on to succeed are said to be an inspiration in that they provide a good model for others. This general usage is often misapplied when the writers (rather than the writings) of Scripture are mistakenly referred to as having been inspired (motivated by ideals). (See **REVELATION** and **INERRANCY**.)

**INTERPRETATION** - The attempt to transfer meaning from one language, culture, or setting to another. When we read the Bible in the original languages, we must interpret the meaning to modern people (or to ourselves). More is involved than just translation of the vocabulary (though in a real sense this is also a form of interpretation). Interpretation usually involves the explanation of context, meaning, purpose, and related ideas.

To discover the original meaning of a written text may require not only linguistic, literary, and grammatical understanding, but also awareness of context, history, cultural factors, and the author's intent. The transfer of the original meaning from one setting to another is the act of proper interpretation.

Because the application of the original meaning to the new situation is sometimes called interpretation also, some view the process as subjective, lacking in objectivity. Application and interpretation should be distinguished, however. Interpretation, then, would be an effort to objectively evaluate the evidence and gain understanding of original intent. Application would admittedly be more subjective, and would be an effort to take the correct interpretation and find points of relevance to the contemporary scene. Both are needed, however, as we try to understand the meaning, the message, the relevance, and the value of God's Word for today's world. (See **CONTEXTUALIZATION, HERMENEU-TICS.**)

**INTUITION** - The act of direct and immediate perception or apprehension; the flash of insight that arrives at knowledge or "certainty" without going through a systematic reasoning process; the power of gaining knowledge without a conscious process of inference.

Intuition is frequently suggested as a means of knowing God. No doubt many do have an awareness of God at a young age. Thus, knowledge of God cannot exclusively be based on formal, fully worked out, logical arguments. Moreover, this "direct knowledge" of God is not limited to our youth. But it is also true that pure intuition could not be objectively verifiable and thus would have only subjective validity.

The biblical view would not downplay the role of intuition in knowing God, but it should not be considered as the primary means of knowing in the Bible. Intuition is private. God's self-revelation was frequently public, and it was always capable of being communicated to the masses. This objective aspect of revelation provides the possibility of verification at least to some degree.

**IRRATIONAL** - Not rational; not in accordance with reason. An action is irrational if it is done for no reason or in spite of good reasons.

Existentialism is characterized by irrationality, because it calls for decision but has no objective basis on which to make a decision. All true communication between two or more minds is based on some form of rationality. If people spoke without any logical connections between their words or sentences, there would be no communication of real knowledge and all would be absurd. Thus the "Theatre of the Absurd" grew directly out of the attempt of existentialism to be consistent to its own principles.

But the effort to be consistent is itself a rational process. No one lives consistently by a strictly irrational theory. Many evangelical Christian philosophers believe that rationality is a part of humanness, a part of the image of God. To act or believe in an irrational manner would, therefore, be to rebel against God's intent for human beings. According to Romans 1:18-20, pagans suppress what they know to be true, and deny things of God that are plain to them. Rebellion against the known truth is, by definition, irrational.

**IRRELEVANT** - Not relevant; foreign, extraneous, not applicable; unrelated to the matter at hand; having no bearing on the subject. Frequently, the term is used to describe an argument or a set of reasons offered as a proof when in fact it does not prove the point in question because it is not properly related to the issue. It is irrelevant to argue that since we cannot see him from a rocket ship in space that God does not exist.

**ISLAM** - The theistic religion based on the 6th century A.D. teachings of Mohammad, an Arabian prophet born in Mecca who opposed all forms of idolatry and immorality. Friday is the Holy Day, and the *Qur'an (Koran)* is the Islamic Scripture. Islam is one of the fastest growing religions in the world today, having approximately the same number of adherents as Roman Catholicism.

**JUDAISM** - The modern religion based upon the Hebrew Bible (the Old Testament). Judaism has an orthodox form that finds its meaning and purpose in the desire to take the Hebrew Bible strictly, even to the point of seeking to renew temple worship. Conservative Judaism seeks to remain faithful to the spirit of biblical teachings but denies the necessity for literal applications of Old Testment ceremonial practices. Reformed Judaism seeks to implement humanistic ideals drawn from Scripture but does not adopt traditional interpretations as binding. Some Jews are non-religious, even atheistic, but Judaism is essentially religious, not nationalistic or political. Gentiles may adopt Judaism as a religious faith.

**JUDGMENT** - The intellectual process of forming an opinion or drawing a conclusion. Particularly for Kant, judgment has to do with relating "particular" to "general" terms in logical analysis. Or it may refer to the result of such a process; that is, a judgment would be the proposition advanced to explain something. Example: it is the professor's judgment that the student who studies the most will learn the most, all other things being equal.

In Christian theology the Judgment is a great event at the climax of history when God will "express his opinion" about every human being. We must all stand before the Lord to receive rewards or punishments. All Christians believe in a final judgment at the end of this present age (Revelation 20). Premillennial eschatology teaches that there will be two judgments, one before the millennium to determine who will be allowed to enter the kingdom age, and then the final judgment at the end of history. Some dispensational scholars will make distinctions within the first judgment. They often conclude that the pre-kingdom judgment will have a Christian aspect (the judgment seat of Christ, 2 Corinthians 5:10), a Gentile aspect (Matthew 25), and a Jewish aspect (Ezekiel 20).

**KALAM** - The term refers to Medieval Arabic philosophy or theology. However, the usage that is most relevant to Christian apologists is as a designation of one of the stronger versions of the cosmological argument for the existence of God. The Kalam cosmological argument was popular in the late Middle Ages among Islamic Arabic philosophers (e.g. al-Ghazali, 1058-1111). It is a logical argument based on the fact that the universe had an actual beginning in time and thus needed a cause (God).

Aquinas rejected this version of the argument because of his belief that the universe may be eternal. He believed that God did not and could not change. If God, then, were a Creator, he must always have been a Creator. If he were eternally a Creator, then there would be an eternal creation, and thus the universe would not actually have an absolute beginning.

Because of Aquinas' influence, most Christian philosophers have in the past rejected the Kalam argument. In recent years, however, the argument has been revived by some Christian philosophers who see in it a way to take advantage of the modern scientific discoveries pointing to the real likelihood that the universe did have an actual beginning. (Compare **BIG BANG COSMOLOGY.**)

The Kalam argument can be stated very simply:

(1)   Everything that has a beginning must have been caused [i.e., "Out of nothing, nothing comes"];

(2)   The universe had a beginning [i.e., "big bang" cosmology is correct];

(3)   Therefore, the universe was caused.

A line of reasoning, then, is offered to show that the universe could not cause itself, that this cause must therefore be other than a natural cause, and finally that this cause must be personal. Thus a successful argument points to an original, supernatural, personal cause of all the substance and form of the universe. Such an existing being would quite naturally be called God.

As with other "theistic proofs," this does not absolutely prove that the God of the Bible exists, but it does provide rather strong evidence for theism. The evidence that the God who exists (as the Creator of all things) is in fact the God of the Bible is provided by further apologetic efforts of Christians philosophers and theologians. The evidence they produce (centering on Jesus Christ) is really quite strong. The Kalam argument is only as strong as the evidence for a real beginning for the universe, however. If steady-state theories are revived, the Kalam version of the cosmological argument will be weakened. (See **COSMOLOGICAL ARGU-MENT.**)

**KARMA** - Belief (in Eastern religions) that every act produces an effect on the soul. Good works "clean" the soul. Evil works add "weight" to the soul. Thus karma is the moral law of cause and effect.

**KINGDOM** - The realm ruled over by a king (or by a "king-like" ruler with some other title).

In the Old Testament the term is used 118 times with an exclusively political reference. The other 29 uses of the term in the Old Testament speak of God's kingdom. Frequently the "Kingdom of God" is associated with the coming of the Messiah. Some understand the kingdom of God to be God's rule itself rather than a realm.

In the New Testament the term "kingdom" is found more than 160 times, by far most frequently in the Gospels (128 times). The phrase "kingdom of heaven" is used only by Matthew. The phrase "kingdom of God" is used in all four Gospels. Some scholars distinguish between the two phrases, but most think they are synonymous. (Matthew, as a Jew, may have used "heaven" as a circumlocution out of reverence for the name of God.)

Some dispensationalist scholars believe that Jesus offered a literal, earthly, political kingdom to the Jews when he came the first time, but that his offer was rejected. Thus the kingdom was postponed until his second coming when it will be established. Others teach that Jesus never intended to set up an earthly kingdom when he came the first time but that he always intended to establish the kingdom at his second coming. Still others believe that an earthly, political kingdom was never God's intention at all, but that the kingdom is the spiritual rule of God in the hearts of men. Thus the kingdom was established when Jesus came the first time and it is presently in force. Careful exegetical study is necessary to decide which view is actually taught in the Bible.

**KNOWLEDGE** - The sum total (or any part) of truthful and/or correct information possessed by an individual or by humanity. The term can properly be used to refer to things that are false or that do not exist, but such usage demands that some appropriately descriptive adjective be used. By itself, it is assumed that the reference is to true facts or true insights.

It is common (and correct if properly understood) to distinguish between simple factual knowledge and personal knowledge. We know a person and a thing on different levels and in different ways. Knowledge of the true God is always personal knowledge. This does not mean that we can have no factual knowledge about God. (We can surely have factual knowledge about people.) What it does mean is that our knowledge of God (just as with people) is more than mere facts. The knowledge we have of God depends upon the nature of the relationship involved.

**KORAN** - Islamic Holy Scripture. (See **QUR'AN**.)

**LANGUAGE ANALYSIS** - Language is the system of signs, sounds, and symbols that communicate ideas from one mind to another. Because language is so crucial to thinking and to the study of ideas, philosophers have in recent years turned more attention to the analysis of language. Efforts have been made to identify types of discourse and to isolate linguistic clues that help to provide meaning and sense to the discourse. (See **LOGICAL POSITIVISM** and **VERIFICATION PRINCIPLE**.)

**LAW** - A a rule to which compliance or conformity is expected. This rule is either a proposition duly established by a recognized authority, or it is a generalization based upon observed phenomena. A scientific law or a natural law fits the latter description. A politically developed or a divinely revealed law fits the former description. God's law (summed up in the Ten Commandments) requires moral righteousness. *Torah*, the Hebrew word for "Law," often refers to the first five books of the Old Testament (the Pentateuch), because in those books we have the story of the revelation of the covenant law to Israel. The Old Testament era from Moses to Christ is thus sometimes referred to as the Age of the Law (contrasted with the New Covenant in Christ, sometimes referred to as the Age of Grace, cf. Gal 3:17–19 and Eph 3:2–12).

**LIBERALISM** - While this term often refers to a generous attitude, it also has a special political meaning. In governments dominated by autocratic rulers it refers to the philosophy of political freedom, individual rights, and personal autonomy. In more democratic political systems, "conservatives" usually defend individual freedom, and the term "liberalism" tends to imply the philosophy of using government resources to provide for human needs, thus fostering a benevolent but strong central government that creates a dependent citizenry. This ultimately robs the individual of his or her freedom.

In theological circles, liberalism is usually identified by its use of "reason" (the "autonomous freedom" of the mind) to judge the truth content of Scripture itself. For a theological liberal, religious freedom includes the freedom to disbelieve and disobey even clear biblical teachings. Conservative theologians believe biblical freedom is freedom from the demands of the Old Testament law (due to the perfect substitutionary atonement of Christ) and freedom from slavery to sin. Conservatives believe true freedom comes in willing submission to the absolute authority of God and to the lordship of

Christ. This submission to God's authority is properly expressed both morally and doctrinally.

Classical liberalism (a 19th- and early 20th-century movement) taught the universal salvation of all humans and often emphasized the humanity of Jesus at the expense of his deity. For them Jesus was a great moral teacher. Therefore, Christianity was essentially a system of ethics that emphasized love and forgiveness but did not include an ultimate judgment on "sin" (human weaknesses) or absolute standards of conduct or of thought. (See **CONSERVATIVE**.)

**LINGUISTIC ANALYSIS** - A somewhat anti-metaphysical movement dedicated to refuting philosophical idealism and replacing it with a scientific philosophy. The idea was to eliminate many major philosophical debates by showing that they were linguistic problems only. Key figures are Ludwig Wittgenstein and A. J. Ayer, and Rudolph Carnap. (See **LANGUAGE ANALYSIS** and **LOGICAL POSITIVISM**.)

**LOGIC** - The principles of correct thinking; the science of inference; the philosophy dealing with proper definition, classification, and correct use of terms as well as a systematic setting forth of the formal principles of valid reasoning. "Correct" is defined in terms of conformity to established principles of reasoning. Correct reasoning is that which is true to the facts. The very fact that generally accepted rules of logic exist is testimony to the correctness of the belief that the world is not random but that it has form and order. Christians would contend that this order is there because God created it. Logic is possible because God is purposeful, and he created our minds to be rational, purposeful, and orderly. (See **DEDUCTION** and **INDUCTION**.)

**LOGICAL POSITIVISM** or **LOGICAL EMPIRICISM** - The philosophy arguing that meaningful propositions are either *apriori* or *aposteriori*. Therefore, according to logical positivism, all metaphysical theories (including Christian philosophy or theology) are meaningless because, in the very nature of the case, they are not verifiable strictly by reference to logic or empirical facts. (See **VERIFICATION PRINCIPLE**.)

The basic thesis is that no statement could be meaningful (much less true or false, since these evaluations cannot even be made unless the statement is meaningful) if the propositional content of the statement could not be tested scientifically or else be shown to be self-evidently true. Unfortunately, the thesis (that meaningful propositions must be empirically verifiable) could not meet its own criteria for meaningfulness. Early proponents of logical positivism were trying to build on an assumption that was itself technically meaningless according to their own definition.

Later theorists of this school of thought agree that the original form of the criterion for meaningfulness was not itself a meaningful proposition, but they argue that it nevertheless defined the basis on which any proposition could be verified. Thus logical positivism as such no longer exists in its early form. But it is very common for philosophers today to be involved in language analysis using exclusively empirical criteria for assessing the meaningfulness of individual propositions. (See **LANGUAGE ANALYSIS.**)

Most philosophical analysts will say that only empirical statements can be verified. One may "believe" religion or metaphysics, say these philosophers, but one could not claim that one's beliefs are true, because they are inherently incapable of being verified. Neo-orthodox theologians seemingly have no defense against such an analysis except to deny the relevance of verification procedures for theology. Evangelicals, on the other hand, contend that the historical character of divine revelation is sufficient to guarantee the meanfulness of theological discourse.

**MATERIALISM** - The belief that matter is the ultimate reality. Thus all values are physical values and morals are simply statistical averages or sociological norms. Marxism is a form of dialectical materialism based on economic values. Materialism cannot adequately account for non-material realities such as personality. Materialism simply denies that personal categories are non-material. The materialist will try to explain all spiritual realities in terms of matter. Pure behaviorism is a materialistic theory.

If matter is the ultimate reality, then how did self-conscious, observant minds develop? Why should reason be trusted if its origin is matter alone? Does matter organize itself and increase its own complexity? If not, then how could materialism be true? (See **NATURALISM.**)

**MATTER** - That which has weight and occupies space and can be perceived. In another sense, "matter" is the substance or the essence of an expression of thought. The same idea may be expressed in various ways and in various languages. The form varies but the matter (the essential meaning) remains constant. (See **FORM** and **SUBSTANCE.**)

**MAYA** - The physical world (in Eastern religious thought) viewed as an illusion, a "dream" of "God." The Brahman is the only reality. All else only appears to exist but is not ultimately real. (See **BRAHMAN.**)

**METAETHICS** - That branch of philosophy that seeks to analyze moral terms such as: right, wrong, ought, good, bad, worth, value, etc.

**METAPHYSICS** - As a philosophical category it includes ontology, cosmology, and epistemology, yet it is broader than any one of these alone. Metaphysics refers to speculation concerning philosophical matters beyond the strictly physical or experiential. It asks the question: "What is the essential nature of reality as such?"

The term was coined by Andronicus of Rhodes (1st century b.c.) as a descriptive title of the section of the works of Aristotle which in his edition came "after (*meta*: beyond) the *Physika*;" in other words: "the last volumes in the set." This is quite different from modern usage.

The term is frequently misused today. In general, however, "metaphysics" is that branch of philosophy concerned with the nature of reality. The metaphysical question is "What is ultimately real?" Modern textbooks on metaphysics will deal with such issues as the mind/body problem, the issue of freedom vs. determinism, the existence of God, the nature of space and time, and other fundamental problems of this type.

**METHODOLOGY** - Basically the term is a general word referring to "how something is accomplished." As an academic discipline it most often refers to the study of various procedures for arriving at truth or knowledge. Of course, the term may refer to one particular process.

Philosophers are especially concerned with methodology. Christian apologetics to a large extent is concerned with the examination, critique, and evaluation of alternative epistemological methodologies, including various theological methods. For example: natural theology and revealed theology are two major methodological options among Christian theologians. Both groups of scholars conclude that God is the Creator of all things and that the Bible is true, etc., but they arrive at those conclusions using two alternative starting points and different forms of reasoning. While they may happen to agree on many conclusions, they use different methodologies.

On the other hand, methodology does somewhat determine the types of conclusions which will result from various patterns of reasoning, and a rigid methodology can easily mold ideas into its own pattern. One must not be misled by the fact that some particular neo-orthodox theologian or existentialist philosopher may at times express ideas which seem at first to be in substantial agreement with certain conclusions of traditional biblical theology. The overall conclusions drawn from non-biblical methodologies will always compromise biblical truth at some point.

Which methodology one uses is vitally important for true Christian faith. More than one variety of theological method may be acceptable, but not all methods are equally biblical.

**MIDDLE AGES** - Designates the historical era in European civilization that connects the "Classical Period" and the "Renais-

277

sance." Key figures include Anselm, Aquinas, Charlemagne, St. Francis of Assisi, and Mohammed, the founder of Islam.

Some claim that this period of time simply stands in the "middle" between the Greco-Roman world and the rebirth of classical art and learning in Europe. Technically dated from the fall of Rome, the Middle Ages are generally said to have begun around 500 A.D. For convenience, some think of Augustine as the last theologian of the Classical Period, and Aquinas is seen as the transitional figure at the earliest beginning point of the Renaissance. Others tie the Renaissance to the Gutenberg printing press, or to the work of Copernicus. Thus the beginning of the Renaissance (the end of the Middle Ages) is disputed but is generally dated no later than 1500 A.D. A true beginning of the Renaissance is in place by the 14th century, however. Nevertheless, as a matter of common reference, the Middle Ages are said to last for a "thousand years."

Platonic philosophy dominates the period. Religion became increasingly "other-worldly," and this can be seen in the rise of monastic orders, Gregorian chants, cathedral architecture, and Medieval art. The spiritual life was identified with the intellectual life. Thus arose scholastic theology and lengthy intellectual debates over theological issues. Europe was essentially united as "Christendom" despite the individual differences between local areas. The pope in Rome was seen as the spiritual head of all Christian churches. (See **RENAISSANCE**.)

**MILLENNIUM** - *Mille* in Latin means "one thousand" and *annum* in Latin means "year." The term is commonly used to refer to any thousand-year time period. For example, someone might speak of Abraham's day as being at the beginning of the second millennium before Christ.

When the term is used independently ["the Millennium"], it usually refers to an expected time of unlimited peace and joy along with material and spiritual blessings. The origin of this common connotation is the identification of the thousand-year period mentioned in Revelation 20:2-7 with the Old Testament passages that speak of material blessings associated with the Messiah or with God's kingdom.

A great deal of controversy has surrounded the various interpretations of the relevant Scriptural passages. These passages do, however, mean something, and a serious student of the Bible will seek the true interpretation with great care. (See **POSTMIL-LENNIALISM, PREMILLENNIALISM,** and **AMILLENNIALISM**.)

**MODEL** - Commonly refers to a small-scale replica of something (such as a model car), but in the vocabulary of philosophical studies, a model most often refers to conceptual theory.

In the philosophy of science we often need a framework (even if it is strictly hypothetical) on which to "hang" our conceptions. This framework provides a structure that can be analyzed to discover what evidence would be needed either to confirm or to refute the hypothesis that originated the model. The model also enables the philosopher of science to understand what a theory means, what it implies, and how it would actually explain the observable data. Models then may be compared and evaluated on the basis of their conformity to fact and on the extent of their explanatory power.

Someone might propose a heliocentric model of the universe, as Copernicus did. This was opposed to the geocentric model. Later on, a revised version of heliocentrism was offered that applied only to the solar system, not to the whole universe. Several competing naturalistic models for explaining the origin of the solar system exist today. No single one of them makes sense of all the data. Thus the issue of planetary origins remains problematic for the naturalist. The notion of an expanding universe is one model that has been proposed to explain the significance of the observed shift toward the long end of the spectrum of the spectral lines identifying the chemical composition of stars and galaxies.

Creation and evolution are competing models, since both offer reasonable explanations of much of the geological and biological evidence concerning the origin of life forms and the formation of the universe itself. By comparing these models we can better understand the two theories, and perhaps we can test the two models against the available data to see which one is better. Evangelical Christians believe that the creation model will ultimately prove to be correct. (See **CREATION, WORLDVIEW,** and **EVOLUTION.**)

**MONISM** - The metaphysical theory that all reality is basically of one substance. This was the theory of Parmenides, who had a strong influence on Plato. Monism denies any distinction between God and the world. Plato ultimately moved to affirm dualism, the existence of both spiritual and material reality, but his sympathy with Parmenides led Plato to affirm material reality in a secondary way. The real was the rational, the spiritual, the ideal.

**MORAL ARGUMENT** - Moral concepts exist. These express moral laws. The existence of those laws implies a moral lawgiver as their source. A lawgiver must be the ultimate judge. God is the moral Judge. His standards alone are ultimate.

**MOSLEM (MUSLIM)** - A follower of Muhammad; an Islamic believer. (See **ISLAM.**)

**MOSQUE** - A Moslem house of prayer. Usually without furniture, and decorated geometrically and/or with Arabic writings from the Qur'an. The center of attention is the prayer niche on the wall that from the center of the mosque is in the direction of Mecca. Thus worshipers face Mecca to pray.

**MYSTICISM** - Three basic meanings:

(1) The reported experience of direct knowledge of supernatural reality (sometimes related to occultism);

(2) The philosophy that intuition is the proper way of attaining a knowledge of ultimate reality or direct knowledge of God;

(3) A vague and unfounded speculation based on so-called intuitive knowledge of matters that are inexpressible in words

**NAÏVE REALISM** - The metaphysical and epistemological viewpoint of common sense; that is, that the world in reality is generally as we perceive it: our mental perception is generated by our five senses in such a way that it is in essence a direct copy of the external world. This is the viewpoint which most people assume to be the case. It is by far the most common theory among the general public in the stream of western civilization. It cannot be absolutely correct, because upon reflection it is obvious that our senses sometimes present illusions as if they were real. But based on the doctrines of creation and of the nature of God, Bible-believing thinkers frequently use this theory as their basic framework, and then delineate appropriate modifications so as to be able to state a consistent epistemology. (See **COMMON SENSE REALISM**.)

**NATURALISM** - A worldview that denies and rejects any theistic or supernatural explanation of reality. This theory affirms that the universe is self-explanatory and self-operating. All reality is located in space and time. Nothing exists which is not within the network of relationships which makes up the universe.

Naturalism's fatal weakness is that all theories must be generated by the same system of cause-and-effect relationships (since there is only one such system), and thus all theories have equal standing if they are empirically based and consistently stated. But this would allow contradictory ideas to be true. Thus it is that atheism and theism both arise from equally valid experiences. But if that is so, one cannot say that the other is false. There is no standard beyond space-time reality by which to judge these matters, and thus naturalism itself fails to be able to claim truth for itself. If reason is strictly a product of nature, then why should it be trusted? Reason, on this view, cannot stand apart from nature and thus claim to be able to describe nature objectively.

**NATURAL THEOLOGY** - Theology that is not dependent

upon special revelation for its starting point. The theory is that God's existence, and other important doctrines, can be demonstrated from a rational examination of the content of ordinary sense experience. The knowledge of God, then, originates from nature (cf. Romans 1:19-20). The theology of Thomas Aquinas is often described as natural theology. He carefully formulated a theological system based upon sensory evidence and analogy. Use of various collections of evidence characterize mainline natural theology, especially in 19th-century British writings. Many evangelicals believe that theistic evidences provide the necessary rational element for Christian theology. Others believe that the use of such arguments compromises our total dependence upon initiative through revelation. Differences here result in different attitudes toward and methods in apologetics.

**NECESSARY** - That which must be; that which does not depend on other things. God is a necessary Being. All things depend upon him, but he does not depend on anything other than himself. God is self-existent and thus exists by necessity.

A premise or a condition that is required for a conclusion is said to be necessary. Whatever has to be is necessary. (Cf. **CONTINGENT.**)

**NEO-ORTHODOXY** - A 20th century movement in Protestant theology characterized by rejection of the immanence theology of liberalism, a renewed emphasis on many orthodox Reformation principles, and a new interest in restoring vitality to faith. Karl Barth is usually considered the father of neo-orthodoxy. Central features of his theology would be: (1) stress on the transcendence of God, (2) the utterly desperate fallen state of humanity, (3) the inevitability of sin yet one's human responsibility for it, and particularly (4) the radical discontinuity between time (history) and eternity. The attempt to maintain an optimistic faith in eternity over against a pessimistic view of humanity and history is made by using a dialectical methodology. Neo-orthodoxy is often referred to as "crisis theology" or "dialectical theology"—the latter particularly. Hegel's dialectical methodology and Kierkegaard's "leap" of faith greatly influenced European theology in the first half of this century. (See **CRISIS THEOLOGY.**)

**NEOPLATONISM** - Platonism after it had developed over seven or eight centuries; platonism as Augustine knew it; platonism modified by Plotinus and others: (1) God is the ultimately perfect Being; (2) Mind and matter (in that order) emanate from God; the whole universe is a series of emanations from God, matter being much further away from God than mind; (3) People approach God by strict asceticism and by meditation, not by ritual or by works.

**NEW AGE** - A late 20th century coalition of mystical, occult, and "gnostic" groups have proclaimed themselves to be part of a "New Age" movement. Heavily influenced by astrology, they believe they are participating in the "Age of Aquarius," supposedly an era of love and world peace. The movement is eclectic, combining eastern religious ideas with western entrepreneurship. Often using the rainbow as a symbol (representing the combination of many colors), the "new agers" teach that a transformation of world consciousness is taking place. Across national and ethnic barriers, the new agers join together in the expectation of a coming world leader who will unite all people and bring everlasting peace to the world. The movement rejects traditional Christianity, however, claiming that Christianity oppresses the people by restricting their freedom. The "new consciousness" advocated allows in some cases spiritual beings from other worlds (or other dimensions) to manifest themselves through human channels.

Forerunners of this movement include transcendental meditation, astrology, and many of the pacifist and environmentalist youth groups of the sixties. Many see this new spirituality as a reaction to the pure secularism and the scientistic naturalism of the mid-20th century, but it may be an even greater threat to orthodox Christianity than it is to secularism.

Essential beliefs include the idea that all people have a divine nature. Collectively human beings are "God." By "resonating" with the pantheistic universe, evil can supposedly be merged with good to produce a better world. Movies, TV, and popular literature often convey facets of these themes. (Compare **MYSTICISM, NATURALISM, CHRISTIAN.**)

**NIHILISM** - The belief that no beliefs have meaning, that no objective values exist and that subjective values are meaningless. It entails the absolute destruction of meaning and purpose. All is "nothing" and "nothing" is all.

**NIRVANA** - The extinction of all individual existence and personal elements of life. The state of nothingness; the void. To achieve nirvana is "salvation" for Buddhists.

**NOMINALISM** - A theory developed in the Middle Ages which suggested that universal ideas are not ontologically real but are only class names or vocal sounds. This is opposed to Platonic idealism which says the universals are ontologically real and do have independent existence. (See **REALISM** and **IDEALISM.**)

**NORM** - A standard, pattern, type, regulation, or authoritative model; a definite rule or an imperative statement; an ideal standard; an absolute. Usually the term refers to a principle of right action or ethical value, but it also refers to a set standard of achievement.

In some cases a norm refers to a behavioral or sociological pattern taken to be typical.

A norm is a rule of evaluation, and something is "normative" if it meets the expectations. Evangelical Christianity is known for its unswerving allegiance to the Scripture as the infallible norm for faith (doctrine and other religious knowledge) and for practice (church polity, ethics, and Christian social life).

**OBJECTIVE** - Characterized by reference to something existing independently of thought or mind. To say that something is objective is to say that the thing exists as an object in its own right apart from any necessary sensual perception or personal evaluation. To speak of an objective idea is to speak of an idea that is capable of permitting observation and/or verification. To be "objective" is to be something that rational minds can agree is real or true. Objective is the opposite of subjective.

"Objectivism" is a theory stressing objective reality and validity of knowledge. "Objectivism" in psychology excludes all nonquantitative data: for example, behaviorism is a form of objectivism. It is the opposite of subjectivism.

In history it is important for Christians to argue for the possibility of objective knowledge. Some apologists have followed modern theories of historiography and have contended for historical relativism. But if history cannot be known, if events cannot be verified, then it seems that Christianity could not be known to be true. It would have to be accepted strictly on "faith." However, faith without an objective base is not biblical faith. (See **SUBJECTIVE.**)

**OCCAM'S RAZOR** - William of Occam (1300–1349), an outstanding late-medieval philosopher, stated a principle of parsimony that opposed the ever-increasingly complex explanatory theories of his day. The principle of economy in explanation can be stated in various ways. One common formula, which William may never have used, is: "Entities are not to be multiplied without necessity." He has been quoted as saying with regard to assumptions: "What can be done with fewer is done in vain with more." In other words, one should claim only those things that are necessary to explain the actual data.

Naturalists accuse Christians of not obeying this principle. God is not needed in the explanatory process, they say. The universe is self-explanatory. It is wrong, they claim, to argue for an immaterial soul in man. If the universe can be adequately explained without the concept of God, then theists have violated Occam's Razor.

William himself considered the articles of Christian faith to be binding, and thus he did not see them as being cut out by his "razor." But many modern theories of the universe and of humanity do believe that theism does violate the "razor." The Christian apologist tries to show how Christianity avoids Occam's

283

Razor, and he attempts to justify the necessity of each part of the Christian system.

**ONTOLOGICAL ARGUMENT** - An attempt to prove the existence of God from pure reason alone. Most of its proponents have believed it to be a rationally inescapable argument. The existence of God was thought by Augustine (and by Descartes) to be more certain than the truths of mathematics. An early, explicit proponent of the argument is the Augustinian monk, Anselm of Canterbury (1033-1109). He said that God is by definition "that than which nothing greater can be conceived." We clearly have the idea of God in our minds. It is greater to exist objectively in reality than to exist only subjectively in the mind. Therefore God must exist both in our minds and outside our minds.

Anselm's reasoning was that if God did not exist outside our minds, we could conceive of a God who did, and that God would be greater than the purely subjective God. By definition God is the greatest conceivable Being. Therefore God must exist objectively as well as subjectively.

The first serious challenge to the argument came from a fellow monk called Gaunilo. He supposed that the logic of the argument required the existence of all kinds of imaginary ideas. Anselm replied that the logic only applied to God since only God is a being than which no greater can be conceived.

Later, in the seventeenth century Descartes restated the argument to conclude that God, who is an absolutely perfect Being, logically could not lack existence. Leibniz includes a restatement of the argument in his writings.

The major critic of the argument was Kant who contended that existence is not a predication of a characteristic of a thing at all but simply an instance of a thing. Existence, he said, is not a part of essence. It is not a perfection that can be predicated of a thing.

In recent days Charles Hartshorne and Alvin Plantinga have reopened the discussion by restating the argument in modern terms. It remains to be seen how successful they will be in making their case.

**ONTOLOGY** - Similar to metaphysics; specifically, a branch of metaphysics dealing with the study of what existence itself is. In general, ontology deals with "being" as such apart from the study of any particular existent being. An ontologist asks, "What is real? What is there, and what is its nature, or what is it made of, or what is the essence of reality?" (Compare **METAPHYSICS**.)

Ontology is concerned with the fundamental categories of all being, the nature of being itself, and the relations and essential properties of being. Ontology may also refer to a particular system of thought or study which investigates problems relating to the nature of being. The term is often loosely used: for example, to ask what is one's ontology may be simply to ask if one is an idealist, naturalist, realist, etc. To study the ontology of history is to look at the actual content (the facts, events, etc.) rather than to deal directly or primarily with methodological questions such as epistemology. (Of course it is to be noted that "methodology" is there whether examined or not, and unexamined methods are more likely to distort the truth than are openly recognized methods.)

**PAGANISM** - technically, polytheistic religion. Sometimes, in popular speech, it refers to a lifestyle given to sensual pleasure and materialism that disdains traditional theistic religion.

**PANENTHEISM** - The theory and belief that God is in everything and everything is in God. God includes the universe in his being, but God and the universe are not equal terms because God is more than and is not exhausted by the universe.

This view identifies the world with God but not God with the world. Exactly what "more" God is has been left undefined. This non-rational "more" is unknowable. In practice this has become only a semantic mysticism that seems to make the universe less impersonal.

Panentheism presents itself as a view of God which is supposed to be a balanced synthesis between the extreme transcendence of deism and neo-orthodoxy and the extreme immanence of pantheism.

This view has been offered as an alternative to classical theism, especially by modern process thinkers. However, in many cases it seems that process theologians have mistaken the view of God in neo-orthodox theology for the classical view. The historical-biblical view of God is not the God of Aristotelian immutability nor is he a Greek Absolute nor is he "wholly other" in terms of his personal nature and relationships (though he is transcendent in his essence). The biblical view of the Reformers (or of Aquinas for that matter) is not built on Greek substance philosophy exclusively and has always had a biblical-dynamic acting God. But process thought has given up any claim to immutability or absoluteness within God's essence, and thus has denied specific and clear teachings in Scripture.

Panentheism is not an acceptable theological option for biblically oriented evangelical theology. This is not to say, however, that we cannot benefit by careful study and interaction with this very prominent theological movement of the modern day. (See **PROCESS THOUGHT**.)

**PANPSYCHISM** - A type of idealism which holds that reality consists of living atoms, and therefore everything has a mind or a soul.

**PANTHEISM** - A worldview which identifies God with the

universe. In this view, God is totally immanent and in no way transcendent. The universe conceived as a whole is God and is an extension of God's essence rather than a special creation.

The Christian basis for interest in ecology is the belief that God created this world and put human beings here to have dominion over it. Dominion is to be understood as humanity's place of leadership and guardianship as it works to please God and do his will. We are to use nature properly so as to bring all things under one head, even Christ.

However, the most common and most popular secular ecology movements usually tend toward a form of pantheism, especially when they place "natural" values above "human" needs, or when they so personalize the natural universe that it is thought of as actually being "Our Mother Nature." This is, of course, pure paganism.

**PARADOX** - Two statements that may be adequately justified by experience, reason, revelation, or some combination of evidences that nevertheless seem to affirm contrary propositions. When one's experience seems inexplicable in light of clear truths given by divine revelation, the mind encounters a paradox.

How can it be true that the infinite and unlimited God could become fully human in the Incarnation? This is not a contradiction (see **CONTRADICTION**), because this is a true description of what actually occurred in history. Neither affirmation (deity or humanity) necessarily excludes the other in the way necessary for true contradictions. Nor is the doctrine of the Incarnation an antinomy (see **ANTINOMY**) since the issues are not in conflict due exclusively to a truth that is contrary to logical deductions. But it is a mental conflict, a truth that is contrary to received opinion (foolishness to the Greeks). The incarnation is paradox, a belief that seems to be affirming a contradiction but in actuality is not.

A paradox may also be a conclusion that seems to be self-contradictory even though it is based on a valid deduction from well established and acceptable premises.

**PARTICULAR** - A single, definite thing; an individual fact; one specific case distinguished from a group, a class, or a general category of all other cases. (Compare **UNIVERSAL**.)

**PERCEPT** - An impression from sense experience; sense datum. When a person attempts to gain knowledge about the world by means of the senses, that which is "before the mind" (that which is immediately present to consciousness) is known as a percept. The total process of gaining knowledge through the senses is known as perception. (See **CONCEPT**.)

**PERSON** - A human being; the self. That which is personal is that which pertains to a specific individual. Personality is that

286

quality and quantity of distinctive traits which define an individual human being. God is a personal God. Humankind was created in his image and thus partakes of personhood.

Persons are self-conscious beings who have a rational nature (though it may be distorted in some particular case), who can and do make choices, and who then act on the basis of those choices. Choices are not always purely logical or rational; they often are based upon that which is valued. Persons may exhibit a variety of attitudes and emotions in very sophisticated ways toward a complex variety of things.

Persons are individuals, yet they are not completely defined in isolation from their community relationships. They do act in keeping with reasons and purposes, at least some of the time, and their nature is balanced by both responsibilities and freedom.

**PERSONALISM** - The theory that reality consists of persons and their experiences; the belief that human beings are persons; that personality is the basic explanatory principle; that personhood is the ontological ultimate; and that personality is the highest good.

With one notable exception (J. M. E. McTaggart), personalism has always been connected with theism. Personal idealism is the most typical form. God is the ultimate person, the divine personality, and the source of all reality. Thus, reality is ultimately personal, yet it is pluralistic: it is made up of a society of persons. Though it has a valuable premise, personalism does not always lead to a fully biblical view of God or humanity. Biblical faith places a very high value on the person as being in the image of a personal God. Modern scientific theories often deny the traditional concepts of a personal God. Modern scientific theories also often deny the traditional concepts of personhood, and thereby lead to the destruction of institutions (such as marriage and the family), educational systems, and moral traditions, all of which are based upon biblical forms of personalism.

*PETITIO PRINCIPII* - Begging the question; the fallacy of assuming the conclusion of an argument and using that conclusion as a premise. (Compare **LOGIC** and **FALLACY**.)

**PHENOMENON** - The result of sensory perception; an occurrence that can be perceived by the senses.

In Kantian thought, the term refers to the "appearance" of a thing as opposed to the "noumenon" which is defined as the "thing-in-itself" (the unknowable reality, according to Kant, behind the phenomenon). This Kantian distinction between what is perceived and what is actually there leads to a deep and pervasive agnosticism or skepticism. Nevertheless, the separation between the subject (the one perceiving) and the object (the thing perceived) has been a dominant factor in modern philosophy. It has led directly to the belief that no absolute knowledge can exist in any area.

Phenomenalism, on the other hand, is a view that the very reality of any physical object depends upon that object being perceived by some perceiver (not necessarily a human being). This view would argue that the physical world does not exist apart from the actual or possible perceptions of some perceiver.

Evangelical theologians usually assert that biblical references to nature use phenomenal language; that is, biblical descriptions of nature use the language of appearances. The heavens are above and springs come from the water below the "earth" (the ground on which we stand). Thus scripture is not properly interpreted as if it were teaching scientific theories. Scripture describes nature as it appears to the eye. In that, it does not err.

**PHILOSOPHY** - It is impossible to stop people from thinking. It is, therefore, of some importance to lead people to think correctly in every area of their intellectual life. That is the basic task of all true philosophy. A philosopher is one who "thinks about thinking" and who tries to lead others to enhance and clarify their thoughts.

The word "philosophy" is a combination of two Greek terms: (1) *philos* - love; (2) *sophia* - wisdom: and originally meant simply "the love of wisdom." The word came into general use in the fifth century before Christ.

The specific meaning of the term has not been constant in the history of thought. Plato thought the philosopher was one who understood the essence of things as opposed to one who knew only the shadows of the material world. Aristotle considered philosophy to be the universal science, and all types of knowledge as branches of philosophy. Metaphysics was considered "first philosophy" because of its foundational importance as the study of the nature and structure of all reality and of the origin and general structure of the known universe. As knowledge increased, philosophy became the unifying factor of all specializations, and the term "philosophy" more and more ceased to be applied to the various sciences and became limited to metaphysics.

In modern times, the meaning has changed even more. In popular terms, philosophy is often used as a synonym for "theory" or for that which is abstract rather than practical. Scholars also attach special meanings to the word. Bertrand Russell tried to limit its current usage to "logic" and to questions of methodology. E. S. Brightman (a personalist of Boston University) proposed to define philosophy as the attempt to think coherently about the whole of experience.

A short definition in keeping with modern usage would be: "Philosophy is the critical evaluation of all kinds of data for the

purpose of discovering and establishing valid (and true?) beliefs."
The most widely accepted meaning of the term would seem to be
one which emphasizes philosophy as an intellectual discipline of
critical examination and evaluation relating to the basis for "beliefs"
about anything, as a part of humankind's instinctive desire to
search for the ultimate and true nature of reality.

*Philosophy of religion* is the analytical study of religious ideas
and concepts with a view toward discovering their presuppositions
and implications.

To be valid a philosophical system or viewpoint must use
sound and accurate procedures of reasoning and must be based on
the whole range of human experience with the broadest possible
inclusion of data. The goal is to provide an integrated, persuasive,
believable worldview. Its method, then, is to build a synthesis of
learning.

Many people have the impression that philosophy is necessarily profound and abstract. They think that only the very wise and
scholarly can even comprehend the subject, but this is far from
being necessarily true. Some philosophical writing, like that found
in any other intellectual pursuit, will be more difficult to comprehend than the rest. But everyone should be able to survey the main
ideas and grasp the central issues.

The term "philosophy" also refers to the sum of a person's
ideas, convictions, and attitudes, whether justifiable or not. In this
sense everyone has a philosophy, whether they articulate it or not.

As Christians we are interested in knowing all of God's truth.
Thus we seek to articulate our thoughts and submit them to serious
examination and evaluation. This is at least part of the task of a
Christian philosopher.

**PLATO** - Greek philosopher (427?–347 B.C.) and Socrates' most
famous student and the teacher of Aristotle. Plato's writings
provide accounts of the philosophical discussions and debates of his
day. Plato was an idealist, believing that mind precedes matter in
importance and that universal mental concepts have their own
independent existence. The mind/body dualism and the value
placed upon Goodness as the supreme universal made his philosophy quite appealing to early Christian theologians. (See **PLATO-
NISM**.)

**PLATONISM** - The view (and the development within the
tradition) of the philosophy taught by Plato. Essentially a rationalist
tradition; an emphasis on the universal ideas that were imperfectly
represented by particular things; emphasis on the spiritual, the nontemporal, the immutable concepts grasped by reason alone as the
epistemological starting point. Mind/body dualism and other-
worldliness characterize Platonism's influence in the religious

community. A government run by the educated elite was Plato's political dream. (See **IDEALISM**.)

**PLURALISM** - The belief that reality is multiple, that there is no single truth, that there is no ultimate right, that absolutes in every area must be destroyed or overcome. The many is better than the one. In a less strict sense, the term is sometimes used merely as a synonym for legitimate diversity. Thus we might affirm pluralism as a way of indicating a willingness to accept and work with those who differ from us in non-essential matters.

**POLYTHEISM** - the belief that many gods exist, that more than one god should be worshiped. No one god is all powerful.

**POPULAR CULTURE** - That which is the controlling element for the mass media, especially the entertainment industry (magazines, pop music, TV, movies). These imitations of the cultural arts represent the moral standards and the philosophical beliefs of the people (the target group). Those concerned about the integrity of the gospel and about the effectiveness of gospel proclamation will often study the popular culture as a window into the current mindset of the masses. Popular culture carries, promotes, and reconfirms the cultural beliefs of the age. In western society, these cultural beliefs include ideas such as that evil is always from outside the community, that "good guys" win, that individual effort succeeds where groups and institutions fail, and that evil is only effectively overcome by force and by excessive violence that can somehow "pay back" the "bad guy" for all the evil he has caused.

**POSITIVISM** - The rejection of metaphysical knowledge. Positivism ultimately reduces philosophy to science. All knowledge requires convincing empirical proof. Consistent positivists reject all non-empirical knowledge claims. Religious beliefs are classified with superstition and myth.

**POSTMILLENNIALISM** - A system of biblical interpretation that identifies the millennium of Revelation 20 with the church age and thus expects to see a continuing growth of Christian influence in the world. A variety of theological viewpoints may be found within postmillennial ranks, but by far the majority of modern postmillennialists are found within the conservative Reformed tradition and thus are strongly Calvinistic. As a summary of this interpretive system, the following points should be noted: (1) The millennial kingdom is understood to be a period of growth and maturation of righteousness, peace, and prosperity for the church (which is Christ's kingdom on earth) as well as for the saints in heaven. (2) Christ will visibly and personally return at the end of the millennium. (3) The return of Christ will coincide with a general resurrection of both saved and lost followed by a general judgment to determine each one's final destiny (heaven or hell). (4) Old

Testament prophecies of earthly peace and prosperity during the messianic reign are taken to be partially figurative and partially literal depending upon the context. They apply to the internal spiritual condition of the church, but they also apply to the visible prosperity of Christ's kingdom. (5) There is a distinct continuity between but no simple identification of the New Testament church and Old Testament Israel. The final stage of the kingdom will include converted physical Israel. (6) A long range perspective will demonstrate an extraordinary growth of righteousness through the triumphant preaching of the gospel. By the power of the Holy Spirit, the nations will be discipled in accordance with the purpose of God as expressed by Jesus in the Great Commission. However, for a short time at the very end of the age, Satan will no longer be restrained, and there will be a great apostasy from the blessed millennial conditions. (7) The millennium of Revelation 20 is a present reality with an optimistic future for the church. The kingdom was inaugurated by Christ and has continually grown since that time. Wars and other great catastrophes were promised by Christ and thus must not be taken as nullifying the proper concept of the kingdom's growth. The first resurrection is the spiritual new birth of the true believer. Christians are to "watch" and thus be ready to seize every opportunity to establish God's law in society, but the "any moment" hypothesis about the return of Christ is not accepted. (See **MILLENNIUM** and **RECONSTRUC-TIONISM.**)

**PRAGMATISM** - The epistemological theory that makes the practical consequences of a belief the ultimate test of truth. As developed by C. S. Peirce (1839-1914), it is a theory that the idea produced by the "sense effects" of an object is the sum total of the idea of the object. Further, the sum total of practical consequences which might conceivably result by necessity from the truth of a conception is the entire meaning of the conception. This was developed by William James (1842-1910), the famous American psychologist, into a theory of truth, arguing that the function of thought is to guide action, and therefore truth is preeminently to be tested by the practical consequences of belief; that is, an idea is true if it leads to validly anticipated experiences or results. This involves the conception of truth as relative. The popular phrase: "It's true if it works" has little to do with pragmatism as a philosophy, but it is correct to explain pragmatism as a philosophy concerned with the practical results of a theory. John Dewey (1859-1952) applied pragmatism to educational philosophy and developed many modern educational methods. Dewey was a naturalist and a humanist who applied Darwinian principles to the learning process. Dewey's pragmatism dominates modern educational philosophy.

**PREDICATION** - The act of making judgments or forming propositions. From the Latin *praedicare*: to affirm or proclaim. Something that may be stated is said to be "predicable." To "predicate" an argument is to base or establish the argument. To state that something has certain attributes or qualities is to predicate those qualities of that thing. Thus that part of a sentence that expresses whatever is being said about the subject is known as the predicate.

**PREMILLENNIALISM** - A system of biblical interpretation that identifies the millennium of Revelation 20 with a future earthly manifestation of the kingdom of God. All premillennialists would be essentially conservative in theological perspective though real differences do exist within their overall conservative stance. Premillennialism is a designation for what essentially are two interpretive systems. Dispensational premillennialism has its roots in a distinct theory of progressive revelation and includes some notable emphases that are unique to that system. Historical or classical premillennialist interpretation is rooted in the theology of the Bible as it was understood by the second-century church fathers. Key points of the interpretive system are as follows: (1) The millennial kingdom is understood as being a future period of righteousness and peace that will be established on the earth by Christ personally. (2) Christ will return at the end of the church age and will then personally establish the kingdom of God on the earth. Thus Christ comes "before the millennium." The millennial kingdom is not established until Christ personally and visibly returns to earth. (3) The return of Christ will coincide with the first resurrection (of those who have died in true faith), and there will be a judgment upon the nations to see who will be allowed to enter the millennial kingdom, but there is no general resurrection nor general judgment at the time of the return of Christ. The final resurrection and the final judgment will take place at the end of the millennial kingdom of Christ. (4) Old Testament prophecies are taken seriously and the emphasis is on literal interpretation. Classical premillennialists are more apt to see spiritual applications to the church, but the expectation in both kinds of premillennialism is that a literal kingdom will be established at the return of Christ. (5) Dispensationalism is characterized by a strict and universal distinction that is maintained between Israel and the church. In fact, dispensationalism characteristically teaches that the church will be raptured (caught up into the air and removed from the earth) and will thus be in heaven (or at least in paradise or in the New City of Jerusalem in the sky) during the millennial era. The millennium is thought of as being a material blessing upon a converted physical Israel. Classical premillennialism will tend to identify the church as spiritual Israel so that both converted Israel and the church together will participate in the historical reign of Christ on earth. (6) The world is moving toward a climax that will be characterized by increased lawlessness. Most expect a personal antichrist that will persecute the nation of Israel (according to dispensationalism) or the church (according to classical premillennialism) during the great tribulation. In dispensationalism the church is raptured just before the tribulation begins (this is the "pre-tribulation" rapture). In classical premillennialism the church goes through the tribulation before meeting Christ in the air (this is the "post-tribulational" rapture). At the end of the millennium Satan is loosed for a short time and a great and final apostasy occurs. Christ is, nevertheless, undefeated. He wins the victory by supernatural power, raises the dead, and judges them to determine their final destiny (heaven or hell). (7) The millennium of Revelation 20 is a future reality. The kingdom was established in its mystery form (that is, in a manner not prophesied in the Old Testament) in the days of the incarnation of Christ but will be established in its physical manifestation at the return of Christ. The first resurrection is the literal bodily resurrection from the dead of believers at the return of Christ. The second resurrection is of the rest of the (wicked) dead at the end of the millennium. Dispensationalists believe that the rapture of the church may take place at any moment. Classical premillennialists do not expect an "any moment" rapture. All premillennialists, however, believe that the actual visible return of Christ will not take place until after the rise of the antichrist and the time of great tribulation. Thus the visible, personal return of Christ cannot take place at any moment but will be expected by those who read and understand biblical prophecy. (See **MILLENNIUM** and **RAPTURE**.)

**PREMISE** - A proposition already proven (or assumed) on which an argument is based. A presupposition: a stipulation. Technically, a premise is either of the first two propositions of a syllogism from which a third proposition (a conclusion) is inferred. In popular speech, a premise is a hypothetical statement that is used to set forth an idea or to provide possible evidence for a conclusion. The premise of an "if-then" affirmation is the "if-clause." (Compare **PRESUPPOSITION**.)

**PRESUPPOSITION** - A starting point; a postulate; an assumption made in advance. It refers to any belief or theory which is assumed at any point in the explanation of a system of beliefs or in a logical argument which is attempting to validly draw a conclusion. This may be a conscious or an unconscious assumption, but it affects the subsequent pattern of reasoning.

Some people have the mistaken notion that a presupposition

must be viewed on a "take it or leave it" basis. In other words they think that by definition presuppositions must be accepted or rejected on *apriori* grounds. But that is not exactly correct. No presupposition should be accepted if it cannot be justified. We should be able to give some reason for anything that we believe. Our reasons may not be absolutely conclusive, but no assumption could be maintained as true if it had no rational basis at all.

Sometimes a presupposition is said to be self-evident, necessary, or irresistible. "I exist" is an affirmation that cannot meaningfully be denied. "Out of nothing, nothing comes" is another affirmation that irresistibly seems to be true. The self-evident presupposition is a special type, however, and it is not necessary for a presupposition to be irresistible in order for it to be considered as valid.

Often a person argues or tries to persuade others on the basis of hidden or unspoken presuppositions. In order to adequately evaluate the rationality or validity of the argument or explanation, it is essential that one "do philosophy"; that is, do critical analysis so as to discover the basis of the conclusions drawn. This would include isolating all presuppositions for analysis and evaluation. It is essential that the Christian learn to challenge the non-Christian presuppositions that underlie alternative worldviews. At the same time we should learn to defend our own presuppositions.

**PROBABILITY** - An argument is said to have a high probability of truth when it is based on adequate or fairly convincing evidence yet lacks absolute certainty. Something is probable if it is reasonably certain but not undeniable. Absolute certainty (undeniability) is only obtainable in logical systems based on definition and/or valid deduction, such as the systems of geometry or mathematics. All conclusions reached by scientific (empirical) and inductive logic must be expressed in varying degrees of probability.

It is often debated whether theological ideas can attain the status of certainty or whether they must remain in the realm of probability. Those who use presuppositional apologetics will argue that we must presuppose the Bible to be true. Then, they claim, we will have religious certainty. It seems blasphemous to those thinkers to suggest that affirmations of the existence of God are merely probably true. Those who follow a more empirical or evidential approach to Christian apologetics claim that religious truth has the logical status of high probability. This does not reflect upon the necessary existence of God, they say, since the problem is with human epistemology, not with divine ontology. For many, the logical status of theistic belief does not affect one's God-given ability to have psychological certitude.

**PROCESS THOUGHT** - A modern philosophy based on

contemporary theories of reality growing from modern physics. Substance is not reality. The constant motion of energy fields (and the interactions of polarized electro-magnetic forces) is reality. Process theology suggests that God is the process itself, the existing flux of the "now." (See **PANTHEISM.**)

**PROOF** - When the evidence and/or the reasoning is sufficient to establish the truth and/or the validity of something, we say that we have proof. The evidence and/or the reasoning must be conclusive even to the point of demonstration. A logical proof is a set of propositions leading irresistibly to an assured or a necessary conclusion. (See **EVIDENCE.**) One is also said to be proofing (or proofreading) when one is marking a document for correction using a standard (such as an original version).

**PROPOSITION** - The meaning of a declarative sentence; a verbal expression capable of being affirmed, doubted, or denied; a declaration of judgment expressed in logical form; the simplest unit to which the law of contradiction may be applied.

Technically the proposition is the "meaning" of the sentence rather than the sentence itself, but of course the meaning cannot be known or understood apart from the words of the sentence.

**PROPOSITIONAL REVELATION** - One often hears debates over whether or not the Bible contains propositional revelation. In other words the question is raised as to whether or not God revealed himself in ways that can be accurately expressed in words and sentences. The debate is not whether God is limited by the words (he is not), nor whether the words exhaustively convey God's nature (they do not). The question simply is whether or not Scripture itself *is* revelation. Propositional truth is defined as truth which can be communicated in declarative form.

Non-propositional views usually define revelation strictly in terms of God's "activity" of self-revelation. This activity is frequently thought of as being in the form of personal encounters with men. Historical events may provide the context for conveying general impressions of God's character, according to this view. Scripture, then, is seen as the recorded "witness" of spiritually sensitive men who were involved in significant events of what is now seen as redemptive history. Thus Scripture is not considered to be truth from or about God, but rather it is viewed as a source or a means for the reader to personally encounter God, and it is thought of as a record of other's encounters with God.

Those who affirm a propositional view of biblical revelation frequently counter the non-propositional theories by asking questions such as these.

(1)  Were the writers of Scripture merely *witnessing* to what *they believed* to be true when they said, "Thus saith the Lord. . ."?

(2)  Were they merely reporters with no special information unavailable to other persons by which to interpret the historical events of Israel's history?

(3)  Did they possess the inspiring Spirit of God in more fullness but in no qualitative difference from other men?

Historic evangelicalism answers those questions "no" and has affirmed in some degree a propositional view of revelation as a part of its insistence on a strong view of special revelation. The Holy Spirit did deal with the biblical writers in a qualitatively different way, and he did reveal cognitive information though not in a mechanical way. Belief in propositional revelation does not by any means deny the essential element of personal encounter with God through Scripture, nor does it deny the value of the insight and indispensableness of a personal relationship with a personal God. In fact, a consistent "propositionalist" must take his own propositional Scripture seriously when it declares and puts emphasis on these elements.

The weakness of a propositional view is that it may degenerate into a "textbook" or "rule-book" approach to the Bible. It may ignore the human element in the Bible and is often guilty of invalid "proof-texting." These weaknesses, however, are not inherent in the view, and they can be overcome with proper hermeneutics. The strength of the propositional view is the emphasis on Scripture as normative for faith and practice. A properly defined concept of propositional truth in Scripture will always support orthodox doctrine and will enable the believer to discover biblical guidelines in ethical issues.

**QUALITY** - Any characteristic or special distinguishing feature. Frequently the term is used to refer to inherent traits. A logical proposition may have the quality of being affirmative or negative. A quality would also be that something which enables someone to identify a subject of perception.

**QUR'AN** - Moslem Holy Scripture (also known as the Koran). Mohammad supposedly could not read or write, but the angel Gabriel is said to have come to him and enabled him to produce the Qur'an. Moslems believe that this book is, therefore, the infallible, verbally revealed Word of God. It teaches about one God, submission to God, a final judgment, and gives warnings about the fires of Hell for the wicked.

**RAPTURE** - This word does not appear in the Scripture as such but the concept is there. It refers to the "catching up" of believers to meet the Lord in the air at the time of his coming. Rapture is an old English word derived from the Latin *rapere* (to seize or to transport). Almost all conservative, Bible scholars believe in a rapture, but there is quite a bit of controversy over its exact time and nature. Some believe the church will be taken to heaven prior to the great tribulation at the end of the age. This is the belief in a pre-tribulational rapture. Others hold that the rapture coincides with the visible coming of Christ (post-tribulational rapture). Still others hold mid-tribulational or partial rapture theories. But all agree that the church will meet the Lord in the air when he comes. (See **PREMILLENNIALISM.**)

**RATIONAL** - Properly related to or based on reason.

**RATIONALISM** - The theory that (at least some) truths about reality may be known apart from sense experience. Rationalists believe that philosophical knowledge is to some extent independent of experience and may be fully deduced from *apriori* concepts. The history of rationalism begins with the theory of the self-sufficiency of reason. Rene Descartes (1596-1650) is the father of modern rationalism.

Rationalism is sometimes thought of as the view that the true basis for solving problems is always an appeal to reason and personal, factual experience, rather than intuition or emotion or faith or revelation. By definition, then, rationalism limits a person's epistemological starting point to one's own finite self in the quest of a unified, meaningful worldview.

Thus rationalism's great weakness is its ultimate subjectivity. It has no objective criteria by which to establish the validity of its starting point nor to provide checks or establish guidelines for the process of reasoning.

It is important to note that while evangelical Christianity is rational it is not rationalistic. (Compare **EMPIRICISM.**)

*RATIONES AETERNAE* - Greek thought, especially in the Platonic stream, believed that "truth" was eternal, unchanging, and universal. Truth was not identified with the changing world of physical particulars but was found in a transcendent, autonomous realm of unchanging ideas (the Forms, the Ideas). Plato contended that these eternal ideas somehow determine the essential nature of the physical world. Man's true knowledge is knowledge of these eternal truths, according to Plato. Even in the thought of Aristotle and Plotinus, all truth that we know is absolute, because it is the universal and unchanging rational form that is known. These eternal rational truths are the *rationes aeternae*.

The impersonal and autonomous realm of absolute truth in

Greek thought is in direct conflict with Christian theology. But theists do believe that truth exists. Augustine took the position that these eternal archetypes (*rationes aeternae*) were in fact the eternal ideas in the mind of God. God created the world according to his eternal purposes. All of reality is shaped by God's Logos (*rationes aeternae*). Human reason is God's image, and Augustine believed that through the divinely given *rationes aeternae*, humans could come to know God and truth. As Augustine saw it, the divine Logos enlightens every human being.

Modern scholars (such as E. J. Carnell) who are in the Augustinian-Calvinistic tradition may use the term *rationes aeternae* to refer to the eternal rational truths that are the same for all humans because of the nature of God's creation. The laws of logic (such as the law of non-contradiction) are usually seen as part of the *rationes aeternae*.

Christian philosophers who use the *rationes aeternae* terminology are careful to base these eternal truths directly upon an eternal, personal God. The law of non-contradiction, for example, is said to be true only because it is believed to express correctly one aspect of God's eternal, unchanging nature. Man's mind is capable of knowing truth because God has made us in his image and all truth is God's truth, according to the biblical worldview.

**REALISM** - The term is variously defined, but primarily it refers to one of these two concepts:

(1) The theory that universals actually exist outside the mind (for example: Platonic realism). (2) The epistemological viewpoint that physical objects exist independently and that their existence does not depend upon mental processes in any way.

Scientific realism is the belief that a theory-independent world exists "out there" and that we do in some meaningful way perceive it and interact with it, so that our scientific knowledge is progressively advancing toward a secure, rationally justified description of that which is actually there.

**REALITY** - The whole of what actually exists; the true nature of whatever is the sum of real things. Reality is often contrasted with mere appearance.

**REASON** - Two basic meanings:

(1) The ability to think and infer in orderly sensible ways; right mental procedures; a sane mind marked by proper use of intellectual ability; the faculty of knowledge; the essential nature of the self.

(2) A proposition offered as an explanation of some procedure or assertion; an idea or concept that makes some other idea or concept intelligible; a statement offered as a supposed justification of some belief or act; a proposition supporting some conclusion.

**RECONSTRUCTIONISM, CHRISTIAN** - Postmillennialism implemented. Christian reconstructionists believe that the Lord is waiting until all of his enemies are put under his footstool before he will return to the earth. The task of overcoming the Lord's enemies is the task of the church.

Rather than pulling out of politics and worldly affairs waiting for the rapture, Christians should be investing their time and money in Christian causes. The goal is to build a Christian society, one based on biblical law and on Christian principles. These include implementation of economic principles drawn from the Scripture, establishing justice using biblical rules of punishment and reward, a concern for the poor in keeping with principles such as "gleaning," establishing Christian schools as an alternative to the secular statist schools, and opposition to laws that violate or hinder the expression of Christian principles.

Because the secular society will inevitably collapse, Christians must be ready to take over the crumbling financial, legal, and other governmental institutions. To be ready means to understand biblical law and to have practical "blueprints" for developing the kingdom of God around the world when the time comes. Usually orthodox in all historic Christian doctrines, reconstructionists are convinced that only a small, highly trained elite will be ready to rule, but that the power of God will enable them to succeed.

As an example of this kind of thinking, the biblical teaching on slavery is often discussed. Most contemporary Christians believe that slavery is contrary to the will of God, and thus they deny, spiritualize, reinterpret, or ignore biblical passages relating to slavery. Reconstructionists, however, remind Christians that Scripture is the infallible word of God, and therefore argue that slavery is not in all cases contrary to God's law. Slavery in the biblical setting was not based on race, and it was not an inherent status. One might offer himself as a slave, for example, as a means of paying off a debt. Thus this slavery would come to an end when the debt was paid. The declaration of "legal bankruptcy" or the debtor's prison system would not be allowed by reconstructionists. Scripture teaches that all people must pay their debts in full.

The eye-for-an-eye principle is seen as a valid system of formal justice, though a Christian is also expected to go beyond justice to show mercy when the offense is strictly personal insult or injury.

The strict adherence to biblical law is exactly the opposite of the dispensationalists' rejection of any binding authority for Old Testament law. Thus there is a considerable debate in evangelical Christian circles concerning the movement. Undoubtedly some of the controversy arises as result of systematic misunderstanding, but some is legitimately about essential principles.

Reconstructionists believe that the church must be involved socially, politically, and culturally in an aggressive effort to establish biblical principles as the basis for modern society. Characteristics of the movement include support for a return to the gold standard as the basis for economic reform, strong support of constitutional restrictions on government, religious freedom, opposition to secularism, support for aggressive social ministries, opposition to all forms of premillennialism or any theology that isolates the church or implies that it has no role in transforming society. Calvin's Geneva is seen as a model, an attempt at reconstruction that, unfortunately, ultimately failed.

Reconstructionists strongly oppose secular, statist government rule. They strongly support family rights and a cash economy. Key figures include: R. J. Rushdoony and Gary North. The movement is generally Calvinistic and politically aggressive. (See **THEONOMY** and **POSTMILLENNIALISM**.)

*REDUCTIO AD ABSURDUM* - To reduce to absurdity; that is, to prove one proposition by showing that its contradiction involves an inconsistency, or to disprove a proposition by demonstrating that it involves a self-contradiction. (See *AB ABSURDO*.)

**REDUCTIVE FALLACY (REDUCTIONISM)** - One of the most common logical mistakes is to explain a complex idea or thing in terms of only one of its aspects or parts. Reductionism is a misuse of Occam's Razor.

Good theories explain data without being either too simple or too complex. To oversimplify or to reduce an idea to the point of inadequacy in explanation is to commit the fallacy of reductionism. For example, one would commit the reductive fallacy by claiming that music is only sound waves. Music surely is made up of sound waves, but it is false to say music is "nothing but" sound waves. (Some have called this the "nothing buttery" fallacy.)

Christians contend that naturalism is characteristically reductionistic. The universe, according to the Christian, is more than matter. Man is more than an animal. Mind is more than material complexity. Religious experience is more than merely a psychological phenomenon. The Christian apologist attempts to justify belief in that "something more."

Some Christians have suggested that naturalistic evolutionary theories are reductionistic. Someone has humorously suggested

300

that pure behaviorism commits the "ratomorphic fallacy"; that is, it assumes man to be nothing more than a complicated mouse in a maze box. (See **FALLACY, LOGIC,** and **OCCAM'S RAZOR.**)

**REFORMATION** - A general term referring to a complex social and political change that occurred in northern Europe during the 15th and 16th centuries. The roots of this intellectual movement were primarily theological. Major leaders included Martin Luther and John Calvin.

The Roman Catholic Church had institutionalized some things that had not been a part of the apostolic and early churches. For example, the emphasis on good works (works arising from love) as an expected result of salvation had now become good works (works of human righteousness) as a basis for or even as a requirement for salvation. This was clearly a compromise of the biblical principles of salvation by grace and justification by faith. Whereas the Roman Church accepted the authority of tradition, the reformers claimed to look to Scripture only (*sola Scriptura*) as being the authentic Word of God.

Eventually the church formally divided. Some remained loyal to the pope in Rome (believing that he represented the true, historic church). Others protested against the loss of true doctrine in the church; they thus became known as Protestant Christians. Protestants have never been able to find the unity they lost because of their attempt at reformation in the church, but their independence from Roman authority brought a new sense of intellectual freedom that has had a vast impact on Europe and on Western Civilization as well as on modern denominational church life. (See **RENAISSANCE** and **ENLIGHTENMENT.**)

**REINCARNATION** - Hindu belief that the soul, after death, successively returns to earth in new forms or bodies. Life, then, is viewed as a never-ending cycle of birth, growth, death, and rebirth. Some Buddhists and some New Age teachers share this belief. New Agers often believe that it is possible to remember past lives. (See **SAMSARA** and **NEW AGE.**)

**RELATIVE** - The state of being contingent. A thing is relative if it is connected in a necessary way to something else. To be relative means not to be absolute or independent. In some contexts to be relative is to be unstable and changeable. A philosopher speaking of the relativity of truth frequently implies that all knowledge is in flux, and that there is no assurance possible in any conceptual realm (except, of course, in the sense of something being true by definition, as in mathematics or pure logic).

In historiography the dominant modern view is relativism. It is not that there is no agreement about any events of history, but it is believed that no events can be known apart from interpretation, and thus all history is inevitably tied up with fallible human opinion. But it is not clear why all interpretations must be false. Truth can be truly true without being exhaustively true. Relativism is a threat to orthodox Christianity (which depends upon certain doctrines being absolutely true).

**RELIGION** - The practice of worship; that set of beliefs which determines one's attitude toward ultimate reality and toward moral standards; one's belief about God and about sin and salvation. Liberal theologians see all varieties of religion as sub-sets of one single feeling of common dependence upon an ultimate. So for liberalism "all roads" (all religions) "lead to Rome" (a common spiritual destination). Thus all religions enable their adherents to be "saved." All religions ultimately worship the same reality. Traditional Christian orthodoxy, on the other hand, often defines religion as mankind's vain search for God, while biblical revelation is seen as God's divine initiative toward us. Thus only true adherents of biblical faith worship the true God. All others worship idols of their own making. (See **SALVATION**.)

**RENAISSANCE** - The 14th, 15th, and 16th century "rebirth" of learning in Europe occasioned by renewed intellectual contacts with philosophical, scientific, and artistic sources from the classical era of the Greco-Roman civilization.

After the fall of Rome, distribution of literature and communication between parts of the empire was much more difficult. Learning and scholarship were preserved in local centers, but general education declined. The Middle Ages produced skilled artisans and craftsmen, but literacy and the artistic and cultural aspects of life radically declined. The rise of Islam drove many Christians to join crusades to try to recapture the Holy Land from the Moslems. This conflict (and economical and political conditions) eventually (as an unintended by-product) restored trade and communication between Europe and the Middle East (where the writings of Aristotle and others had been preserved).

This reintroduction of classical sources into Europe produced a "new birth" (a rebirth, a renaissance) of classical culture. Aquinas is often seen as a transitional figure. He is clearly a Medieval theologian, but he established an Aristotelian framework for theology, replacing the Platonic worldview of the Middle Ages, and thus opened the doors for "Renaissance" thinking.

Key figures include Michelangelo, Raphael, Leonardo da Vinci, and Copernicus. Pivotal elements were a new sense of individualism, freedom, self-esteem, and nationalism. Centered in southern Europe (Italy), the Renaissance coincided with the voyages of Columbus and the age of scientific awakening. It is parallel to the Reformation in the North, though the Renaissance was not primarily theological. It was a cultural awakening. Most scholars see this era as the beginning of the modern world. (See **MIDDLE AGES** and **REFORMATION**.)

**REVELATION** - Something disclosed which was not previously known. The word "revelation" means either the process of unveiling or that which is unveiled or communicated. Revelation is something which is opened up to view.

In theology, revelation refers to Divine self-disclosure, God's manifestation of himself and of his will to humankind. The methods by which God has revealed himself have been varied. He spoke and acted in many ways. Evangelical Christians believe that God has uniquely revealed himself in words, visions, and in many other ways including special acts in history. The Scripture is an accurate record of his special disclosures, and thus the content (the meaning) of Scripture is in principle equivalent to the actual space-time (historical) disclosure. This equivalence of meaning is owing to the special work of the Holy Spirit of God, and therefore we may refer to Scripture itself as revelation (the word of God). To speak of equivalence "in principle" is to recognize and call attention to the necessity of proper interpretation. (See **INSPIRATION** and **PROPOSITIONAL REVELATION**.)

**ROMANTICISM** - The demise of strict rationalism in the latter half of the 18th century was partly caused by a shift in the mental life of the Europeans toward imagination, feeling, and emotion as a basis for truth. This "romantic" worldview was initiated by Goethe (1749-1832) in Germany but was carried to the English public by Wordsworth, Coleridge, Byron, Keats, and Shelley. In music we find Beethoven and Mendelssohn writing imaginative melodies that invoke sentiment and passion. Out of this environment arose Schleiermacher, the emphasis on feeling as the common element in all "true" religions, and thus the rise of theological liberalism.

**SALVATION** - Salvation is the state of final freedom from whatever is perceived to be the "religious" problem.

In theistic religion (whether Jewish, Christian, or Muslim), the religious problem is perceived as the moral gap between God and Man. Human beings are sinful, thus deserving punishment by a morally righteous God. By good works that please him or else by his unmerited favor (particularly in Protestant Christianity) we received the gift of eternal life.

In Eastern religions, on the other hand, the perceived religious problem is that one inherently has eternal existence (through reincarnation or through avataric forms), but life is full of suffering and hardship. The burden of Eastern religion is the belief that humans have everlasting existence. Salvation in this case is nirvana, the cessation of individual self-consciousness or the merging with the infinite spiritual realities of the universe. (See **RELIGION** and **NIRVANA**.)

**SAMSARA** - The wheel of life, the cycle of birth, death, and rebirth. Common to Eastern and other non-theistic religions. One can break out of samsara only by "faith" and by meditation (i.e. union with the One). (See **REINCARNATION**.)

**SCHOLASTICISM** - A name given to a type of Medieval philosophy. Building on "fixed religious dogmas," some of the theologians attempted through rational and speculative methods to solve basic philosophical issues, not the least of which was the attempt to prove God's existence. They also debated many seemingly inconsequential matters of theological detail.

Those who seek a rational basis for faith today are often accused of scholasticism by those who prefer to base faith on existential decision or intuition. The term is used pejoratively by neo-orthodox scholars to characterize the thinking of evangelicals (because of their emphasis upon history and fact as a basis for faith). Pejorative language does not settle issues, however. The question of whether or not we need to rationally justify faith must be addressed directly by scholars from various viewpoints.

**SCIENCE** - It is very difficult to define science. Some suggest that it must be defined as a method of observing the world. Others prefer to think of science as a mood in which such observations are made. Our English word comes from the Latin *scientia* which means "knowledge" in general, but today the term is restricted to certain types of knowledge. Even so the field of general science is so vast that one can hardly conceive its limits.

Science includes (among many other things) the study of the stars, the study of animal life, the study of the earth, the sea, and the air, the analysis of subatomic particles, mathematical laws, ecological balance, geological strata, chemical molecules, mental processes, blood chemistry, quasars, motion, sound and light, disease germs, carbon compounds. . . . What is the one definition that sets the limits of meaning for the term "science"? Science is a constantly developing (not a static) body of knowledge. It is "sophisticated curiosity." It is a mental search for truth (or at least for the universal consent of the "experts").

Traditionally, science has operated at the level of appearance. Sense perception has been assumed to be reality. Science generally ignores the epistemological issues raised by philosophy or religion. The abstraction of the phenomena into symbols or mathematical formulas is usually for the purpose of making predictions about the phenomena. Much of science, even today, such as atomic physics or microbiology, depends upon indirect perception through technological devices, but the phenomena are still central.

Science, for the Christian, may be defined as the study of God's creation. Secular humanists would argue that science cannot be defined in terms of God or creation but that it must be strictly "neutral" (by which they mean naturalistic). In the opinion of a great number of scientists, concepts like creation or even theism have no place in scientific vocabulary at all. The Christian argues that God does in fact exist as the Creator, and that the observable universe is contingent upon God's existence. Thus the Christian contends that science can never achieve the ultimate truth about the nature of the universe as long as it ignores the implications of theism.

Creationist science and naturalistic (evolutionary) science will function in similar ways in the task of observing and collecting data, in the experimental process, and in the search for practical applications of discovered knowledge. But there will be radical differences in their interpretive frameworks and in their systems of value.

The study of origins is essentially a philosophical question, and science cannot legitimately claim any special insight in this field of inquiry. Origins (by definition) are non-observable and non-testable. To show that life can be produced in a "test tube" from non-living chemicals could never legitimately be construed as demonstrating that life actually originated in that same manner. At best science could claim only that *if* the conditions on the early earth were the same as those in the laboratory, then the reactions produced in the laboratory may have taken place on the earth. Even so the laboratory must be considered as a planned environment in which certain processes were produced by the deliberate intention of the investigator. Thus science cannot rule out the biblical creationist's contention that life began by a planned intentional act of God. To show an alternative possibility for the origin of life is not a disproof of a creationist theory. All theories of origins are statements of faith. Naturalism vs. creationism cannot be resolved by science alone.

Science has developed a very effective means of gathering data, however, and the Christian should have no hesitancy about using it. All truth is God's truth for the Christian. Nevertheless, naturalistic bias has so come to dominate "scientific" explanations today that the Christian is justified in avoiding a mindless acceptance of scientific theories. The Bible is and must remain the norm for our faith. That means that naturalistic interpretations of the empirical data can never be Christian interpretations.

It is a complex and difficult task to work out the relationship between science and faith. Christians will not all agree since they will have different levels of awareness regarding philosophical analysis and both scientific and biblical data. But we must not allow the prestige and the influence of the naturalistic scientific community to intimidate us.

Naturalistic bias is not limited to evolutionary theories of origins. It shows up especially in modern behavioristic psychology, in medical research, in ecological studies, and in the life sciences. But naturalism is not a necessary part of science, and it must be challenged. The biblical alternative is still a viable option, and it deserves to be adequately presented within the scientific community. (See **CREATION** and **NATURALISM**.)

**SCIENTISM** - A philosophy based upon the assumption that all truth is derivable by the scientific method. The basic assumption of this viewpoint is that science gives ultimate and complete answers to all kinds of questions. Supposedly there is no area that is not open to investigation by the strict methodology of the natural or physical sciences. When science speaks, it provides the last word, the final truth, the exact and total description of the true nature of reality itself.

Technically, this view is sometimes called the "unity of science" theory. This is not merely an assertion that one methodology should be applied to all the sciences, but it is a deliberate attempt to limit science to a search for causal laws of the mechanical or naturalistic type.

The idea is that all truth must be of the type that lends itself to empirical verification in the strict sense. Scientism is the positivism of August Comte applied to all aspects of reality. Scientism is very much opposed to biblical personalism. Scientism carries with it an almost religious fervor, though it has no deity except science itself. (See **NATURALISM**.)

**SECULAR, SECULARIZATION, SECULARISM** - The conscious shift away from all religious or theistic beliefs: worldly, not spiritual. Thus secularism attempts to build a society upon principles drawn exclusively from human rationality and natural law.

The "age of secularity" refers to the post-enlightenment era, usually centered in the 19th century and carrying over into the 20th century. Key figures included Marx, Darwin, Herbert Spencer, and John Dewey.

Secularism is a post-Christian phenomenon; that is, it assumes and attempts to maintain many Christian values in moral, legal, social, and cultural aspects of life, but no longer accepts the theistic foundation for those values. Christians believe that these values cannot be maintained apart from their spiritual roots. Thus Christians believe that secular society is unstable, heading for an inevitable collapse. Secularists, on the other hand, usually speak optimistically of humanity as having come of age, as having finally achieved autonomy, and as having finally reached the last stage of evolution where we truly become self-reflective, understanding our origin without benefit of myth or religious illusions about God and supernatural saviors.

There is also a form of non-evangelical theology that calls for a "secular Christianity." The idea is to move away from an other-worldly emphasis and try to find meaning from within the concerns of modern society. Usually this is either an outgrowth of modern urbanization or related to the rejection of traditional worship patterns.

For evangelicals in the mid-20th century, secular humanism was the greatest intellectual enemy facing the church. (See **HUMANISM, LIBERALISM,** and **NEW AGE.**)

**SELF-STULTIFYING; SELF-DEFEATING** - Any assertion that undermines its own claim to truth is said to be self-defeating or self-stultifying. This is not necessarily the result of a logical contradiction, but it is something that no one would ever have an occasion to accept.

The most famous example of this type of statement is the assertion: "I am telling a lie." This is not a logical contradiction, but it could not be true. If it were true then the speaker would be telling a lie, which means the statement would be itself a lie and, thus, be false. If it is a true statement, then it is a false statement, because it would itself be a lie. The statement is self-stultifying.

Another example would be the assertion: "I do not exist." If the statement is true, then there is no speaker. No one would ever have an occasion to truthfully utter such an assertion. The statement defeats itself.

Another case that is more difficult to recognize, yet falls into this same category, is the assertion: "I am a machine." If such a statement were true, then the assertion would not be governed by any rational considerations at all. A machine might equally be programmed to assert that it is a person. Such an assertion would be due to mechanical programming in the computer's memory banks, but such programming (though explaining why the assertion was made) could not justify the truth of the assertion. There would be no necessary reasons for accepting my conclusions if I were a machine (since I would be following my programming whether for good or ill). Thus there would be no reason to think that the assertion that I was a machine should be believed. If it were true, then there would be no way of knowing that it is true without some source of independent knowledge. Affirmations that by their own nature cannot be meaningfully affirmed are self-defeating. (See **CONTRADICTION.**)

**SEMANTICS** - The study of meaning; the attempt to analyze language and linguistic forms in order to discover and classify the normal meaning of, and any changes in, the signification of linguistic elements (such as, for example, words), and further to explore the meaning of those linguistic forms with full understanding of all denotations, figurative usages, connotations, and possible ambiguities.

**SHINTO** - Shinto mythology attributes the creation of Japan to the gods from whom emperor and people traced their descent. Shinto possesses neither creed, code, nor authoritative written canon. Concerned with ceremonial purity, its teachings concerning sin and salvation have remained rudimentary. Elements in Shinto have historically included emperor worship and sensitivity to the divine in nature.

**SKEPTICISM** - The philosophical position either that knowledge is not possible, or that certainty in knowledge is not possible, and that all knowledge is merely more or less probable. Whereas agnosticism questions the human ability to know, skepticism goes further by denying the possibility of truth in any objective sense. Agnosticism says we cannot know truth (though there may be such a thing as truth) but skepticism says truth as such does not exist. The skeptic may argue as follows:

(1) All rationalistic systems are based on some presuppositions. The truth of these assumptions cannot be established by any means. Deductive truth is no better than its postulates and, therefore, cannot be finally established. Thus truth as such is impossible.

(2) Inductive conclusions are based on experience and sense data. The senses can be proven to be unreliable sometimes; therefore, how could one prove that his or her senses were not at any given moment (if not always) deceptive? One cannot be absolutely sure one is not being deceived even when one has reliable information, and so can never by induction be sure one has any certain truth.

Thus, according to the skeptic, valid knowledge is impossible. Interestingly enough, a skeptic seems to "know" that rational assumptions are undemonstrable and that sense experience is most untrustworthy, and further he seems to "know" that skepticism is valid. Nevertheless, this logical refutation does not solve or remove the questions raised. It does indicate, however, that skepticism is not a real answer, and people do not ever live consistently as if it were. (See **AGNOSTICISM**.)

**SOCRATES** - Greek philosopher (470?–399 B.C.), Plato's teacher. Engaged the citizens of Athens in dialogue forcing them to think about values and other issues. Socrates asked questions rather than giving lectures in hopes of getting his students to think clearly and find answers from within themselves.

**SOLIPSISM** - The belief that only one's self (mind) exists and that all other apparently existing things are merely illusions perceived by that self. It is likely that no philosopher ever actually held this view consciously, but quite a few have been told that this is the logical conclusion of their basic theories.

**SOPHISM** - Deceptive reasoning or argumentation. Thus a sophist is one who emphasizes success in winning a debate even at the expense of moral or intellectual integrity.

**STOICISM** - Students of Zeno of Cyprus (333–261 B.C.) who sat with him on a porch (*Stoa*) to study. Stoics rejected dualism and affirmed that only physical objects were real. God was reason itself. God (Reason) was the soul of the universe (the body). People then should live rationally and in harmony with nature. All men possess reason (a spark of the divine fire), and thus all men are equal. Reason, not emotion, enables us to live a meaningful life, but we must at the same time adopt a fatalistic attitude (in contrast to **EPICUREANISM**). We are each like a wave in the sea, temporarily distinct but ultimately merging with the one reality. Stoicism was popular in New Testament times, and Paul seems to have been quite familiar with Stoic philosophy and literature.

**SUBJECTIVE** - Relating strictly and exclusively to the thinking mind or personal consciousness; that reality which is determined entirely by mental operations; something characteristic of reality only as it is perceived rather than as it exists objectively; arising strictly within the individual as contrasted with modification by an external environment.

George Berkeley (1685–1753), an early and influential subjectivist idealist, argued that all qualities of objects exist only in the mind of the perceiver. His famous theory may be summarized by the phrase *esse est percipi*, "to be is to be perceived," and his theory remains an interesting apologetic for theism as he tried to demonstrate the necessity of an eternal Perceiver. Nevertheless, subjectivity is generally considered a weakness in an argument except by the existentialist who sees subjectivity as a strength. (See **EXISTENTIALISM** and **OBJECTIVE**.)

**SUBSTANCE** - The basic reality; that which has properties, qualities, attributes, or accidents; the system of properties considered in abstraction. Substance in Greek thought refers to the material out of which a thing is made.

Greek philosophy emphasized the description of a thing in terms of substance categories alone. Some early Christian theologians were influenced by this type of thinking, and many early attempts to define the Trinity or the nature of the Incarnation ended up by affirming seemingly contradictory statements (100% God and 100% man = a 200% person). The Trinity, for example, in terms of substance categories has three persons (three substantial entities) in one God (in one substance). This conceptual problem can be resolved by modalism or by affirming a seeming contradiction, neither of which is a happy stance. Some theologians have tried to develop non-substance relational and spiritual categories in order to meaningfully affirm the existence of the Trinity. But the existence of God's trinitarian nature is known to us because God has revealed himself in this way, and that remains whether we are able to explain it without using substance categories or not. (See **ACCIDENT**.)

*SUMMUM BONUM* - The highest good; that which qualifies as the supreme goal of human endeavor; that which is most worthy of being sought for its own sake. Classical Christianity has often taught that the *summum bonum* will be to stand in God's presence unashamed.

**SYLLOGISM** - A logical deductive analysis of a formal argument consisting of a major premise, a minor premise, and a conclusion. For example:

[Invalid]

| | |
|---|---|
| All horses are four-legged. | All H are 4L |
| My dog is four-legged. | D is 4L |
| Therefore, my dog is a horse. | Therefore, D is H |

> This syllogism is invalid not because it is false. We all know that dogs are not horses, but this syllogism is not valid because of its form. The middle term is not properly distributed. Let us look at another invalid syllogism that most people might suppose leads to a true conclusion.

[Invalid]

| | |
|---|---|
| All horses are four-legged. | All H are 4L |
| My friend Flicka is four-legged | MFF is 4L |
| Therefore, my friend Flicka is a horse. | Therefore, MFF is H |

> While this conclusion may be true, the logic is still invalid. But study the valid syllogism that follows:

310

[Valid]

| | |
|---|---|
| Every human being is rational. | All H are R |
| Melvin Elmer is a human being. | (ME) is H |
| Therefore, Melvin Elmer is rational. | Therefore, (ME) is R |

Notice that the term "human being" is the universal term. Thus anything true about the entire term (the category as a whole) is true about individuals that are properly classified by that term. Notice also that the first term (H) in the first premise is the second term in the second premise. Now compare that to the structure of the two invalid examples above.

Any good textbook on logic will provide illustrations of many different types of syllogisms, most of which are more complex than these examples. Definite rules apply by which one can distinguish valid from invalid arguments. Many times the difference is not as obvious as in the examples above. A valid syllogism will yield truth if the premises are correctly stated and true. An invalid syllogism may have a factually true conclusion. Nevertheless, only valid arguments are ultimately acceptable.

Syllogisms are helpful logical tools if one knows that the premises are true, but without a solid basis in truth with which to start, a syllogism does not serve the cause of truth. Deductive logic is only capable of being as true as its first presupposition. This deductive method is most helpful in critically analyzing the arguments of others to find out where possible error lies. But syllogisms are not the most adequate way to investigate factual reality. An inductive method is better and more scientific in that regard. (See FALLACY, LOGIC, and VALID.)

SYSTEM - A coherent, articulated understanding of certain phenomena which is used to explain the phenomena.

For example, an ethical system would claim to provide a context for understanding and explaining ethical phenomena. Various systems have been proposed to explain supposed patterns or the supposed lack of them in history.

A system is usually a set of propositions relating to the subject in question. A system is tested by its comprehensiveness and its coherence. Very few people state the propositions that underlie their beliefs in an organized fashion. (Those who do are the true philosophers.) But most people do work and think within a definite framework of ideas. Systems may be more or less rigid.

Helping people to recognize and evaluate their own framework of ideas with regard to religion is a major task of the philosopher of religion.

311

*TABULA RASA* - Meaning "blank tablet," a term (not original) used by John Locke (1632-1714), the British empiricist, to refer to the mind at birth as being without innate ideas. If that is true, all knowledge must come into the mind after birth, and the means by which all knowledge is gained must be experience (and, of course, reflection upon that experience). For Locke experience was not just the best teacher, it was the only teacher. (See **EMPIRICISM.**)

**TAOISM** - Chinese religion based on the teaching of Lao-Tzu (also Lao-tse or Lao-taze), 604?–531 B.C. The stress is on meditation and serenity in spite of the troubles of life. The word *Tao* signifies a way, a road, a course of action. In the *Analects* of Confucius it usually refers to the way in which and individual, a ruler, or a state ought to go, the way which heaven has laid down as regulative for human conduct. In the religion of Taoism the word *Tao* acquires metaphysical meaning as the unchanging unity underlying all phenomena, and the impetus which gives rise to every form of motion and life.

Religious Taoism, with its monasteries, temples, and priests, was despised by the Chinese scholar class, but its philosophical basis has exerted a perennial appeal. In modern times Taoism encourages temperance, frugality, almsgiving, meditation, and the study of Taoist writing.

**TAUTOLOGY** - Usually a tautology is a needless and meaningless redundancy, because it consists of the repetition of terms or ideas in close association. A tautology is something that is true by virtue of the meaning of the terms used. For example: "All husbands have wives." This is tautological because if a man did not have a wife, by definition he would not be a husband. The major value of such a statement would be to illustrate or define the meaning of some term.

**TELEOLOGY** - The most common meaning of the Greek word *telos* is simply "end." It refers to the last item in a series, or the limit at which a thing ceases to be. But in Greek the word could also carry the connotation of the goal, the aim, or the purpose to which something must relate. It is this latter meaning which produces the modern English usage.

A number of philosophical questions come under this general category. In a general sense, teleology is the philosophical study of evidences of design, function, or purpose in nature or in history. A teleological explanation would be one that views the activity being studied as having a discernable reason for its own existence. By way of contrast, the universe could be thought of as being controlled by impersonal and arbitrary forces (natural law) or as being undetermined, random, or chaotic. Teleological explanations, however, would attempt to provide criteria by which purposive activity could be identified. Teleological ethics proposes to determine the rightness of an act by its end result.

Any theistic affirmation of providence would be teleological. One who denied providence might still affirm a teleological view on the basis of man's free will. However, apart from theism, free will seems to be difficult to sustain. The Christian contends that only biblical theism adequately provides criteria for recognizing and affirming that either nature or history is teleological. The Bible itself provides a teleological view of creation and of history. Christians believe that the question "Where is history going?" is not only a legitimate question, but that it has an answer.

**TELEOLOGICAL ARGUMENT** - In essence this argument maintains that evidence of purpose and design in the universe is of such a quality and is strong enough to suggest that a cosmic designer exists (which is God).

This "design implies a Designer" approach was popularized in the 18th century by William Paley (1743-1805). The essential argument, however, had been used by theists for many centuries (See Psalm 19:1, 104:24). Some theologians believe Paul used a teleological approach in Romans 1:20 and others think it is a cosmological approach. (Of course Paul is speaking about knowledge of God, not merely the fact of God's existence.)

Teleological reasoning is found throughout the history of theology. Athanasius, in his *Contra Gentes* (See especially Part III, Ch. XXXV and XXXVIII) uses explicit teleological reasoning. Aquinas included teleology as the "fifth way" in *The Summa Theologiae* (Question II, Third Article). Even Calvin uses teleological reasoning (*Institutes*: Book First, Chapter V).

The Darwinian theory of evolution based on the principle of the "survival of the fittest" and "natural selection" destroyed the teleological argument in the public mind, because evolution (supposedly) explained the appearance of design without the necessity of any personal designer at all. Evil and ugliness also challenge the teleological approach.

Nevertheless, teleological evidence is still meaningful if carefully used. Such evidence has frequently supported those who wanted to challenge naturalistic science. Biological theories of evolution are technically irrelevant to design arguments based on phenomena in the physical universe.

Belief in God is not based on teleological arguments according to the Bible, but it is not antithetical to them. The teleological approach is a useful apologetic tool if used with caution and insight. (See **COSMOLOGICAL ARGUMENT**.)

**THEISM** - The philosophy that is grounded on belief in God as the Supreme, Necessary Being. Christianity, Judaism, and Islam are the three great theistic religions, but one may be theistic without belonging to any of these three religions. "Classical theism" is biblical theism as it has been elaborated primarily by Christians such as Augustine, Aquinas, or Calvin.

**THEISTIC EVOLUTION** - The interpretation of standard evolutionary theory as being "the way God did it." This is a nebulous position from the viewpoint of both scientist and theologian. At the very least it demands that the opening chapters of Genesis be taken in a figurative or a mythological fashion rather than as a narrative history. Scientific weaknesses are not overcome, nor are the scientific strengths of the evolution hypothesis increased by theistic affirmations of this type.

There is no doubt that many dedicated and believing Christians hold various forms of theistic evolutionary views, but it seems that some form of creationism should be an essential part of any fully biblical theology. It is not just the general concept of God which must be included in a theory of origins, but the content of Genesis 1 must be dealt with by careful exegetical analysis and a well worked-out hermeneutic. If harmony can be found between scientific data and theological truth, then the interpretation promoting harmony is to be preferred. Our hermeneutic should be controlled by factual textual data, however, and not merely by the most popular current theories in science. (See **CREATION** and **EVOLUTION**.)

**THEODICY** - From the Greek *dike* meaning order or right and *theos* , thus a defense of the rightness of God. Gottfried Wilhelm von Leibniz (1646–1716) chose *Theodicee* as the title for his attempt to defend the justice of God in light of the pervasive existence of evil in the world. The term has been widely used since that time as a technical term for theistic justifications of God's actions in the world. The particular reference is usually to the intellectual problems raised by evil and suffering. How can God be good if he allows so much suffering in the world? Why should we believe that God is all powerful if he does not act to eliminate evil and suffering? A theodicy is an attempt to explain the ways of God (usually to believers who face these issues in their own lives). A theodicy defends the goodness and the justice of an all-powerful God in spite of the evil in the world that God has made and over which he rules.

**THEOLOGY** - The study of God, and the attempt to answer or solve questions or problems relating to belief in God. "Natural theology" is the study of God as he has been revealed through the natural world that he created. "Revealed theology" depends on a valid revelation that comes to the human mind from God through history or through direct encounter.

In modern semantics, theology has come to be used in the

314

same sense as the term "doctrines." Thus in the modern evangelical Christian seminary the Department of Theology is normally the department of "Christian doctrine" (though the history of doctrine and the analysis of contemporary theological methods and systems may also be taught in such a curriculum classification). Not only do theologians study and attempt to formulate a doctrine of God, but they also discuss ecclesiology, eschatology, soteriology, Christology, etc. The connotations of the term "theology" are extended by some to include anything religious. A school of theology will teach doctrine, but it will also teach biblical studies, practical ministry, and other related subjects.

**THEONOMY** - "God's Law": Theonomists assert that God's revealed law in the Bible (both moral and civil statutes) remains normative and binding upon Christians as well as non-Christians. Civil authorities should enforce biblical law including making adultery, sodomy, rape, kidnapping, witchcraft, blasphemy, sabbath-breaking, persistent juvenile delinquency, etc., capital offenses. (See **RECONSTRUCTIONISM**.)

**THEORY** - From Greek *theoria* (the act of viewing or considering something). A theory is a belief or a hypothetical explanation of some set of facts. Used frequently to describe well-accepted scientific data, theories do not always explain, but they usually organize data in useful ways. The term "theory" refers to ideas which are considered to be better attested or confirmed than similar explanations called "hypotheses." (See **HYPOTHESIS**.)

**THERMODYNAMICS** - The study of the role heat plays in the transformation of matter and energy. Essentially a mathematical discipline, it has practical relevance in almost all fields of science and engineering, and readily lends itself to philosophical discussions about cosmology, time, history, and the broad questions of meaning, order, and purpose.

Basically all thermodynamic applications derive from three general laws. The first two of these laws are so thoroughly based in experimental observations and they are so rationally consistent that they are virtually accepted as absolute principles that underlie all physical, chemical, and biological processes. There is less agreement about the possible application of these laws to psychology, sociology, economics, or any of the social sciences.

The first law is correctly known as the law of the conservation of energy, but it is often linked with the parallel principle of the conservation of matter. Work is the movement of a body against an opposing force, or the transfer of energy from one body to another. Energy is the source of this movement and of the opposing force and/or of the temperature of anything. Energy may be potential or kinetic. The flow of heat produced by work of any kind is found by measuring changes of temperature. The heat absorbed by one body is found to be equal to that given up by the other. Technically, *for all changes in an isolated system, the amount (not necessarily the kind) of energy remains constant.* In other words, the amount of energy (and matter) in the universe remains constant. No new energy (or matter) is coming into being, and no energy (or matter) is ever actually lost. God is sustaining his creation. Of all that he has made, nothing has been forgotten or lost. God continues to uphold all things by his power. Matter and energy can be transformed, but they are never destroyed.

The second law is based on the observed result of countless experiments. Energy gained by conduction or by radiation is called a heat flow. Energy exchanged by other mechanisms is called work. In ideal, isolated systems, the first law (the law of conservation) applies both theoretically and practically. Most environments are not ideal gasses or perfectly thermocoupled reactions, however, and in the real world there are no totally isolated systems. Thus when energy exchange and work is performed, there is a dissipation of heat that is "wasted," that is, it does not do any work. A portion of the potential energy is never transferred perfectly. Work is done, but less heat is absorbed than is generated. In other words, *it is impossible to operate a system in such a way that the only net effect of the energy exchange is the production of work.* There is always some reduction in the amount of energy exchanged that is still available to do work. The energy is all still existing (the first law), but some of it inevitably is converted to heat and dissipated into the surrounding systems (the atmosphere, the water, the soil, the universe, or whatever). **Entropy** is the measure of this dissipation. In an ideal system, a heat flow or work process would be totally reversible and thus would have an entropy of zero. For any irreversible process, however, the entropy can be defined as a positive number. (Technically the heat, $q$, is divided by the temperature, $T$, so that $q/T$ defines the entropy of a given process, and $q/T + q/T$ will be zero in a perfectly reversible process but will be a positive number in any irreversible process.) Therefore entropy depends only upon the initial and final states of a process, and essentially is a measure of the disorder, the loss of potential, the degree of irreversibility of the energy exchange. The higher the entropy the less available the energy is at the end of the process being measured. A simple example is the sun. Heat and light are being generated and are radiating in all directions out into space. The energy that strikes a green leaf on earth is used in photosynthesis, but most of the sun's energy is being dissipated into space. That extremely small amount of the sun's total energy which is absorbed by the leaf is used to fuel the photosynthesis process, but even some of that energy is also imperfectly exchanged. An abundance of energy normally reaches the leaf, however, providing all that it needs to do its sugar producing work. Thus the imperfect exchange does not ordinarily hinder the process unduly. Under normal conditions, at every stage of energy exchange there is a sufficient amount of the proper kind of energy available to accomplish the necessary task. (Theists see this as an evidence of design.) The point is, however, that there is never a perfect energy exchange. Thus a seemingly inevitable consequence of this is the fact that the universe (and everything in it) is rapidly moving toward a real end for all work processes. Work can only be done as long as a sufficient amount of energy is available in a usable form. There is only a finite amount of energy in the known universe, and it is changing through time from available and useful forms to unavailable forms. Most of the sun's useful energy is flowing out into space, and eventually the sun's total amount of energy will be dissipated. Thus ultimately, from the scientific point of view, there will someday be a final cessation of all work being done anywhere and everywhere in the universe. Ultimately all motion will stop, no work will be done, and the entire universe will have dissipated its energy evenly throughout all available space. There will be no longer any potential for doing work. This is when entropy will be at a maximum. This entropy principle seems to be universally true and incontrovertible, thus it clearly implies that there must have been a true beginning of this one-way process, and anything that has a beginning must have a cause. Theists often see this as a rather strong piece of evidence supporting the theistic worldview. (See **KALAM**.)

The third law of thermodynamics was formulated primarily by W. H. Nernst (1864-1941), a German chemist. By no means is the third "law" as defensible as the first two, and it is often so heavily qualified as to lose its practical usefulness for science. In general, however, it recognizes that every substance has a positive entropy (the second law) but *at the temperature of absolute zero the entropy of a substance will (or may) become zero*. Zero entropy is sometimes affirmed only for perfect crystalline substances at absolute zero temperature. For most substances, entropy, as currently measured, approaches a limit other than but near zero. For example, in metals with free electrons entropy will approach a small but nevertheless still a positive value. There is of course a problem in the math since one cannot get an answer if one divides by zero ($q/T$), and the only hope is to show that the q (heat) of a substance actually goes to absolute zero. The principle has some practical value in scientific research, but it has several anomalies (particularly in the case of hydrogen). Hydrogen usually exists as a mixture of parahydrogen (with nuclear spins aligned in opposite directions) and orthohydrogen (with nuclear spins in the same direction). At near zero, however, the gas becomes nearly pure parahydrogen (if certain catalysts are present), and the calculations are affected. In the absence of the catalysts, on the other hand, measurements of heat capacities are also apparently in disagreement with other means of calculating entropy in hydrogen. Many substances do seem to approximate the third law, but others (such as hydrogen) do not fit the expectations as clearly as one might expect. Thus the third law is still the subject of thermodynamic research, but it is clear that God's world runs by heat exchange (an evidence of design). When there is no heat (at a temperature of absolute zero), there is no work. It is not surprising, then, to discover that modern instruments measure a small temperature even in deep space. God's dynamic creation is at work.

Even more clearly can we see that the first law is consistent with theistic expectations. God created a definite quantity of matter and energy and he maintains that quantity without loss.

The second law is also consistent with theistic belief. God has always planned to bring this world to a conclusion. Thermodynamic processes are the essence of time itself. Some relate the principle of increasing entropy to the curse of death and disorder imposed on the universe by God due to man's sin. The moral judgment of God goes beyond physical processes of energy exchange, however, and perhaps the second law is God's good plan for his universe independent of that judgment. It is not unreasonable, though, to speculate about possible relationships between energy loss, decay, and information loss, and human sin. (See **CREATION** and **ENTROPY**.)

**TRANSCENDENT; TRANSCENDENTAL; TRANSCENDEN-TALISM** - The verb "to transcend" means to go beyond the usual limits. The reference is often to exceeding the limits of ordinary human experience. Sometimes the idea includes something that is prior to as well as beyond or above. This is especially true of references to things that transcend the material universe. God is transcendent. He existed prior to the universe, and thus is greater than the universe. He is not contained within the universe, and thus he exists beyond and above the universe.

Kant used the term to refer to that which lies beyond ordinary sense experience. Transcendental knowledge was possible, but it related to experiences that grew out of the internal structures of the human mind, not out of sensory experience. Thus God, for Kant, could be known as a mental category, but one could not offer rational proofs for God based on evidence found in the universe, because the universe could never transcend itself. Since we can only know the universe through sensory perception, we could never go beyond the limits of sensory perception if we base our faith on it.

A philosophy that emphasizes the "unknowable" character of God or of ultimate reality may be called transcendentalism. The term also applies to a philosophy that affirms ultimate reality to be transcendent. Transcendentalism asserts and affirms the primary importance of the spiritual over the physical. In that sense, Platonic idealism is a form of transcendentalism.

Sometimes a philosophy that emphasizes the *apriori* conditions for knowledge or for experience, or a philosophy that affirms the supernatural, will be described as a transcendental philosophy. Transcendentalism would be the opposite of an empirical or a materialistic philosophy. Christian faith, technically speaking, has transcendental characteristics, but most theologians do not empha-size this terminology because of the historical character of biblical revelation and the incarnational Christology of biblical faith. (Com-pare **IMMANENT,** and see **IDEALISM** and **EMPIRICISM.**)

**TRIBULATION** - This biblical word means distress or oppres-sion. It refers to times of persecution, anguish, and trouble. The term is frequently used in the New Testament in a variety of contexts. The controversial aspect of this term as it is used in doctrinal studies comes when it is related to the time of "great tribulation" at the end of the age. Will the church be raptured prior to the tribulation (pre-tribulational rapture) or will the church remain on earth through the tribulation (post-tribulational rapture)? Bible scholars differ on that point, but all true believers will experience some tribulation in this life.

**TRUTH** - Generally, truth is that which corresponds with reality as it is. Truth is the opposite of falsehood.

Truth is variously defined, depending on one's epistemology and ontology. In the Bible truth is related to God. Truth about some fact corresponds to God's knowledge of that fact. All truth is God's truth. Therefore truth is absolute, unchanging, and universal. At the same time truth is intensely personal. One cannot separate what God says propositionally from who God is personally.

In a similar way man as a whole person is involved with truth. Truth relates to the human's reason, values, experiences, and activities. Truth relates to the universal laws of logic and to public evidence.

Perhaps the most significant aspect of the biblical view that truth is grounded in God is that, since God is one, truth is a unity. Distinctions between sacred and secular are challenged by the biblical view of truth.

A full discussion of truth giving all the various theories will not be attempted here, but further information will be found in comments made in the discussions of the following terms: **ABSO-LUTE, ABSTRACT, COHERENCE, CONTRADICTION, CORRE-SPONDENCE, DEDUCTION, EMPIRICAL, GOD, IDEALISM, INDUCTION, KNOWLEDGE, LOGIC, MATERIALISM, MYSTI-CISM, NAIVE REALISM, NATURALISM, NORM, OBJECTIVE, PRAGMATISM, PROBABILITY, RATIONALISM,** *RATIONES AETERNAE,* **REVELATION,** and **VERIFICATION.**

**UNIVERSAL** - A general category or concept capable of denoting every item in a class; an abstraction. For Plato, the universals were "Ideas" with actual existence. Others have argued that the universals are only class names and have only a subjective existence. (See **IDEA.**)

**UNIVOCAL** - Having only one meaning; something which is unambiguous and has an unmistakable meaning. Contrasted to equivocal which means having two or more meanings. The term is frequently used in discussions concerning the nature of religious language. Are our words capable of being understood univocally when we speak about God? Aquinas argued, "No!" and taught that all "God-talk" is analogical. Others have argued that without at least one univocal element, all language about God reduces to pure equivocation. This debate is a major issue in the philosophy of religion. (See **ANALOGY** and **EQUIVOCAL.**)

**UTILITARIANISM** - An ethical theory that actions should be measured or evaluated by the goal of doing the most good for the greatest number.

**UTOPIA** - From the Greek *ou-topos,* the land of nowhere. An ideal community, hoped for but not yet in existence. Utopians believe and promise that a better life awaits us as soon as we implement their plan of action, which usually includes the destruction of norms and institutions currently in place.

**VALID** - From the Latin *validus* (strong). Something authenticated by proper rational procedures and confirmed by sufficient evidence. The strict, technical, and formal meaning is "the state resulting from correct inference." The term often refers only to logical relationships, in which case something may be formally valid but materially false. Arguments that do not follow the rules of correct inference are invalid, even if the conclusion drawn happens to be true.

In another sense, something is valid which has legal strength, proper authorization, or sets forth a position or a viewpoint correctly. Baptists, for example, argue that immersion is the only valid form of baptism. (Other Christians may hold other views, of course.) A legal contract is a valid argument. A valid objection is one based on sound evidence. A valid passport is one that is legally accepted internationally.

**VALUE** - Relative worth or importance; the relative rank in a list of preferences. The measure of how much something is desired. The concept of value is closely related to "worth." Philosophically we are interested in the criteria for determining value, and we ask whether intrinsic value exists. That is, we seek to discern whether a desirable principle or quality inherently resides in some object or activity. Moral values are ethical principles that produce good results.

**VERIFICATION** - The procedure for establishing whether or not a statement is true or whether or not a descriptive sequence is accurate or whether or not some fact or some series or set of claimed facts actually obtain; the use of evidence (of various kinds) to authenticate ideas or concepts. In ordinary scientific terminology, the experimental or empirical evidence will serve as adequate verification of some theory. Theology raises a whole different set of issues because it seems that no simple empirical test will serve to establish the truth of some statement about God. Thus the question of how to verify theological claims is a very serious one.

**VERIFICATION PRINCIPLE** - As stated by A. J. Ayer in *Language, Truth, and Logic* (1936): "We say that a sentence is factually significant to any given person, if, and only if, he knows how to verify the proposition which it purports to express–that is, if he knows what observations would lead him, under certain conditions, to accept the propositions as being true or reject it as being false." Statements that fail to lend themselves to this kind of analysis and/or verification procedure were considered by Ayer to be pseudo-propositions, meaningless statements having no literal significance. This criterion of empirical testing was the chief weapon of the logical positivists against biblical and religious language about God or about any theological truths. It fails to meet its own test, however, and even if it were a self-consistent principle, the Bible (as understood by Protestant orthodoxy) is not rendered meaningless by it. There is empirical evidence for New Testament teachings, and in principle we do have ways to verify many aspects of Christian faith. Most evangelical Christian philosophers, however, do not accept the idea that meaning resides only in empirical propositions.

**VITALISM** - Belief that the functions of living organisms (specifically the production of organic compounds) are due to a special force (an "élan vital") that is distinct from other physico-chemical processes. Modern science has produced organic molecules from inorganic compounds, however, and vitalism is no longer commonly held. Theists, on the other hand, continue to affirm that life is not completely explicable strictly in terms of the laws of physics and chemistry. Life is divinely originated and thus has a measure of self-determination and self-continuation apart from mechanistic cause-and-effect processes.

**VOLUNTARISM** - The theory that the basic reality is the human will. People act under their own free will, and the will is more significant than the intellect (Pascal). Under certain conditions, truth can only be found by an act of the will (William James, *The Will to Believe*, 1847).

**WORLD PICTURE** - The world as we see it scientifically or as it appears to the senses. Medieval philosophers thought the world was flat and four-cornered. Modern human beings view the world as round (or slightly pear-shaped) and spinning in orbit around the sun. That illustrates a change in humankind's world-picture. (Contrast with **WORLDVIEW**.)

**WORLDVIEW** - One's basic philosophy of reality. A comprehensive system by which one attempts to understand and classify everything of which one is consciously aware. That set of assumptions (whether consciously recognized or not) by which one orders one's thoughts, responds to experiences, and interprets reality.

Communism and capitalism have essentially the same world-picture but different worldviews. Communist rule is atheistic and follows Marxist dialectical materialism. The United States, a major non-communist nation, is moderately theistic and follows a form of democratic capitalism.

Christians may hold the same world-picture as other modern people, but their worldview is essentially supernaturalistic and revelational. One's world-picture may change with any new discovery, but one's worldview is less likely to shift with changing empirical facts. A worldview is a basic and fundamental attitude toward and understanding of the nature of ultimate reality.

Worldviews are changed by a radical process known as conversion. People can be converted to non-Christian views as well as to Christianity.

Phenomenological descriptions of nature (using the simple language of appearances: "the sun rises. . .". etc.) in Scripture are to be interpreted as a part of the possibly changing world-picture. The most important feature of the biblical material, however, is its worldview, its basic explanation of how things really are and what our attitude or obligation should be.

The biblical worldview sees all mankind as fallen and in need of redemption and forgiveness. That same Bible reveals a way of salvation and everlasting relationship with God through faith in and acceptance of the lordship of Jesus the Christ.

**YOGA** - A physical discipline designed to allow one to manipulate one's body to increase awareness and to prevent sleep. The purpose is to enhance meditation in the effort to unite with the divine (usually "the Brahman"). There are various yogas (ways of acting). Not all relate to sitting crosslegged, but all claim to enhance one's mental well-being. All relate to Eastern forms of religious consciousness, but some do not explicitly require the practicer to affirm religious doctrines.

**ZEITGEIST** - The ethos, the outlook, the life-style and individual characteristics of a generation or an era.

# SUBJECT INDEX

*Ab absurdo*, 215
Absolute, 215
Absurd, 216
Absurd evil, 169
Accident, 217
Acquired Immune Deficiency
    Syndrome (AIDS), 174
Actual cause, 96
*Ad absurdum*, 217
*Ad hoc hypothesis*, 217
*Ad hominem*, 217, 256
*Ad infinitism*, 217
Advancement, the, 218
Advent, 218
Aesthetics, 104, 218
*Afortiori* argument, 60–61, 64
Agnostic, 218–19
Agnosticism, 219, 249, 308
Aguillard vs. Edwards, 118
Ambiguity, 219
Amillennialism, 219
Analects, 235, 312
Analogy, 220
*Analogy of Religion*, 244
Analysis, 60–61
Ancient earth, 137
Ancient Near East, 220
Animism, 221
Anthropomorphism, 221
Antinomy, 222
Antithesis, 223
Apologetics, 189; Christian,
    233, 240–41, 277;
    defined, 223; evidential,
    294; of Paul, 116; philo-
    sophical, 114; pre-

suppositional, 294; revela-
    tional, 102
*Aposteriori* argument, 103,
    105–10, 223–24
*Apriori* argument, 103–5, 224
Archaeopteryx, 129
Archetype, 224
Argument, 39, 46, 48, 57,
    224, 310; *aposteriori*, 103,
    105–10; *apriori*, 103–5;
    cosmological, 107, 109–
    11, 230, 239; deductive,
    49, 50, 52; false, 215; in-
    ductive, 51–54, 57; in-
    valid, 59; logical 64, 270;
    moral, 103, 113; ontologi-
    cal, 105; rational, 85, 201;
    teleological, 104, 108–9;
    theistic, 107, 111; valid,
    58, 60, 84
Aristotelian, 169
Aristotelianism, 224
Asceticism, 224
Assumptions, 70–71, 225
Astrology, 161, 257, 282
Atheism, 98, 151, 225
Atheistic existentialism, 165
Atman, 163
Augustinian theodicies, 209
Authority, of the Bible, 191,
    225
Axiology, 225
Axiom, 226

Baptism, 226
Being, 84, 195–204. *See also*
    Necessary Being.

325

"Believed interpretation," 128
*Bhagavad-Gita*, 262
Bible, the, 35, 101–2, 128, 172, 182, 227; authority of, 191–93, 225; and contradictions, 238; and error, 53, 267; and eschatology, 177; and existence of God, 112; infallibility of, 30; logic in, 64–66; and revelation, 96–97, 99, 295; and science, 305; and teleological arguments, 313; and truth, 52, 215–16, 319. *See also* Scripture.
Biblical creationism, 147
Biblical criticism, 267
Biblical theism, 78, 95, 100, 151, 313. *See also* Christian Theism, Theism.
Biblical theist, 109, 112
Biblical worldview, 230
"Big Bang" cosmology, 25, 108, 120, 139–41, 227
Blessed hope, 178
Brahman, 163, 228, 262, 276
Buddhism, 98, 162–64, 228

Causality, 230
Chance, 72, 146
Chaos, 120, 230, 240
Christian, the: defined, 230; evangelical, 227, 270–71, 303; and biased statistics, 55; and miracles, 87, and morals, 74; and truth, 82
Christian apologetics, 233, 240–41, 277
Christian apologists, 82
Christian life, 176
Christian theism, 70, 72–74, 78, 82, 84, 86. *See also* Biblical theism, Theism.
Christian worldview, 115, 151

Christianity, 69–70, 78, 87, 89; and coherence, 232; evangelical, 204, 268; as logically consistent, 85; and rationality, 84; relevance of, 90
*Christianity as Old as the Creation*, 244
Coherence theory, 232
Combinationalist, 100
Conclusion, 53–54, 57
Consistency, rational, 85
Contingency, 133
*Contra Gentes*, 313
Cosmogony, 239
Cosmological argument, 107, 109–11, 230, 239, 272
Cosmology, 25, 108, 241
Cosmos, 241
Creation, 113, 124, 127, 132, 173, 241
Creation *ex nihilo*, 125
Creation model, 117–18
Creationism, 305, 314
Creationist, 228
Creator, 96, 240, 305
Cross, the, 186–87, 191

*Das Nichtige*, 207
Deductive argument, 49–50
Deductive logic, 58
Deism, 123, 244
Demiurge, 158, 167, 245
Demon possession, 176
Design, 108, 253
Determinism, 73, 160, 245
Devil, 175, 178
Dialectic, 26
Discipline, 180
Divine revelation, 98, 114, 242
DNA molecule, 121, 136
Dualism, 166, 248

Ecology, 286

Eden, 211
Eighteenth-century, 193, 244, 303, 313
Election, 162
Empirical, 86–88, 98, 100, 127
Enlightenment, 249
Entropy, 120, 144–45, 249–50, 316
Epistemological nihilism, 165
Epistemology, 30, 41, 45, 71, 82, 85, 97–98, 138, 191–93, 250, 295, 304
Error, 53, 69, 85
Eschatology, 177–78, 209, 251, 271
*Esse est percipi*, 309
Essence, *See also* Being.
Ethics, 41, 252. *See also* Moral.
Evangelical Christianity, 204, 227, 236, 252, 268, 270–71, 276, 283, 303
Evangelicalism, 296
Evidence, 72, 98
Evil, 148; "absurd," 169; a Christian response to, 187; existence of, 153–56, 165; and the fall, 206; overcome by God, 169; problem of, 171; and suffering, 25, 109, 151–57, 175; and the teleological approach, 313; in western thought, 157–60. *See also* Suffering.
Evolution: and "the Advancement," 218; and animals, 212; defined, 253; naturalistic, 109, 119–20; and science, 124, 127, 132; theistic, 121–23, 314; theory of, 128
Evolutionary excess, 133
Evolutionary model, 118
Evolutionary philosophy, 212

Evolutionist, 172–73, 250
Excluded middle, law of, 65
Exegesis, 66, 221
Existence, 14–15
Existential undeniability, 109–10
Existentialism, 78, 255, 270
*Ex nihilo* creation, 139, 254
Experience, 14, 83, 102, 191–93

Facts, 86–87, 100
Faith: biblical, 98; defined, 255; fideistic, 98; and knowledge, 115; and logic, 64, 66; and reason, 100; theistic, 240
Fall, the, 205–6, 211–12, 233
Fallacy: defined, 55–54; naturalistic, 74
False, 65
False philosophy, 38
Fatalism, 160–62, 166, 257
Fideism, 98–99, 257
Fifteenth-century, 301–2
First Cause, 107
Foreknowledge, 162
Fossils, 188, 131, 133
Fourteenth-century, 302
Free will, 165, 211
Free-Will Defence, 205
Fundamentalism, 253

Garden of Eden, 174
"God beyond God," 96
Greek religion, 161
Gregorian chants, 278
Gutenberg press, 278

Hedonism, 261
Hellenism, 261
Hermeneutics, 261
Hindu, 228
Hinduism, 72, 162–64, 262
History, 22–23, 74, 78, 103, 188, 262

Humanism, 77, 263
Human Knowledge, 36
Human nature, 75–76
Hypothesis, 100

Idea, 14–15, 86, 157–58, 264
Idealism, 72, 77, 79, 81, 85–86, 157, 265–66
Idealist, 86
Idealist theodicy, 160
Image of God, 35, 63, 76, 89, 90
Immortality, 178
Induction, 54–55
Inductive argument, 51–54, 57
Inductive logic, 51
Inference, 48, 51, 84, 268, 270
Infinite regress, 107
*Institutes*, 313
Intermediate state, 177
Interpretation, 128, 221, 267, 269, 303, 314
Intuition, 71
Invalid argument, 59
Invalidity, 48
Islam, 78, 161, 188, 257, 271, 302

Jehovah, 201
Judaism, 78, 271
Judgment, 178, 271

*Kalam*, 108, 241, 272
*Karma*, 163, 273
Kind, 129
Kingdom of God, 74, 248, 273
Knowledge, 37, 71–72, 100, 138, 270, 273, 304. *See also* Epistomology.
Koran, *See Qu'ran.*

*Language, Truth and Logic*, 321
"Laws of thought," 47

Liberalism, 274
Lifestyle, 69–70, 76
Logic: in biblical exegesis, 56, 64; as a branch of philosophy, 47; for clear thinking, 171; deductive, 51, 58, 243; defined, 45–46; inductive, 51; and the problem of evil, 151; and rules of inference, 48; to test a worldview, 82
Logical analysis, 61, 66
Logical argument, 64, 270
Louisiana Balanced Treatment Act, 118
Love, 187–88

Marxism, 276
Materialism, 77, 276
Matter, 79
Maya, 163, 276
Meaning, 74
Meaninglessness, 84
Messiah, 50–51
Metaphysics, 25, 40, 45, 71, 277
Middle Ages, 272, 278, 302
Millennium, 248, 278
Mind, 86
Miracle, 87, 100, 200
Model, 118
Modern science, 95
Moksha, 164
Moral: argument, 103, 113; laws, 174; philosophy, 45; standards, 70; value, 73. *See also* Ethics.
Mystery, 184

Natural laws, 96
Natural selection, 148, 156, 313
Naturalism, 71–73, 77, 79, 81–85, 87, 89, 95, 100, 138, 250, 280, 305

Naturalistic evolution, 119–20
Naturalistic fallacy, 74
Naturalistic origin, 128
Naturalists, 146
Nature, 84–85, 286; created
    by God, 90
Necessary Being, 108, 239,
    281, 314. *See also* Being.
Neo-orthodox theology, 207,
    242, 258, 276, 281
New Age, 83, 282, 301
"New Consciousness," 282
Nihilism, 78, 164–66, 282
Nineteenth-century, 26, 37,
    74, 218, 223, 275, 281
Nirvana, 163–64, 282

Objectivity, 39
Omnipotence, 168
Order, 72, 120
Ontological argument, 105,
    284
Ontology, 284
Optimism, 74
Original text, 267
Ozone layer, 145–46

Panentheism, 96, 285
Pantheism, 26, 72, 77, 87, 95,
    113, 254, 286
Particular, 49, 52
Pessimism, 162, 164, 166
Philosopher, 27–29
Philosophical nihilism, 165
Philosophy, 23, 36; and criti-
    cal reflection, 45; defined,
    22, 288; evolutionary,
    212; false, 30, 38; how to
    study, 33; and questions,
    28; terminology of, 39; as
    a tool, 29. *See also* Phi-
    losophy of religion.
Philosophy of religion, 9, 13–
    15, 22, 36, 289
Platonic idealism, 282

Platonic ideas, 158
Political nihilism, 165
Polytheism, 73
Positivism, 77
Post-millennialism, 26
Pragmatism, 73
Predestination, 162
Premise, 48–49, 52–54, 57–
    58, 311
Presupposition, 39
Primary sources, 36
Probation, 182
Problem of evil, 172–75,
    187–89
Process philosophy, 78
Process theism, 78
Process theology, 95–96
Process thought, 96, 168, 295
Progress, 37
Propositions, 82
Punishment, 179
Purpose, 74

*Qu'ran*, 161, 271, 280, 296

Random, 72, 84
Rapture, 248, 297
Rational, 82, 85, 100, 111,
    127, 201
Rationality, 46, 84, 111–12
Reality, 37, 71–72, 76, 88,
    163, 203, 322
Reason, 82, 84–85, 98–100,
    111, 138, 201–2
Reconstructionism, 299
Redemption, 185, 190
*Reductio ad absurdum*, 64
Reformation, the, 26, 301
Reincarnation, 262, 301
Relative, 215
Relativism, 192–93, 223
Religious experience, 101–3
Renaissance, the, 26, 278, 302
Resurrection of Christ, the,
    66, 86–87, 190

Retribution, 179
Revelation, 183, 238, 269; divine, 96, 98, 114, 242; general, 202; propositional, 295; special, 97, 99, 202
*Ryrie Study Bible*, 248

Salvation, 191
Samsara, 163
Scholasticism, 220, 304
Science, 87, 127
Scientific method, 56, 72, 77
Scientific laws, 195
*Scofield Reference Bible*, 248
Scripture, 56, 153; authority of, 191, 193; and logic, 63–64; and the problem of evil, 171; as revelation, 303. *See also* Bible.
Secular humanist, 305. *See also* Humanism, Secularism.
Secondary sources, 36
Secularism, 78
Self-cause, 198
Self-contradiction, 70
Seventeenth-century, 244, 249
Sin, 49, 52, 176, 179–80; doctrine of, 74, penalty for, 202
Sixteenth-century, 301–2
Skepticism, 111, 193
*Sola scriptura*, 301
Son of God, 191
Sources, 36
Special creation, 123, 127–28, 134, 141–42. 149
Special revelation, 97, 99
Stoicism, 246
Stoics, 161
Substance, physical, 196–98
Suffering: substitutionary, 185–86; a Christian response to, 187. *See also* Evil.
*The Summa Theologiae*, 313
Syllogism, 243, 293, 310
Synthesis, 223
Systematic consistency, 100

*Tabula rasa*, 249, 268
*Tao*, 312
Tautology, 65
Teleological argument, 104, 108–9
Teleology, 110, 312
Television, 37
Testimony, 191–92
Test: of comprehensiveness, 96; of logical consistency, 82–85; of empirical adequacy, 86; of explanatory power, 88; of practical relevance, 89; rational 97; of a worldview, 81, 91
Textual criticism, 267
Theism: biblical, 95, 151, 313; Christian, 72–74, 78, 82, 84, 86; compared to deism, 244; defined, 314; as a major worldview, 79, 81; and miracles, 100; process, 78, 96; and science, 305; and the test of explanatory power, 89; traditional form of, 96; trinitarian, 84; as a worldview, 195–204
Theistic faith, 240
Theistic finitis, 165–66, 168–69
Theistic evolution, 121–23, 119, 212, 314
*Theodicee*, 314
Theodicy: biblical, 171–72, 175; defined, 153, 314; Irenaean, 205–13

Theology, 14; Christian, 193; defined, 314–15; neo-orthodox, 207; process, 95
Theory of knowledge, 30–41
Thermodynamics, 142, 146, 199; defined, 315; first law of, 143–44; second law of, 144–47
*Timaeus*, 166, 245
Torah, 274
Trends, 37
Truth, 37, 76; absolute, 215–16; defined, 319; and experience, 102; God's 9, 29, 138, 149; and logic, 48, 51, 53, 82; permanence of, 151; and personality traits, 217; and rationality, 46, 85–86; and relativism, 140, 302; and science, 304; and sin, 69; and syllogisms, 311; test for, 86, 88, 97; ultimate satisfaction of, 90
Twentieth-century, 75, 83, 85, 95, 108, 218, 227, 275, 281–82, 307

Uncaused Cause, 107
United States Supreme Court, 118

Universal statement, 49, 52
Universe, 84, 106–9, 111–13, 125, 148, 157, 198–99, 227, 239, 318
Upanishads, 162, 262

Valid: argument, 58, 60; defined, 320; logically, 49
Validity, 48, 50–51, 64, 84, 138, 270
Value, 63, 77
Waste, 145
*The Will to Believe*, 322
Word of God, 191
Worldview: biblical, 230; Christian, 116, 151; defined, 70–72, 322; elements of a, 79; empirical test of a, 86–88; and faith, 98–101; idealistic, 76; and meaning in life, 74; naturalistic, 77–78, 85; pantheistic, 87; pessimistic, 75; philosophical, 139; and reason, 138; testing a, 81–91; theistic, 78–79, 195–204

Yahweh, 201
Young earth, 136

# NAME INDEX

Abraham, 181, 248
Adam, 52, 135, 173, 176, 179, 190, 205–6, 210–12, 248, 259
Alexander the Great, 224, 231, 261
Al-Ghazali, 272
Allah, 161, 188, 219
Ananias, 179
Anaximander, 238
Anaximenes, 238
Andronicus of Rhodes, 277
Anselm, 278, 284
Antichrist, 293
Antisthenes, 242
Aquinas, Thomas, 26, 39, 108, 217, 224, 272, 278, 281, 285, 302, 313, 314, 320
Aristotle, 28, 224, 231, 246, 265, 277, 288–89, 297
Asimov, Isaac, 139
Augustine, 26, 158–60, 165, 205, 231, 255, 278, 281, 284, 298, 314
Ayer, A.J., 275, 321

Bacon, Francis, 249
Barth, Karl, 207–8, 255, 258, 281
Beethoven, 303
Berdyaev, 255
Berkeley, George, 266, 309
Bohlin, Raymod G., 129
Boyle, Pierre, 167
Bradley, Walter L., 144
Brightman, E.S., 168, 288

Brown, Colin, 43
Browne, M. Neil, 43
Bruce, F.F., 87
Buddha, 164, 228
Bush, L. Russ, 43
Butler, Bishop, 244
Bultmann, 255
Byron, 303

Cain, 52
Calvin, John, 205–6, 301, 313–14
Carnap, Rudolph, 275
Carnell, E.J., 100, 298
Chapman, Colin, 87
Charlemagne, 278
Christ: the answer, 29; death of, 186; devotion to, 164; and false philosophy, 38; life of, 84; philosophy built on, 30; resurrection of, 66, 86, 190; as Son of God, 191. See also Jesus.
Coleridge, 303
Columbus, 303
Comte, August, 306
Confucius, 234, 312
Copernicus, 278–79, 303
Craig, William Lane, 43
Cunningham, Richard B., 43

Daniel, 21, 177
Darwin, 26, 37–38, 306
David, 175
Denton, Michael, 136
Descartes, 26, 28, 268, 284
De Vinci, Leonardo, 302

Dewey, John, 38, 291, 306
Dunn, James D.G., 87

Edwards, W.D., 87
Epicurus, 250
Evans, C. Stephen, 43

Flew, Antony, 225
Freud, 260

Gabel, W.J., 87
Gabriel, 296
Gaunilo, 284
Geisler, Norman, 43, 189
Gleick, James, 121
God: and anthropomorphism,
        221; authority of, 63; and
        the "best," 189–90; bibli-
        cally theistic, 83; charac-
        teristics of, 172; consis-
        tency of, 57; and cre-
        ation, 125, 257, 286; dis-
        cipline of, 180–81; doc-
        trine of, 315; essence of,
        85; and evil, 151, 171–90;
        existence of, 37, 72–73,
        87, 95–116; as force, 157;
        goodness of, 24, 153,
        159, 174; image of, 35,
        63, 76, 89, 90; and Job,
        31; limitations of, 176;
        and matter, 79; and na-
        ture, 90; in pantheism,
        77; as person, 78, 89; as
        potter, 181; power of, 65,
        153, 187; in scientific
        theory, 141; as source of
        moral standards, 74; sov-
        ereignty of, 184; as tran-
        scendent, 318; worship
        of, 69, 201
Goethe, 303

Habermas, Gary, 87
Hartshorne, Charles, 284

Hegel, 26, 28, 86, 215, 223,
        246, 266, 281
Heidegger, 255
Henry, Carl F.H., 87
Heraclitus, 222, 259
Hick, John, 205–12
Hoffecker, W. Andrew, 43
Holmes, Arthur F., 43
Holy Spirit, 64, 84, 269, 296,
        303
Hosea, 183
Hosmer, F.E., 87
Hume, David, 167, 230, 234,
        249, 265
Hunnex, Milton D., 43

Irenaeus, 210
Isaiah, 177, 186

James, 69, 181
James, William, 291, 322
Jesus, 49, 231, 236; curses
        the fig tree, 179; deity
        of, 86; and evil, 187, 189;
        as God in the flesh, 202;
        and healing, 167; and
        logic, 56, 59–63, 65; lord-
        ship of, 323; the Mes-
        siah, 50; obedience of,
        181; personal relationship
        to, 164; resurrection of,
        51, 86; and suffering,
        178, 185–86; temptation
        of, 176; and the testi-
        mony of others, 193–94;
        and truth, 69. *See also*
        Christ.
Job, 24, 31, 177, 180, 182,
        184
John, 186
Jonah, 181
Joseph, 185
Jung, C.G., 224

Kant, Immanuel, 26, 111, 167, 229, 246, 249, 268, 271, 284, 287, 318
Keats, 303
Keeley, Stuart M., 43
Kierkegaard, Søren, 28, 216, 255, 258, 281
Krishna, 164, 192

Ladd, George Eldon, 87
Lao-Tzu, 312
Lazarus, 51, 178–80, 189
Leibniz, 284
Lester, Lane P., 129
Locke, John 26, 28, 249, 265, 268, 312
Luther, Martin, 301

McTaggart, J.M.E., 287
Marcel, 255
Marsh, Frank L., 129
Marx, Karl, 26, 28, 247, 306
Matthew, 273
Mendelssohn, 303
Michelangelo, 302
Mohammed, 271, 278, 296
Moore, John N., 129
Moreland, J.P., 43, 126
Morrison, Frank, 87
Moses, 191–93, 247–48

Nash, Ronald, 43
Nernst, W.H., 317
Newport, John P., 43, 175
Newton, Isaac, 65, 249
Noah, 173
North, Gary, 300

Paley, William, 109, 313
Parmenides, 222–23, 246, 279
Pascal, Blaise, 249, 255, 258, 322
Paul, 30, 38, 65, 107, 112–15, 173, 181–82, 184, 191, 205, 222–23, 236, 309, 313

Peter, 178, 186, 223
Pharaoh, 192
Pharisees, 58–59, 65
Pierce, C.S., 291
Plantinga, Alvin, 284
Plato, 28, 77, 86, 157, 166, 223–24, 231, 245, 259, 264, 266, 279, 288–89, 297, 309, 320
Plotinus, 158, 248, 254, 281, 297
Protagoras, 263

Ramm, Bernard L., 43
Raphael, 302
Reid, Thomas, 234
Robinson, H. Wheeler, 175
Rousseau, 26, 249
Rushdoony, R.J., 300
Russell, Bertrand, 288

Sagan, Carl, 133
St. Francis of Assisi, 278
Sapphira, 179
Sartre, 165, 255
Satan, 102, 175–76, 184
Schleiermacher, 303
Seth, 52
Shelley, 303
Slusher, Harold Schultz, 129
Smith, Gary Scott, 43
Socrates, 24, 231, 246, 289, 309
Spencer, Herbert, 306
Streeter, B.H., 168

Tertullian, 233
Thales, 238, 245
Tindal, Matthew, 244
Tyron, Edward P., 139

Van Til, Cornelius, 257
Voltaire, 249
Von Leibniz, Gottfried Wilhelm, 314

Wellnhofer, Peter, 130

Whitehead, Alfred North, 78
Wilder-Smith, A.E., 129
William of Occam, 283
Wittgenstein, Ludwig, 275

Wordsworth, 303

Zeno of Cyprus, 245, 309
Zeus, 192

# SCRIPTURE INDEX

**Genesis**
1 ...... 124–25, 314
1–3 ............. 212
1:1 ............. 228
1:14 ............. 126
1:20 ............. 63
1:24 ............. 62
1:26–30 ......... 125
1:27 ............. 63
2:1–3 ........... 126
2:7 ...... .62–63, 126
219 ............. .62
3 ...... 176, 179, 233
3:17–19 ......... 147
3:19 ............. 63
8:22 ............. 126
9:6 ............. 63
37–50 ........... 185

**Leviticus**
22:3 ............. 59
23:3 ............. 57

**Deuteronomy**
14:4 ............. 61
22:1–3 ........... 62
22:4 ...... .57–59, 61
28 ............. 179

**1 Chronicles**
21:1 ............. 175

**Job**
1 ............. 175
38–42 ........... 177

**Psalms**
1 ............. .177
19:1 ............. 313
37 ............. 182
73 ............. 177
104 ............. 127
104:24 ........... 313

**Proverbs**
3:11–12 ......... 181

**Ecclesiates**
3:19–20 .......... 63

**Isaiah**
24–27 ........... 177
40–55 ........... 186
65:17 ........... 144

**Jeremiah**
18–19 ........... 181

**Ezekiel**
20 ............. 272

**Daniel**
7–12 ............. 177

**Zechariah**
3:1 ............. 175

**Matthew**
5:27–28 .......... 60
12 ............. 64
12:1–8 ........... 64
12:11–12 .......... 56
12:26 ............. 64

12:28 ............. 65
12:30 ............. 65
24–25 ........... 178
25 ............. .272

**Mark**
10:45 ..... ...... 186

**Luke**
16 ............. 179
16:19–24 ........ 178

**John**
3:16 ............. 188
4 ............. 69
5:16–17 ......... 126
9:23 ............. 180
14:23 ............. 188
16:33 ........... 187

**Acts**
5 ............. 179
8 ............. 186
18:24–28 ........ 126

**Romans**
1 ............. .223
1:18–20 ......... 271
1:18–2:16 ... 113–14
1:19–20 ......... 281
1:20 ... 107, 112, 142, 313
3:1–4 ........... 114
3:21–26 ......... 114
4:9–5:1 ......... 115
5:2–5 ........... 184

8 ...........173, 178
8:18–23 .........147
8:28 .......211, 186
14:5 ..............66

1 Corinthians
15 ...............178
15:12–18 .........65

2 Corinthians
5:10 .............272

Galatians
1:4 ..............186
3:17–19 .........274

Ephesians
3:2–12 ..........274

Colossians
1:16–17 .........126
2:8 ...............30
2:15 .............186

Hebrews
1:3 ..............126

1 Peter
1:18–20 .........213
2:21 .............186
3:15 ..............30

4:19 .............178
5:10 .............178

2 Peter
3:10 .............144

Revelation
1:9 ..............186
13:8 .............213
20 .....219–20, 271,
290, 292
20:2–7 .........278
21:1 .............144